AN INHERITANCE

AN INHERITANCE

The Memoirs of

DHANVANTHI RAMA RAU

HARPER & ROW, PUBLISHERS
NEW YORK HAGERSTOWN SAN FRANCISCO LONDON

FIRST EDITION

Designed by Gloria Adelson

Library of Congress Cataloging in Publication Data

Rama Rau, Dhanvanthi, 1893–
An inheritance: the memoirs of Dhanvanthi Rama Rau.
   1. Rama Rau, Dhanvanthi, 1893–   2. Birth control
—India—History. 3. Feminists—India—Biography.
I. Title.
HQ766.5.I5R298 1977   301.42'6'0924 [B]   76–26248
ISBN 0–06–013508–5

77 78 79 80 81 10 9 8 7 6 5 4 3 2 1

Acknowledgments

This book could never have been completed without the constant encouragement and effort of my daughter Santha, to whom I wish formally to express my devoted thanks. I should also like to thank my sister Kamala, whose prodigious memory, unimpaired at the age of 93, has corrected and extended my own sometimes hazy recollections of the past.

Preface

Not so long ago, with advancing age, my abounding energies began to flag and I became more and more convinced that one approaching the age of eighty should make way for younger workers in the many areas of social welfare that have interested me, especially in the family planning movement, the major focus of my work in recent years. Until 1973, I visited London at least twice a year to attend meetings of the International Planned Parenthood Federation as one of the former presidents of the organization. On each occasion I stayed with my beloved granddaughter, Asha Waglé, who had made her home in London soon after she graduated from Oxford in 1966. Asha is my oldest grandchild and has lived away from India for many years, first as a schoolgirl, then as a college student, and later as a young working woman. She used to listen with wonder to the many stories of my own childhood days I related to her at various times. From her expression, I might have been describing a totally foreign land in a remote period of history. In a sense I was, so much have India and even the smallest details of Indian family life changed in the course of my lifetime. Asha paid frequent, though brief, visits to her parents in Bombay, but she felt she would like to have some sort of close and permanent record of the family and the many revolutions her old grandmother had witnessed.

Last year she began to pester me to write my memoirs for her generation and the next generation after hers. Only then, she said, would she feel that she could link up the past that I had known with the present she was living in and the future I could not live long enough to see and assess. Therefore, I must dedicate this memoir to my grandchild Asha Waglé and link with her name that of my first great-grandchild, Aisha Pearl Waglé, now a year old, the daughter of my older grandson and his American wife.

To Asha: Here is the story you urged me to tell.

To Aisha Pearl: Here is over a century of family history which you may one day read to learn something of your Indian heritage.

D.R.R.

The author and her first great-grandchild

AN INHERITANCE

CHAPTER 1

FOR THE FIRST sixteen years of my life, my home was in the small provincial town of Hubli in the southwest of India. Although I, like all but two of my eleven brothers and sisters, was born in Hubli, our parents came from North India, and many of my earliest memories concern the differences between my family, who were Kashmiri Brahmins, and the people who surrounded us in the South. I remember, for instance, an incident that must have occurred when I was about three years old. One of my mother's two maidservants, Chodabai, had taken me into our garden and was chatting with a friend over the gate. I couldn't understand very much because they were talking in Kanarese and our own home language was Hindi, but I did catch the words *"Sone ka oonda"* ("Lump of gold"). Immediately, Chodabai caressed my face with her hands, then cracked her knuckles on the sides of her own head, rushed me into the house, picked up a few chilies from the kitchen basket, waved them over me, and threw them into the kitchen fire. At the time I was merely bewildered by this performance, but much later I realized that Chodabai's friend had expressed aloud her admiration of my unusually fair-skinned baby face—like "a lump of

1

gold"—so Chodabai felt she had to perform the whole ritual to ward off the evil eye.

I was born in 1893, the sixth child of my parents, and because my father was an official of the Southern Maratha Railways, which had its headquarters in Hubli, we lived in a little white-washed bungalow in the Railway Colony a couple of miles outside the town itself. It was furnished in a pseudo-European style quite unlike the traditional Indian homes in the town proper. We had a small garden in front and a path that led from the gate on the roadside to the veranda screened by a trellis. Behind the house there was a well from which water was drawn for household purposes and a leanto at the further corner of the garden, which housed a buffalo for the milk required by the family. On the veranda were two old-fashioned easy chairs that could be extended to form leg rests. From the veranda we entered into a small, sparsely furnished sitting room containing a sofa and chairs, with white crocheted antimacassars, and a round table in the center. One door from the sitting room led into a largish bedroom, which opened onto a small storage-room, beyond which was my mother's prayer room. There was a second bedroom, with a passage between the two leading out to a courtyard, where another small building contained the kitchen, storeroom, and bathroom. We slept two or three on each bed, and, when they were fully occupied, mattresses were spread on the floor to accommodate the rest.

In the storeroom, a month's supply of rice, wheat, lentils, condiments, and so on was stored, a hand mill for grinding wheat stood in one corner, and vessels that would be required for cooking and serving food were arranged on a shelf. The kitchen had a homemade fireplace of mud plastered over brick, built on the floor, and in it firewood and cow dung cakes were burnt for fuel. My mother, who did all the cooking for the family, sat on a low stool by the side of the stove with her tongs, spoons, and the other implements she would need within easy reach. At one end of the kitchen was an open space with cotton mats on the floor, which served as our dining room.

In the bathroom, large vessels full of water stood on a raised platform, where the family bathed in turns in the Indian way, by pouring water over oneself from buckets of hot or cold water, according to the temperature. The courtyard was open to the sky, and we could sit out there in the cool of the evening on mats on the ground or on a small raised wooden platform and sew, knit, or study before the sun set.

The roads in the Railway Colony were all unsurfaced and the bullock carts carrying produce from the villages to the main market in Hubli raised clouds of red dust all day. The only means of transport for those who could afford to ride rather than walk was the *dumni*—a wagonlike vehicle drawn by two bullocks, with two long bench seats inside for as many passengers as could cram in.

Our neighbors were all Anglo-Indians and English-speaking Goans, mostly connected with the railway. The Indian population centered on the market business area, but our family had no occasion to get to know them.

There was very little contact between those who lived in old Hubli and the newer settlement which had grown up on its outskirts, and as my parents were considered part of the "Railway Group," most of whom were Christian, we had virtually no opportunity to get acquainted with the orthodox Hindu families who had lived in the city since before the Railway Colony was established and the city had begun to spread out into the open spaces around.

Our colony had, however, other advantages. A small Roman Catholic Church had been built about a decade or so before my birth, and a school attached to the church had been opened by Catholic missionaries for the children of the railway workers. St. Mary's School was a private school for boys and girls from the kindergarten stage to the pre-matriculation class when my elder sisters were admitted to it. A boys' high school existed in old Hubli and was recognized by the educational authorities, but no schooling for Indian girls was available till St. Mary's was opened. At that time parents did not demand for their daughters the sort of education that was necessary for boys who would have to seek careers under the British Government. Girls were

3

educated at home, for there was no thought that they might want careers or paid jobs in the outside world.

The climate of Hubli was temperate and salubrious, though great care had to be taken when epidemics erupted. Plague, smallpox, and malaria were scourges which periodically ravaged the villages around us. The only doctor we could call upon was a Dr. Braganza, a Goan gentleman, a general practitioner who lived and practiced in our part of the town, though there was also a railway dispensary to which we were taken for small ailments.

My North Indian parents, with their Kashmiri Brahmin heritage, could not become integrated with the Indian community living in the city because they did not speak Kanarese, the language of the South, nor could they fit into the Anglo-Indian social group of the Railway Colony, who spoke English among themselves and culturally aped the British in their way of living, dress, food, and manners. My mother never learned English and could not (and did not particularly want to) conform to foreign ways. No newspapers reached our home and of course radios and cinemas were unknown.

In any case, I can't see how my mother would have had the time for any extensive outside life or social contacts. She had two women servants, who spoke a smattering of Hindi, to help in the house. Each was paid five rupees a month—approximately one dollar at that time—plus their food, for work they did for the family from 7 A.M. till 8 P.M. every day. Their duties included sweeping and dusting the rooms and washing the clothes and the vessels—both the cooking pots and pans and the *thalis* (metal trays) and *katories* (small bowls) used for eating. (We always ate with our fingers and, except for a few serving spoons, owned no Western cutlery.) All the metal vessels were scrubbed with ashes from the cooking stove and coir fibers, which were stored in bundles for this purpose. And then tamarind rind was often used to shine and polish the brass vessels. The large earthenware jars in the bathroom were kept full of water drawn by our women servants from the well. The courtyard and the latrines at the end of the courtyard were attended to by the sweeper, an

Untouchable who came twice a day for his part of the work. The buffalo was milked morning and evening by a milkman, who was paid five rupees a month, and his son took the animal with several others in the neighborhood to graze in the open fields some way off for two rupees a month. Since we had no electricity, our house was lit at night by kerosene lamps, which all of us children, as soon as we were old enough to be trusted, learned to clean and replenish; we learned to trim the wicks and polish the chimneys until the light came through absolutely clear.

My mother supervised all the household work, cooked all the meals, took care of the youngest children and made all their clothes, and planned the lives of the older ones. Because my father's work obliged him to travel constantly, the major responsibility of maintaining our home and keeping us all together fell on her. Her way of life and her outlook were different from everything we saw around us, but her wisdom and affection persuaded us, without our knowing it, to accept her values as paramount. It was not till we were much older that we began to be curious about these differences and seek to find out the origins of our parents' early life that had shaped them so strongly that even so far away in time and space from their own community they retained implacably their own separate identity. Gradually, bit by bit, the fascinating story of our ancestry was unfolded, and before I go on with the events of my own life, I must narrate the events that shaped the lives of my parents, their growth and development, for, after all, I too am a product of that past.

CHAPTER 2

MY MOTHER'S AND my father's families, the Shahs and the Handoos, were Kashmiri Pandits, a small community of Brahmins who had emigrated from Kashmir during the latter part of the Moghul period, about A.D. 1700. They settled in all parts of northern India from the Punjab to the United Provinces but never really integrated with the other Brahmins in their new homeland. History does not record, definitely, what caused them to uproot themselves, though various theories attribute the exodus to famine, Moslem oppression, or the seeking of job opportunities away from the beautiful but impoverished countryside of Kashmir. They arrived and learned to live in what was almost a different country to them. They were obliged to alter their dress from the loose robes and distinctive head coverings of Kashmiris to the Hindu saris for women and pajamas and long coats for men, or to the trousers and tunics dictated by the Muslim Moghul court. They had to learn a new language, adopt a new cuisine, and get used to the flat, dry landscape of the North Indian plains. However, they continued to cling to their names and the customs, rites and ceremonies that belonged particularly to their community. The marriages of their young men and women were arranged by the elders and kept strictly within the bounds of the Kashmiri families. They all knew each other or were at least acquainted with the histories of each other's families.

In Delhi, the capital of the Moghul Emperors, so many Kashmiri immigrants sought homes in the same locality, using their sense of community as a buffer against homesickness and providing themselves with moral support in this huge foreign city, that there exists to the present day a Kashmiri *maholla* (residential area) and a Kashmiri *galli* (street) where all the residents on both sides of the street are Kashmiris. They liked to be within easy reach of each other, to depend on neighboring families, to share in communal functions and special Kashmiri festivals, to keep an eye out for marriage possibilities for the younger generation, and so on.

The men, of course, were forced by circumstances to enter more freely into public life, to understand and work with other groups, both Hindu and Muslim, outside the Kashmiri community. The women remained far more conservative and maintained traditional observances and special Kashmiri practices in their general living, and especially in their religious and ritualistic ceremonies. It took much longer for them to become integrated or even to establish friendly relations with non-Kashmiri women living in their neighborhoods.

My mother belonged to the Dhar family, originally settled in Delhi though her parents had moved to Moradabad, about 90 miles away. She was the eldest of four children and was named Bhagbhari. Her grandfather was a scholar and a poet in the court of the Moghul Emperor Bahadur Shah, who reigned in the early eighteenth century. Bahadur Shah was himself a poet. He wrote under the pseudonym "Zafar" and his poetry still thrills Urdu scholars.

My great-grandfather, on one occasion, took part in a poetry recital at a court gathering. He was awarded the highest prize, a *khilat,* or ceremonial robe, which he wore over his own costume. The *khilat* suited him so well, the story goes, that when it was on the Emperor turned to the audience and said, "Doesn't

7

he look like a shah?'' The name stuck to him, and since then he and his family were known as the Shahs rather than the Dhars. Even today members of my mother's family are known as the Shahs and it is only on ceremonial occasions that their real Kashmiri surname of Dhar is used.

The Handoo family had settled in Delhi, and their eldest son was named Rup Krishna. He was born when his mother was sixteen years of age, and in the course of time had five sisters and seven brothers. In accordance with custom, a marriage was arranged by the elders of these two families between Rup Krishna Handoo, aged ten and a half, and Bhagbhari Shah, aged eight years.

And so, one morning more than a hundred years ago, my mother, Bhagbhari, or Bhaggo for short, was told that she would be married in a week. She did not know then of the elaborate negotiations that had gone on for months beforehand, the exchange of astrological charts, the consultations with gurus, with friends of the family, with go-betweens expert in the diplomacy of matchmaking. For her the whole affair was not much more than a marvelous party in her honor.

From her own reminiscences and from the many orthodox weddings I have attended, I can easily picture my mother as an eight-year-old bride running excitedly from room to room in her home greeting the large number of relatives and guests who had assembled to spend a week with her parents. She was the center of attention, the wonderfully fortunate girl for whom all the preparations were being made, for whom all the rites and ceremonies would be performed throughout the week till the wedding day and after, when her bridegroom's party would return with her to Delhi. Although at that age she knew nothing of the full significance of marriage, she was delighted by her sudden importance in her family, and the dizzying deluge of rich-colored silks and satins, necklaces, bracelets, earrings, rings, and even a small diamond nose stud, all part of her trousseau, and the many other presents showered on her by relatives and friends.

Like girls in most Indian communities, my mother was married in her parental home, and I can follow her in my imagination through the crowded days of her wedding week. She could only think of Rup Krishna impersonally as her "bridegroom" because she had never met him, but knew that he and his party, consisting of his parents, family members, and friends, had traveled by train from their homes to Moradabad and were met there by her relatives with great honor and respect. They were garlanded, presented with bouquets of flowers, and taken to the lodgings where they would spend the few days before and after the wedding. More of my mother's relatives were waiting to receive them there, to see to their needs and comfort, and to present them with fifty-one large *thalis* (round trays) of sweet and salty preparations, with tea and sherbets. Of course, the whole party was invited to a meal. An important member of the bridegroom's entourage was the guru (priest) who performed the premarriage ceremonies in the bridegroom's lodgings and was joined by my mother's family guru at the second part of the wedding in her own home.

As soon as the younger members of the bridegroom's family recovered from the fatigue of the journey, they carried a large decorated casket containing jewelry woven from flowers and tinsel to the bride's house. There, surrounded by her friends, my mother was decked in this symbolic jewelry, a foreshadowing of the ornaments and jewels to be given by her in-laws. Necklaces, bracelets, armbands, rings, earrings, head ornaments, a floral belt—all were made from jasmine blossoms, rosebuds, and sweet-scented frangipani.

Only after this ceremony did the gurus begin the preliminary religious ceremonies of the wedding in their separate houses. Sacred fires were lit, fed with clarified butter, incense, dried fruits, and sandalwood. Sanskrit verses were recited with each addition to the fire of the ingredients considered sacred. Prayers were offered to all the Hindu gods and goddesses, each representing one of the elements, and to the mythological heroes and heroines of the great epics of India, invoking their blessings.

Before the next serious stage of the prayer ceremony or *puja* began, as in any fully orthodox marriage, both the bride in her home and the bridegroom in his temporary home were given a public ceremonial bath, to the accompaniment of Sanskrit recitations. They were dressed in their oldest clothes and rubbed all over with curds and a paste of chickpea flour, both supposed to be cleansing agents. There is usually much merriment during this ceremony—a relief from the solemnity of the earlier part of the *puja*—and my parents' wedding was no exception. All the relatives and friends may join in smearing the head, ears, face, arms, hands and feet of the victims with the sticky mess. My parents, still children then, sat patiently enduring—even enjoying—all this raillery until at last they were allowed to go to their baths and emerge cleaned up and in new clothes. In their day the women relatives of the bride helped to bathe her and the men relatives of the bridegroom helped to bathe him—but now it is no longer the practice.

Before the *barat,* the arrival of the bridegroom's procession, could take place, my father's guru had to take the *nakal*—a copy of the chart of the position of the stars in my father's horoscope —to be presented to my mother's people. He was accompanied by a party of friends and relatives carrying a large basket of toilet requisites for the ceremonial decking of the bride—a mirror and a set number of silver boxes containing powder, rouge, *kumkum* powder (for the scarlet spot on the forehead of the bride), and attar—as well as flowers and sweets and nuts. All this was carried in procession and accompanied by musicians and, in the olden days before my parents' time, by dancers. The mirror is still of special significance, as the orthodox bride sees her husband for the first time reflected in the mirror when it is held up under her veil, at the actual marriage ceremony.

In the meantime, the decking of my father as a bridegroom was performed by his near relatives. He was helped into his best *achkan,* the long, high-collared jacket, and jodhpurs and a gay-colored turban decorated with flowers strung to fall like a curtain to cover his face. He was then ceremoniously led to a grandly caparisoned white mare, her bridle embellished with flowers, on which he rode to the bride's home. With him was a young lad, a relative, as his "best man." Musicians marched in front of him playing their instruments, and there were displays of fireworks at various stages along the route. Behind his mare followed all the relatives and friends belonging to his party, and when they all arrived at the bride's house, they were warmly received with garlands by the bride's relatives.

The bridegroom always waits at the door of the bride's house while she is brought out closely veiled for a ceremony known as the Dwar Puja, or "entrance prayers," which must be performed before he may come into the house. The bride's mother holds the *arti,* a tray of auspicious things such as coconut, the red *kumkum* powder, sugar candy, betel leaf, and an oil light. She circles the tray around both the bride and groom to keep away the evil eye on the momentous occasion of the entry into the bride's home. Both my parents, carefully drilled in these observances, then exchanged garlands. After this, my mother returned to her room to await the astrologically propitious hour for the wedding ceremony to begin, while my father retired to another room to enjoy the teasing, the music, laughter, jokes, and pranks of all the younger members of both parties.

The sacred fire, symbol of purity, has to be kept alive from before the actual marriage, and as the appointed time approaches, the parents of the bride and of the bridegroom sit around the fire. My mother's parents then performed the *kanya dan* (giving away of the bride), repeating the chanted Sanskrit words after the guru. They put her hands into the hands of her bridegroom, after which his guru performed the marriage ceremony according to Vedic rites. In those days it usually took a couple of hours or more of chanting and prayers to complete the marriage ceremony, while the bride sat with her face covered all the time. Nowadays many of the rites have been simplified, shortened or omitted, but the most sacred part, the Sapta-Padi, always remains the same. These are the seven steps taken by the couple hand in hand around the sacred fire, stopping at each step to repeat in order one of the seven marriage vows. Once this is over, the bride and the bridegroom, usually exhausted by now, are allowed a short rest, though they are still not allowed to talk to each other.

11

The following morning the traditional floral blessings, in my opinion the most beautiful part of an old Kashmiri wedding, were given. The priests, as always, invoked all the gods and goddesses to bless the newly married couple, who sat opposite each other, each covered with a light shawl on which the relatives and guests poured flower petals to punctuate each verse of the incantation. After this, my mother was taken to her room, changed, and dressed in her elaborate wedding garments with as much as she could wear of the jewelry given her by her parents and relatives—five or six necklaces, masses of bangles, rings, anklets, toerings, earrings—while the rest of the jewels, impossible to put on, were carried on a tray, to accompany her to her new home.

At the leave-taking, always a very touching affair, even the onlookers could scarcely keep from being emotionally affected. To the parents of a bride the departure of a daughter in the olden days meant a much more complete severance from her parental family than it does today. In my father's day the bridegroom rode on the same white mare back to his own lodgings with his bride following in a covered palanquin. There his mother performed another *arti* ceremony, now formally changing the first name of her new daughter-in-law to give her a new identity as the wife of her son, and fed them both with sweetened rice from the same plate as an auspicious gesture. All the bridegroom's party then examined my mother's dress, all the jewelry she was wearing—openly counting the number of necklaces, bracelets, and the rest of her ornaments, trying to evaluate them, and often deriding or appreciating their elegance and cost.

After refreshments, the young couple were allowed to rest, but the same evening the bride's parents were expected to invite not only the young couple but the whole marriage party to the first of several formal dinners. This provided the occasion for the bridegroom's party to display their gifts to the bride. All the finery she wore when she entered the house was removed and she was decked in new jewelry and wedding garments given to her by her parents-in-law. These were unfailingly admired by

12

her own people, who were naturally less critical since their daughter now belonged to a family in which she would have to win the good will of those around her. As usual, at this first dinner, the trousseau given to the bride by her parents was set out for display before her new parents-in-law and all the marriage party.

But courtesy dictated that several more ceremonial dinners had to be exchanged between the two families before the wedding guests began to leave for their homes.

In my parents' day, when marriages between children were an accepted practice, naturally the young couple were not expected to grasp much of the significance of the ritual or the new relationships which would bind them, and they soon forgot every unpleasantness that may have occurred during the wedding, the criticisms or unfavorable views expressed by this or that relative.

During the first few days after their return to my father's home in Delhi, my mother was on display, decked in her bridal finery, to receive relatives and friends who called to congratulate and give them presents. After that, they were children together in the family with other children, and automatically the newcomer fell in with the ways and interests of her new family and gradually absorbed the teachings of her elders, with the necessary lessons in reading, writing, and simple arithmetic that were considered proper for the girls of a family who had never and would never expose their daughters to the immodesty of being taught in a school or acquiring a formal education. Household duties, cooking, sewing, garment making, fancy needlework, knitting, crochet work were essential and correct. There was no particular emphasis on her new relationship with her young husband. He was just another elder brother—as he was to her new sisters-in-law, who were almost her own age and whom she had to get to know and to whom she had to fulfill the duties expected of her.

In almost all Indian homes, under the system that we call the "joint family," members of at least three and often four generations live in the same house. Grandparents, parents, the sons and their wives and children, as well as other relatives on the male side of the family who are dependent, disabled, or without

13

a job would make up a not unusual joint family. The girls who have married into the family must be taught the proper observances, obeisance due the elders, the care and training of the younger children, what ceremonial gifts are given according to customary patterns on religious or such other occasions as births, marriages, and festivals. The household is ruled by the oldest woman of the family, even if she happens to have lost her husband and has a grownup son with his wife and children in residence. The men of the household earn the money, but it is this woman who decides, often in consultation with other senior members of the family, all important matters relating to the family—the arrangement of marriages, the dowries to be given to daughters, the trousseau suitable for each bride, the general expenditure within the household for food, education, and other necessities, and the assigning of duties to the younger women in the house, while the sons and other men of the family are either at their jobs or at school.

In those days, when bride and groom were usually very young, the girls divided their childhood days between the homes of their parents and their parents-in-law. They were taught the main household duties in the two homes, especially looking after children younger than themselves. The purpose of this traveling to and fro was to keep the young girls from getting too homesick, to give them a change of atmosphere and surroundings, to allow them to keep in contact with friends and relations in their parental home, and, with these frequent breaks in routine, to keep their interest alive in both households. The only drawback to this sensible arrangement was that it required the humane cooperation of a compassionate mother-in-law. To my mother's great misfortune, her mother-in-law was not such a woman.

Many of the living arrangements of North Indians are designed around evading or enduring the heat. From March onward the temperature hovers around 100 degrees, and when the dreaded *loo* blows, the searing wind across the Rajasthan desert, the mercury soars to 120 in the shade and dust storms whirl through the city. Only in October does the heat subside, when the monsoon has cooled the whole subcontinent and Delhi's cold, crisp, and brilliant winter changes the whole style of life in the capital.

The Handoo family was reasonably well-to-do, and the Handoo home in the Kashmiri *galli* (street) in Delhi was a fairly large and comfortable house. Like many homes of those days it had a basement where the family retired for the hottest part of summer days; these basements (known as *thakhanas*) were so built that they kept the heat and dust storms out during the scorching summer months. At this time, the annual retreat to cool hill resorts was quite unknown. Immediately after an early lunch the women of the family went down to the *thakhana*, where the work of the younger members could be carried on as usual until the evening, when the worst of the heat was over. Then they all emerged to prepare the evening meal, and as the heat was still uncomfortable, cots or *charpoys* (light cotlike structures woven with tape and rope) were carried up a narrow staircase and placed on an open terrace, still a typical feature of old Delhi houses. Light bedding was laid on these *charpoys* and the family slept in the open under the stars, where it was much cooler than in the rooms below. It was not the custom then to change into nightdresses or pajamas, and even now most Indians sleep as fully clothed as in the daytime. Privacy was not thought to be essential for family members, who slept side by side on the open terrace.

If, for some reason, the women had to remain on the ground floor in the hot mornings, they used hand fans, and sometimes a large fan was installed in a living room. A four- or five-foot wooden pole with a two-foot frill of stiff material attached along it hung across the room from a beam in the ceiling. A rope tied to the pole passed through a hole in the wall to a servant sitting in the passage outside. He was appointed to pull the rope rhythmically, which moved the frill to and fro to create the breeze that cooled the room. Across windows and open doorways, screens made of *khus*, a sweet-scented grass that was kept damp all the time, filtered, cooled, or perfumed any faint current of air that reached the ground-floor room until the work was done and everybody could seek refuge in the *thakhana.*

The main room in the Handoo household and, in fact, in almost all Kashmiri homes, was furnished with a large *takth,* an oblong wooden platform covered with a light cotton mattress, a clean white sheet, and large bolster pillows and cushions against the wall and along the two ends. On the *takth* there was always a *paan daan,* a highly polished brass or silver box in which were kept the limes, catechu, areca nut cut fine, cardamoms, cloves, eating tobacco, and all the other necessary ingredients that are wrapped in the green, heart-shaped betel leaves to make *paans.* It was an essential courtesy to offer ready-prepared *paans* to all visitors and elders in the family after meals. In another corner of the *takth* was a shiny metal spittoon, for people usually needed to spit out the betel juice, especially if tobacco was used in the *paan.* Nearly always there was a hookah in the room, which stood within reach of men visitors. The hookah is supposed to provide the coolest smoke in the world. The tobacco is prepared with molasses and scented, placed in a clay holder, live charcoal is put on top, and this holder is fitted into a fancy pipe leading into a metal vessel of water. Then the smoke is drawn through water and a long, flexible, decorated tube to the mouthpiece. Each inhalation is accompanied by a gentle, liquid gurgling, and the fragrant aroma of the smoke fills the air.

It was often the duty of the young people in the house to fill and wrap the *paans* for their elders and for visitors, and to prepare the hookah for the men after each meal.

The *takth* was always the focus of the main living room. Family members sat cross-legged on it and spread out their reading, writing, or sewing materials. If visitors entered and the *takth* was already crowded, small round cane stools were pulled up for them. They were light and convenient. People rarely sat on the floor, unless it was well carpeted. To sit on a bare floor would have been considered crude.

For the women of the household, the kitchen was perhaps the most important part of the home. That was where they spent the morning hours preparing the meals, measuring out the required amounts of grain, lentils, cooking oils, dried foods, pickles, spices from the storeroom and preparing the meat, vegetables, and condiments that were to be used. The food was served on *thalis,* each holding several *katories* containing different preparations of meat, fish, or vegetables, with a little hill of rice in the middle of the *thali.* Each person added the contents of the *katories* to the rice in varying quantities and mixtures according to his or her own taste. In most homes men and younger children were fed first, while the women helped serve with glasses of water and second helpings of food. After that, the senior women of the household settled down to eat. Since the food was eaten with the fingers, hands were washed before and after a meal, and mouth rinsed with water afterward.

In most homes there was a *mardana,* a men's quarter or an outside room, and a *zenana,* the women's apartments. This was a system adopted from the Muslim rulers, but while the Kashmiris did not insist on keeping their women in veiled seclusion from the men within the community, no man of another community was allowed in the women's section of the home. Even a Kashmiri man from outside the family was allowed to meet only the older women in the *zenana.* Young women were not permitted to carry on a conversation with young men, even in the presence of their elders, and of course there were no occasions when the young people could meet each other socially, unless they were closely related. When Kashmiri women went out of their houses, they covered themselves with all-enveloping shawls, woolen in the winter and cotton in the summer, drawn up to cover all of the face except the eyes, so that they would not be seen by non-Kashmiri men on the street.

While the women of the household occupied themselves with domestic work during the day, and spent their leisure hours at the temples for the evening worship or visiting each other to exchange gossip and discuss eligible young men and women, with a view to arranging marriages for the sons and daughters of relatives or friends, the men, after their working day, were free to indulge in those activities which found no place in a crowded joint family. In every town there was a red-light area where music, dancing, singing, gaiety, laughter, sentimental or racy conversation, and sex were available. There men sought relaxation from the humdrum life in the domestic circle with the excitements of dancing girls and musicians. No respectable woman could attend such an occasion. Only if a concert was arranged in a private home could she enjoy it—and even then from behind a fretted screen or a curtain.

Women, as a rule, accepted the infidelities of their husbands as a matter of course, no matter how much suffering such philandering might cause. Mothers and grandmothers advised young wives to allow their husbands some latitude. A wife, they said, was the stake to which her husband was tethered by a long rope. If he wandered into pleasant pastures he was bound to return and would give undiminished loving care to his wife and children. A woman should be grateful for this and should learn to pull the rope skillfully enough to prevent too deep an involvement outside his home. Because the performing arts were associated with women of easy virtue, no decent parents would dream of allowing their daughters to learn music, singing, or dancing, no matter how great an aptitude they showed. Love songs, even if they were addressed to the deity, could not be sung by well-brought-up girls. Dance gestures, too easily interpreted as seductive, were unthinkable even within the family circle. Married life was a serious and honorable business which should not be cheapened by the shady frivolity of such arts.

My mother was a strong, healthy girl with large dark eyes, curly black hair, a golden-brown complexion and an affectionate temperament. She soon learned to accept her role as a member of the Handoo family. Her husband, his three sisters, and two brothers were all welcoming and friendly. Her father-in-law was a warm and charming man, but his wife was rather critical and demanding. She was young, fair, and beautiful at that time, but delicate in health. She was still in the child-bearing stage and was constantly either pregnant or nursing a small child, spoiled and fussed over by her husband, always needing rest and care. She soon became very dependent on her new daughter-in-law, along with her own elder daughter, to help with small jobs in the house all day.

18

Boys were never expected to help out with domestic chores. In fact, they were waited on hand and foot by the women of the family. My father and his brothers went to school in the city, where they sat on the floor or on carpets and wrote on planks of wood coated with dried yellow mud. Their pens were reeds cut to certain lengths, pointed and slit to form nibs and dipped in homemade black ink, making the letters stand out in sharp contrast to the yellow planks. At the end of the lesson these planks were washed off and a fresh yellow mud coating was applied to dry in the sun for the next lesson. In the education of boys, there was heavy emphasis on languages, for no young man could get gainful employment unless he knew Urdu, Persian, and Arabic besides Hindi and some English.

Gradually my mother found herself entrusted with a major part of the household responsibilities. At first she only shared in the kitchen work, cutting and preparing the vegetables and serving meals to the younger children. Later she took charge of the cooking, the mending and hand-sewing of clothes, for there were no machines available, the embroidering of saris and shirts, the teaching of the younger children. She accepted all this as natural in a home where she was older, stronger, and more intelligent than the other young girls, and she performed all these duties willingly.

In the normal course of events, she would have returned to her parental home on frequent visits for respite from the relentless pressures of her life in Delhi. But soon after her marriage her father died, leaving her mother with very limited means, a son to educate, and two other daughters for whom dowries, jewelry, and trousseaux would have to be provided. She moved, with her children, into the house of a relative, and could no longer afford to invite her married daughter to visit her. Regrettably, my paternal grandmother never offered to send her daughter-in-law home for a holiday.

The only occasions that lent some color to the uneventful routine of everyday life were the festivals which punctuate the Hindu lunar calendar.

Every year the family guru presented a chart detailing the

festivals, fasts, and religious occasions which should be observed. Almost every month some special day, religious or seasonal, must be celebrated. Some, like the spring festival early in the year, were hardly more than an excuse for young girls to dress up in shades of yellow to represent blossoms of the yellow mustard fields, the first flower of spring, and to show off their finery to their friends. Swings were put up in verandas and gardens, and songs were sung to welcome the spring.

Equally, the Indian New Year, which usually falls in March, was always gay, with new clothes for the elders and the children and special dishes for the midday meal. Holi, which marks the end of spring, was a rowdy, colorful, and lighthearted time, when gangs of boys sprayed colored water or powder on passersby on the streets. Friends visited each other, greetings were exchanged, the younger members of the household squirted the older ones and, in turn, had their own faces smeared with colored powder. Birthdays were celebrated, but rather modestly. There were no "birthday parties," just a special sweet dish made with rice, almonds, plums, and saffron, and served with rich curds, which the whole family enjoyed. The only birthday presents were new sets of clothes.

Most of our festivals are connected with stories from the great epics of India, the *Ramayana* and the *Mahabharata,* and every Hindu boy or girl is taught the significance of each day of celebration and the related story from the epics.

Navrathri, the Nine Nights, ending in Dasera, the Tenth Day, celebrates the battle and eventual victory of the perfect mythological King Rama, hero of the *Ramayana,* over the forces of evil personified by the demon King Ravana. After the nine days of feasting and processions and prayers, on Dasera itself effigies of the defeated Ravana, a monstrous character with twelve heads, are publicly burnt with great rejoicing.

Diwali, the prettiest of the Indian festivals, celebrates the victorious return to their kingdom of Rama and his queen, Sita, the pure, long-suffering, devoted Hindu ideal of a wife. At Diwali, every Hindu home, from the most palatial to the humblest, is lit with strings of lights, small clay bowls filled with oil and homemade cotton wicks; crackers and fireworks explode everywhere. Trays full of sweets are served to the family and sent out to neighbors, and there is general rejoicing at the happy ending of India's best-loved story.

Besides the joyous festivals of those days there were the fasts to be observed. In all homes fasting was considered part of the life of the elders of a family. Some fasts were ceremonial, some religious, and some undertaken with prayer to the gods for some wish to be granted in return. They could last for a day or longer and there were no set rules for them. But a young woman in charge of the daily routine in the family was obliged to remember which one of her elders had to be catered for especially, what was necessary for the observance of each fast or festival, and what prior arrangements she should make for food, flowers, gifts, offerings, so that when the time of the celebration came she would not be disgraced or blamed by her family for negligence.

As my mother grew up into a strong, attractive young woman, her household duties increased even further as the family learned to depend on her more and more. Every evening during the summer months, when rooms the sun had heated all day radiated the heat at night, it was necessary for her, with the help of other members of the family, to carry the light *charpoys* to the terrace, so the family could sleep under the stars. These cots had to be brought down every morning with the bedclothes and put away until it was time to carry them up again in the evening. After the cooking and serving of meals with whatever help was available it was time to settle down to sewing garments for the children, embroidering saris and *kurtas.* Then, of course, there were the younger children to look after.

When she was seventeen, new guidance from her elders began to awaken her to the fact that the boy she had always treated as a brother had, in fact, a different relationship to her. No actual sex education was given in those days, for it was believed that with maturity natural instincts would guide a young couple to discover for themselves the meaning of marital relations. This same pattern continued to my day, and even now,

21

in many Indian homes, sex is never mentioned. Menstruation, the physical changes of adolescence, the development of secondary sexual characteristics were never referred to by the elders. When they decided that the time had come to bring the young couple together as husband and wife, they invited friends and relations to a second religious ceremony conducted by their guru. After this, my parents were assigned a room to themselves and, for the first time, were allowed privacy together—but only at stated hours.

New restrictions were now imposed on them. They were no longer allowed to speak to each other in the presence of their elders, and if one of them wanted to ask a question of the other it had to be relayed through the parents. They could not spend any time together in their room during the day. Only at bedtime, when all the work of the household was done, was my mother given permission to retire. My father, however impatiently he may have waited for his wife, would never have protested to his parents about the long delays. It would have been considered a lack of modesty and decorum for her to retire to their room without permission—no emotion or demonstration of feeling between them was permitted in the presence of other members of the family. Any spontaneous show of affection, even from young parents toward a new baby, was considered improper and strongly discouraged in public.

Soon after my parents had their second "marriage" ceremony, they received an invitation to attend the wedding of one of my mother's cousins in Ajmer, an important railway and administrative center about 250 miles southwest of Delhi. It is easy to understand why they were so excited by the prospect of being wedding guests. For my mother it meant no domestic duties, a real holiday after years of drudgery, and parties with friends and relations whom she had not seen since she first left her mother's home. For my father there would be the added pleasure of spending as much time as he wanted with his wife. He had grown to be a handsome man, tall, very fair, dark-haired, vivacious, and full of the joy of living. My mother, though short in comparison, had beautiful black sparkling eyes and curly hair.

She was more reserved than my father but with a depth of character and an intelligence that gave confidence to those who were close to her and so easily depended on her in all matters of importance. They were, at this time, very happy with each other.

As soon as she received her mother-in-law's permission to go to the wedding, weeks before the date of departure, my mother started making plans for the journey and packing her trunk. For safety's sake, she put all her jewelry into it, wearing only the heavy gold earrings, the typical Kashmiri sign of a married woman, and a thumb ring of gold with a tiny oval mirror embedded in it, called an *arsi*. All young women wore such rings and glanced into the mirror to see that their hair was not untidy, the red *tika* on the forehead or the kohl on their eyelids was not smudged.

As the preparations for the trip were nearing completion, her mother-in-law realized how hard she was going to find the absence of her daughter-in-law, who had become the most useful member of her large household, and how much she had learned to depend on the services she so willingly gave elders and youngsters alike. The evening before my parents were to leave for their holiday, my grandmother began finding reasons for preventing their journey, and after a long argument with her son (for her daughter-in-law had not the temerity to voice her opinion), she laid down her verdict that their journey must be canceled and excuses telegraphed to their hosts in Ajmer.

This was such a blow to their expectations that my stoical mother, who dared not say anything in contradiction to her mother-in-law, burst into tears. Such unbridled emotion so improperly displayed was unheard of in those days, but my father, the eldest and most cherished son of the family, could not bear to see his wife weeping and had the courage to defy his mother. He insisted that they would go to Ajmer no matter what.

Angry and frustrated, my grandmother turned to her son and, according to the story I heard many years later, said, "If you go, I have the right to refuse to allow you to take any of your belongings with you, for until you and your wife are of age all your property belongs to the Handoo family. Bring it all down from your room immediately and I'll lock it up. Then, of course, you will be free to do as you please."

My parents spent a miserable night but they remained determined, and the next morning they came down ready for departure, without luggage, my mother weeping, my father defiant. As they left, my mother stooped to pick up a *lota,* a brass water vessel without which no Indian ever traveled, but her mother-in-law, furious, snatched it from her hand and said, "No, you can't take even this, for it belongs to my family."

They left in an *ikka,* a one-horse vehicle, the cheapest means of transport, for the station. They had already bought their tickets, but because they would need some money for the journey and after their arrival, they stopped at a pawnbroker's. My mother sold the thumb ring she was wearing for fifteen rupees, and it was with that sum that my parents started their independent life together.

CHAPTER 3

THE JOY AND HIGH hopes with which my parents had looked forward to the marriage festivities were badly dampened by their unexpected anxieties. My father immediately began to search for a job. He had already passed the matriculation examination, a great academic qualification in those days, and could speak and write English well, a very useful skill in a country where English was the only lingua franca among dozens of Indian languages and dialects. He was offered a small job by the railway authorities in Ajmer, and accepted it at a salary of fifteen rupees a month. Almost as important as the job itself was the fact that it carried the right to a tenement. Once the wedding ceremonies were over, my parents moved into their new home, and so a new life began for them.

My mother was much too proud to dwell on the hardships, financial worries, and uncertainties of those early years. Probably it would have been easier for them to go back to Delhi, to apologize for their defiance of their elders and receive their forgiveness. But there was a streak of stubbornness and a strong sense of justice in my mother, which armored her against all suffering, so long as she was convinced that she had done no wrong and provided her husband would stay with her. Perhaps a spirit of independence and even of adventure motivated her readiness to face new situations, however difficult. I have never understood from what source she drew her courage—a girl from such a sheltered background, without the smallest knowledge of the outside world. But for her determination, my father might have weakened and returned to Delhi, for he was the pampered and much-loved son of a well-to-do family and was not used to deprivation. And even though my mother was confident of his love and loyalty, still she was afraid that the very simple food, which was all she could afford to serve him, might make him so homesick for the luxurious living of his father's home that he would make her return with him. So she always bought the fine quality of rice and cooked one delicacy every day for him alone, while she subsisted on the coarser and cheaper rice and lentils. She never revealed this to him, but set about equipping her new home with utensils given her by her aunt and collecting sets of clothes for herself and my father from friends.

My father was a very intelligent man with a love of reading. Of all the languages he had studied, Persian was his favorite, and when we were children we loved to hear him recite long passages of Persian poetry. The sound of the language is beautiful, and he used to stop periodically to translate for us and to be sure we understood the rhythmic imagery. My mother on the other hand had never been to school, and her education at home had trained her only in domestic skills, in reading and writing Hindi, and in simple arithmetic. Her reading was confined primarily to the great epics of India, the *Ramayana* and the *Mahabharata.* She was a deeply religious woman, and when she went through periods of anxiety and despair in the early days of her independent life, her faith in God and her own good sense kept her from being overwhelmed by the difficult conditions and unfamiliar problems she had to face in Ajmer.

The first major decision that faced her and my father was whether to accept an offer made by the railway authorities of a transfer to southwest India, where a new extension of the railway was being established. My father at that time was twenty years old and my mother seventeen and a half. Looking back now, it is hard to picture how daunting such an offer seemed. Those Kashmiris who had for generations been established in the North and had adopted the ways of the North Indian communities knew nothing of the South of India. Northerners and southerners spoke different languages, wore different clothes, cooked in different ways, ate different foods, observed different rules and customs in social and religious matters. The climate was vastly different. The intense cold of the North Indian winter and the great heat and dust storms of the summer were unknown to the Southwest. Moreover, all Indians lived and still live, by and large, in tight communities, and any newcomer would find it difficult to fit into and be accepted by the communities of any other part of India. A further hurdle for people brought up in the closely knit joint families of the time was that the distance between them in the South and their relatives and kinfolk in the North was so great that visiting home would entail journeys of six or seven days and nights. The only comfort was that as railway employees these journeys would cost them very little. Perhaps, having made the biggest decision of all when they broke with the family in Delhi, this new uprooting seemed less terrifying. Perhaps a year of living by themselves on my father's earnings, with no outside help, had given them extra confidence. Perhaps my father's prospects for advancement in his work outweighed the misgivings they must have had.

Also they took courage from the fact that two other Kashmiri couples from the Railway Community, one my mother's younger sister, Kailas, and her husband, Niranjainath Hookoo, and the other a cousin of my mother's, Lakshmi, and her husband, Shyannath Gurtu, had also decided to go south because of better prospects. Niranjainath Hookoo was a few years older than my father, better educated, more serious-minded, and intellectually more gifted. He had read about the work done by social reformers of an older generation and was progressive in his thinking. Years later when my mother was also interested in social reforms, he lent her support and encouragement in breaking down old prejudices and outmoded customs.

27

It was a comfort to my parents to think that they would not be going to Hubli, into the wilderness, with no one to help, advise, talk to, and associate with in times of loneliness or distress. But, as it turned out, neither of these families was a source of companionship very long. My mother's younger sister soon died in childbirth and her cousin's marriage broke up in scandal.

In any case, my parents packed their few belongings and left for Hubli, a small town in what is now Maharashtra State south of Poona. When they first arrived, everything around them was strange, new, and exciting, though my mother soon found that friendships would be far from easy to establish for someone who spoke only Hindi. Kanarese was the language of these southerners, and only the working class could manage a few words of Hindi.

Yet life soon took on a new and absorbing dimension for my mother. She became pregnant and looked forward ardently to her first confinement, for which she would, in the conventional Indian way, have to travel north to her mother. Her first child, a daughter, was born in 1883, when she was twenty years old, and to her great sorrow and misery the child lived for three days only. She returned to Hubli sad at heart, but buoyed up by her husband's enthusiasm for his increasingly interesting work and better pay. Two years later her second child was born, also in the North, and she returned this time triumphant, with a lovely little girl, and with added important duties to perform. After that, during the next twenty years, ten more children were born to my parents, in all six girls and six boys, three of whom died in childhood.

My mother had neither the time nor the inclination to seek out a wider world than her family and household provided. Inevitably the horizons of her children were comparably limited. We had no means of knowing about or understanding public affairs, and yet there was an instinctive feeling in all of us that there was more to life than we encountered in our narrow circle. Not that we wanted to launch out on our own, in a spirit of adventure or in defiance of restrictions imposed by elders or society. In fact, a great bond of duty and affection bound us to our home, our parents, our brothers and sisters. Our greatest concern was for their success in all ·their undertakings. I have often wondered, as I look back on my family history, what subtleties of indoctrination or tricks of chance or destiny scattered us across the world and constructed our lives in such astonishingly different designs.

Our days had a certain rhythm and even now remembered details of that long-ago life in our austere and overcrowded house bring back the comforts and excitements of my childhood in Hubli, though I am helpless to explain why they seemed so satisfactory. I would sometimes wake very early in the morning to the sound of my mother chanting prayers or softly singing hymns. She woke every morning at five o'clock, had a cold bath and went into her tiny *puja* room. There she sat on a small square of carpet in front of a shelf holding several images of Hindu gods and pictures of both living and dead saints. She made her token offerings—a couple of flowers, a sliver of coconut—and read from her religious books for half an hour. Then she meditated for a short time and finally recited prayers in the correct chant.

The last verses of her prayers were a signal for all of us to wake up and get dressed. At 6 A.M. she called the older children to their various duties while she looked after the youngest ones and then went to the kitchen to prepare and serve the morning meal. I remember the harsh whisper of the hand mill as one of the maidservants, helped by each of us in turn, ground the wheat each day. I remember the taste of the fresh *chapatis,* the thin unleavened bread, spread with home-churned butter from whatever extra milk our buffalo produced. I remember the special treat of being allowed to lift off the layer of cream which formed on top of the cooled boiled milk, to mix it with sugar and eat the whole rich, delicious mess.

After the birth of her third child, my mother could no longer travel north for each confinement. Without help, heavily pregnant, and with small children to care for, she found the thought of a week-long journey nightmarish. As there were no nursing homes or maternity hospitals in Hubli, all the rest of her children were born in our home with only a *dai,* a midwife with no formal training, to assist her. But she was a strong, healthy woman, and after her first sad confinement, she produced strong, healthy babies. Her three eldest living children were my sisters, Kamala, Bishan, and Kishan, then a boy, Bali, after whom I followed, then my younger sister, Shyama, was born, and after her five boys, of whom one, to our sorrow, lived only a few days. The *dai* charged three rupees for a daughter and five for a son. My mother, who always carried on with her usual household duties right through her pregnancies, could not stay in bed for more than three days after each delivery. She then returned to her normal routine of cooking, cleaning, washing, sewing, marketing, and taking care of her husband and children.

CHAPTER 4

W HEN I WAS YOUNG I took my mother for granted, as most children do. She was the authority in our large and crowded family, and her word was law. She was alert, watchful, and loving, but expected and exacted strict discipline to maintain order in a home in which children of all ages had to be considered. Our welfare was her prime concern, with special emphasis on our health and education. Our activities were tactfully supervised by her constant encouragement to each one of us to confide in her, to relate interesting incidents we might have encountered during the day, quarrels with friends, triumphs or miseries at school.

We believed in her wisdom and accepted without question the rules and regulations she laid down for us. Her pride and satisfaction in our achievements gladdened our hearts, and her disapproval meant we had to strive harder to reach the standards she set for us. The pattern of her ideas for her children had already been set by the time I grew old enough to understand and fully appreciate the codes by which she guided us.

It was not until I was the only daughter in our home that my mother and I became really close. My eldest sister was married when I was six years old, and Bishan and Kishan, my other two sisters, were married when I was thirteen. My younger sister had died at the age of eight. All the other members of my family were boys, one older than myself and the other four younger. There were few restrictions on my brothers' activities. They were allowed to go to the playgrounds or visit friends or join other boys in outings and excursions. But I was allowed only to go to school, return straight home, and care for the younger children in the family. Inevitably my mother became my best companion, and I grew more and more interested in the many and varied incidents in her life as she recounted them to me over the tasks we did together.

Gradually I pieced together the happenings in her story and linked coherently her past narrow orthodoxy with her later mental expansion, the phenomenal progressive growth of her thinking, and the ambitions she developed for her children. Coming as she did from a large joint family, where traditional practices were paramount, where a woman's place was well defined but limited to a domestic circle—the regulation of one's kitchen, obedience to one's elders, care of one's children, observance of religious rites and festivals, attendance at community functions, at the naming ceremony of a baby or the thread ceremony of a boy, arranging of marriages, assessing of dowries received or given, and so on—my mother was unaware of the outer world as she grew to adulthood. She had never met people of other communities (except, perhaps, the servants, who were non-Kashmiris and who only served in the household) and had thus never had the occasion to encounter different views.

It was a three-year-long conversation, frequently interrupted, always resumed in answer to my insistent demand, "Tell me another story." And slowly I learned to respect her courage and strong-mindedness.

She used to say that, in part at least, it was the result of the isolation in which she lived. She had a great deal of time to think. My father was often away; traveling was essential for his work. She was not a demonstrative mother; she didn't fuss and coo

My parents and their children in Hubli, 1895, before the birth of my younger brothers. I am leaning against my father, with my hand on his knee.

over her babies or play games with the small children. Instead, she began to think, question, analyze.

Her reason told her that many of the customs and doctrines which she had accepted as inviolable were meaningless. Her religion taught her that all men were equal. Why, then, should there be a caste system? Why were Brahmins and non-Brahmins not equally entitled to decent treatment and dignity? Why should women be considered inferior to men? Women were capable of handling every sort of problem within the domain of their large households. Why should they not be interested in and consulted about men's work in the outside world? She saw that, among her contemporaries, women clung to old traditions out of fear. They became the custodians of ancient practices, both religious and social, not only from pride in their heritage, but also from terror that their own security, the stability of their society, would be threatened by Western ideas. Very likely it was her solitary thinking through of this thorny position that led her to the most remarkable question of all—why should daughters and sons not have equal opportunities of education and enlightenment?

Father d'Souza, an elderly, gray-bearded, rather portly gentleman, was the priest of the parish and the principal of St. Mary's School in Hubli. He was a Goan Catholic, spoke Hindi, and became intrigued by the only Hindu family living in a Christian enclave and with ways and manners entirely different from those of his parishioners. One day he called formally on my parents. He must have arrived hoping to persuade them to send their children to his school and, knowing orthodox Hindu ways, probably expected firm, even shocked, resistance —especially about the girls. I wish sometimes that I had been present at that scene. It would have been amusing to watch the old man and my parents perched on the only pieces of Western furniture in that spare Indian house, talking at cross purposes and finally realizing that each of them held the most unlikely views.

My mother and, with her insistence, my father had already

34

accepted the idea of formal education for their children even though they had only two of school-going age at that time, both girls. Their chief worry was about the company their daughters would keep at St. Mary's. The school had been established for the benefit of the Anglo-Indian children of the Railway Colony in Hubli. Their fathers were mostly engine drivers, guards, and firemen, and the students were notorious for their fluent use of English slang and swear words. Usually their mothers were Indian, but they identified themselves solely with whatever strain of English blood they could claim, always took English names, and adopted as many of the ways of British life as they could manage. They considered themselves vastly superior to their Indian fellow citizens. My mother in turn considered her family vastly superior to them. Father d'Souza, who surely must have cherished the possibility that he might be able to mold these Hindu children into an acceptance of Christianity, found himself assuring my mother that her daughters would not be required to attend the catechism or Bible classes. She, in turn, replied briskly that she wouldn't think of depriving her children of the opportunity of learning about other religions. A study of Catholicism would only help to widen their vision. She would take care of their Hindu education at home. To this Father d'Souza very sensibly added that she could probably train them in decent Indian manners, behavior, and attitudes too. The ways of their schoolmates need not be a hindrance to their demeanor as respectable young Hindu girls.

Only one problem remained: language. My father was the only member of our family who spoke English. All the rest spoke their North Indian mother tongue, Hindi, but all subjects in school had to be taught in English. With the confidence of wide experience, Father d'Souza told her that language would not prove any great obstacle. Children learned it easily as long as they started young.

My two oldest sisters, Kamala, aged six, and Bishan, aged four, were enrolled in school the following week. They were the first girls of the Kashmiri community to attend school—a coeducational school, at that—the first to be instructed in English, the first to study Christianity, the first to associate with children of all communities and to learn from personal contact the manners and customs of other very different families. To do so was not a matter of pride in those days.

CHAPTER 5

IN THE YEARS that followed, a number of events occurred, some trivial, some tragic, that forced my mother to examine old principles, accepted standards, traditional patterns of conduct. Had she still lived in the cushioned world of a joint family she would never have had to make the kind of decisions that confronted her; neither would she have put her independent mind to work on thinking out the rights and wrongs of long-established patterns of living.

An insignificant incident soon after my sisters started school made her take a small but determining step in the liberation of her thinking. Kamala and Bishan returned home one day complaining not about the language barrier but that the other children laughed at their clothes—the loose trousers, cotton tunics, and bolerolike jackets that all North Indian girls wore. My mother had the choice of taking her daughters out of school rather than allowing them to be figures of fun, telling them to grin and bear the ridicule, or dressing them in English frocks, which, according to the rules of her upbringing, exposed the legs in a thoroughly immodest way. She knew how merciless children can be toward anyone "different" in their circle, but she couldn't afford tailors to make these unfamiliar garments and there were no shops in Hubli that sold them. I daresay that for once she wished she had managed to make friends with her neighbors in the Railway Colony.

However, with considerable ingenuity, she thought up a method of learning something new. She gave a couple of tea parties for her daughters' little classmates and made sure they were served something rather messy to eat, like mangoes, or easily spilled, like one of the more syrupy Indian sweets. She then persuaded them to take off their clean, pretty dresses and petticoats while they enjoyed their tea with as much abandon as they liked. She, meanwhile, took the clothes into another room and quickly cut out paper patterns from them. She had been well trained in cutting and sewing garments in her mother-in-law's house, and that night, after the guests had gone and all the children were asleep, she sat up till the small hours finishing the frocks her daughters would wear to school the next day.

Not long after this time, my grandparents belatedly realized that their son and his wife were reconciled to living away from their relations and the Kashmiri community, that my father was earning enough to support a growing family, that he and my mother were acquiring new interests, and independently planning a future for their children, ignoring family traditions. They decided to bring about a reconciliation and resume contact with their eldest son. They were convinced by then that my parents were not likely to return to the parental home to seek forgiveness or beg for support from their elders. Accordingly, my grandfather wrote to my father, and my grandmother, who had treated my mother so callously, added a note reminding her of the tradition that it was her duty to send a token contribution each month from her son's salary to pay for his mother's *paan supari,* literally her betel leaf and areca nut, though symbolically it stood for her acknowledgment of her duty to her elders.

The one area in which my mother was tradition-bound was in matters where relationship with the elders of her family were concerned. She responded immediately and dutifully sent a small money contribution to her mother-in-law every month, and with that, to all extents and purposes, the rift between them was bridged. Gradually family news began to filter south to my parents. My father's four younger sisters had, in the meantime, been married. The third, Brijkumari, nicknamed Birjo, a little girl when my mother left the house, had been her special favorite. Birjo had been married when she was ten and six months later her husband had died.

Under Hindu law and community tradition, widows were not allowed to marry again. Birjo had only the dismal prospect of growing from a strong, healthy, beautiful child to maturity and to old age carrying the ineradicable stigma of widowhood, though she had never really been a wife. My mother, who had loved Birjo, was greatly distressed by this tragedy. She knew exactly how terrible life would be for Birjo. Her dead husband's parents would be quick to send such a hopeless liability as a child widow back to her own family, and though she would probably be safer there, she could only look forward to living with a hard and dominating mother. Her duties would be around the house, virtually a domestic slave, with no chance of going out without the protection of some elder, and being at the beck and call of her sisters-in-law when her two brothers married. The presence of a widow in those days was considered inauspicious on all festive occasions. At marriage celebrations or other festivities she would be kept in the background, and would always be the last to appear at a reception or party.

Some years later, one of my father's younger brothers fell in love with an Anglo-Indian girl and wanted to marry her. My grandmother was shocked beyond measure. Such a step would ruin the family, she insisted. She would commit suicide, she declared, if her son broke with the family on account of "an Untouchable woman." She succeeded in extricating her son from this romantic entanglement, but she couldn't have got much satisfaction from her victory. This love affair so preyed on his mind that he became melancholic and never again took an interest in work or play, never left his room and ultimately, a few years later, wandered out of the house and never returned.

When I was three months old my maternal grandmother invited all our family to the marriage of my mother's only brother, who was working in Kashmir in the State Government of the Maharaja of Kashmir. Many years had passed since my mother had seen her mother and brother and sisters, and she decided to undertake the long journey with all her children. It was, as usual, a colorful wedding and for her a real homecoming and a wonderfully happy holiday, in spite of the first signs of another pregnancy and the prospect of weaning me, a small baby, and preparing for the next arrival.

It so happened that when my young widowed Aunt Birjo heard that my mother would be returning from Kashmir to Hubli, she wrote to suggest that she should meet us on the way and accompany us to Hubli for a visit with her brother's family. My mother welcomed the suggestion. Apart from the pleasure of having Birjo's company after so many years, my mother would be grateful for the help Birjo would certainly give in taking care of me, the baby, while my mother was preparing for the birth of the next one. Birjo, at that time in her early twenties, took charge of me completely, smothering me with love and rich buffalo milk. The first agreed with me wonderfully well, the second upset my little stomach lamentably.

She stayed with us six months, and became so devoted to me that when it was time for her to leave Hubli she could not bear the thought of parting with me. I was equally devoted to her, for she had given me wholehearted care and attention, and I am sure she meant more to me at that time than my mother did. Just before she was due to leave Hubli she made a serious proposal to my mother: Could she adopt me? She would promise to care for me, to educate me, to give me everything possible for my good, if only my mother would give me to her. My mother had many children and would probably have many more; to part with me would perhaps mean little to my mother but would be the making of her own future life.

Of course it was an impossible proposal. My mother could not give away any one of her children, no matter how many she bore. She often described the heartbreaking scene when my Aunt

Birjo had to part with me. She held me in her arms, sobbing, and I cried to see her distress though I could understand nothing of what was happening. My mother was equally moved, but could not change her mind. At last, Birjo dumped me on a stool and rushed out of the house, where my father was waiting to escort her all the way back to her parents.

Two or three years later my parents heard of her sudden death. Rumor had it that she had become pregnant and had committed suicide with the encouragement if not the connivance of her mother, who could not have tolerated the scandal. My mother remembered with terrible remorse Birjo's last leave-taking and all her sympathies were for the unfortunate girl who could not resist a natural instinct. Birjo's senseless death, more perhaps than anything else, helped to widen my mother's outlook and compelled her to focus her humane intelligence on practices she had accepted from childhood as reasonable and moral. She became convinced that the ancient custom of forbidding child widows from marrying again was pernicious and ought to be abandoned. She even began to wonder whether child marriage itself might not be an evil, though it was many years before she could express so revolutionary a view.

Disaster followed disaster in my father's family. His youngest brother was married to a charming Kashmiri girl; she bore him two children, a boy and a girl. Under the dictatorial regime of her mother-in-law she was subjected to the same observances and requirements of an orthodox home that my mother had experienced. This young woman did not come up to the standard her mother-in-law expected in all matters and was continually plagued by her carping, criticisms, and complaints. This situation began to get on her nerves, especially as she felt she had no ally. Her husband, unlike my father, was not strong enough to stand up to his mother on his wife's behalf. After one serious quarrel with my grandmother she reached the limit of her endurance, poured kerosene on her clothes and set herself on fire. She died a painful death. Once again my mother looked back on the momentous step she had taken years ago of abandoning her home and property in what must have seemed like an explosion of youthful pique and disappointment. Once again she thanked God for a husband who stood by her, supported her, and cheerfully sought a new life for both of them.

CHAPTER 6

IT IS DIFFICULT after such a long time to realize the courage
and the farsightedness of my mother at that time. So much of
what she did in her own small sphere to break the chains of
orthodoxy which she felt instinctively were wrong is now the
most ordinary practice of society. One forgets the almost irre-
sistible pressures on her. She knew that her daughters would
have to be married. No other honorable life was open to them.
She was not yet brave enough (or, perhaps, foolish enough) to
flout the convention of child marriage. In any case she would
find it difficult to arrange suitable matches for them with the new
background they were acquiring in the different surroundings of
Hubli and St. Mary's School.

Marriage to a boy of a lower caste was unthinkable, and of a
different community, impractical. How could one know the
background of a prospective bridegroom unless the complicated network of Kashmiri friends and relations could provide
the necessary detailed information before a final decision was
made? We lived a long way from the rest of the Kashmiri community, and already rumors had spread about the unconventional way in which the young girls of the Handoo family were

being brought up. Naturally enough, my mother's determination to give her daughters an education in school was often shaken by the anxiety of what would happen to them if the community rejected such educated girls and thought them unfit for respectable homes. How, then, would she find good husbands for them within the Kashmiri community?

Whatever uncertainty or misgivings her interior arguments may have caused her, she always presented a calm and confident front to her children. She was a strict disciplinarian, and may well have appeared rather detached from her children, but we all knew that her whole heart and all her time were devoted to the welfare of her family. Most extraordinary was her vigilance over and encouragement of our school activities, even though she herself didn't know what, exactly, a school education required. None of us was ever permitted to skimp on homework. The older ones were expected to help and supervise their younger brothers and sisters. The boys were allowed to take part in the school sports. It was good for their health. The girls had to come straight home and do their share of household chores, looking after the babies, folding and smoothing out the wrinkles in the clothes the servant had washed and dried (we had no iron), tidying the rooms, laying out clean clothing for each child in readiness for the next day. Finally, after we had finished our homework, we could go out to our small garden and play, mainly hopscotch and skipping rope, while we kept an eye on the smaller children.

Any thought of social life with our schoolmates, except for the tea parties to copy dresses, was firmly outlawed. If we had to mingle with Anglo-Indians in the course of our education, that was unfortunate though unavoidable. We certainly did not have to attend the parties and dances that were part of Anglo-Indian life. My mother's idea of a leisure-time occupation was to open one of her big books of epics, the *Ramayana* or the *Mahabharata* in Hindi, lie down on the carpet and start chanting aloud in her beautiful voice. All of us would cluster around her, spellbound by the stories of gods and demons and heroes, listening intently to her explanations of the more difficult passages in the text.

The pattern of living that she imposed on herself and on all her family was simple and rigorous. Rise at daybreak, eat a wholesome meal, work hard all day (work was essential for good health), relax in the evening, sleep at night. The odd thing is that we never resented this spartan regime, never felt abused, never envied our schoolmates—indeed, we felt rather superior to them—and, though we argued with her, we never defied my mother. Above everything else she wanted her children to be diligent and progressive of mind. Her chief dread was that we might give cause for scandal or behave in a frivolous or unbecoming way.

Kamala, my oldest sister, was brighter than any of us at school. She used to carry away so many of the prizes after the annual exams that her teachers called her the "pride of the school." Predictably and promptly, her fellow students called her "P.O.T.S.," not altogether in fun. It was Kamala's future that first presented my mother with the hard choice between reality and painfully formulated social theory.

When Kamala was eleven, my parents traveled north, making some family festivity the excuse for a holiday. They took Kamala with them, a fair, delicate child with enormous brown eyes and an alert, intelligent manner. There they met a Mrs. Kaul, who seemed very taken by Kamala's looks and talk and general deportment. Evidently she decided almost at once to propose her twenty-year-old nephew, whom she had adopted as a son when his father died, as a bridegroom for Kamala.

It was not considered proper by Kashmiri society to approach a mother directly for the hand of her daughter. Accordingly, Mrs. Kaul asked one of my mother's relatives whether she would act as go-between through whom she could send the young man's astrological chart to my mother. Even today it is customary to begin marriage negotiations with an exchange of *nakals*. This provides a convenient opportunity for a girl's elders to inquire into the antecedents, looks, health, behavior, economic position, education, and future prospects of a young man. They may receive several *nakals* and make numerous inquiries through the vast interconnected network of Kashmiri Brahmin families. When they have chosen the most suitable candidate for their daughter, they write to say that his *nakal* tallies with the horoscope of their daughter, and so marriage negotiations may proceed, and they can then gracefully refuse the other proposals by returning each *nakal* with the explanation that the girl's stars are not in accord with the boy's. No one would want to court disaster by pressing for a marriage that might be astrologically uncertain.

When my mother received Mrs. Kaul's son's horoscope, she hesitated for a long time before she could bring herself to consider the proposal. After much thought and many reminders and warnings from friends and relations of how difficult she had made it to find suitable bridegrooms for her daughters, she reluctantly accepted. She was very aware of how many rules of the Kashmiri community she had broken. She herself was young. She had four daughters for whom she must provide Kashmiri husbands, and already objections were being raised to the way she was educating and training them and fears were being expressed as to whether they would fit into orthodox homes on marriage.

The young man, Kishorilal Katju, was well educated, a law student, and owned an extensive landed estate in Gujrat in the Punjab. He was the grandson of Motilal Katju, a learned judge of the Lahore High Court. His father had died young, leaving two sons, the elder of them adopted, and his mother, Mrs. Katju, and a widowed aunt, Mrs. Kaul, who lived in the same house, took charge of the two boys and cared for them. The grandfather, before he died, had divided his money and landed property between the two widows in trust for his two grandsons, who were children at the time of his death. The elder child, Kishorilal, was brought up by Mrs. Kaul, who had adopted him and who moved with him to Gujrat from Lahore, a journey of a couple of hours, where the property left him lay.

She was a powerful, intelligent woman, who was devoted to

Kishorilal and ambitious for him, determined he should follow his grandfather's profession as a lawyer, and perhaps one day, like his grandfather, rise to a judgeship in the Lahore High Court. They lived in a large house in the center of the property in Gujrat, with an orange grove and fields stretching out on all sides where they grew sugar cane, cotton, wheat and corn.

My eldest sister was married to Kishorilal the following year, when she was nearly thirteen years old. Her young husband, aged twenty-one, fell deeply in love with her at first sight. She might in turn have been attracted to him and taken an interest in him if they had been given an opportunity to see more of each other, but she was too much of a child to understand the meaning of an emotional attachment to an adult man whom she scarcely knew even though she was married to him. She called him Bhai Pyaré, Dear Brother, and meant it quite literally. Her mother-in-law made it a point to keep them apart, for fear—as she explained—that the young bride might distract her son from his studies. It was important he should work hard and single-mindedly for his law degree. There were no near Kashmiri neighbors who could be companions and friends to Kamala, nor did the old lady encourage any other girls of her daughter-in-law's age. She expected service from Kamala and gave in return as much loving care as her rigid nature allowed.

Five years went by for Kamala in this great house with no companions of her own age. All her interest was supposed to be concentrated on the dutiful performance of services for her mother-in-law and her household. She received, as well, some teaching in areas that were new to her—the care of the property, the collection of ripe cotton, the setting up of spinning wheels and looms, and the supervision of the spinning and weaving done by the women from the villages around the estate when the cotton harvest was in. Mrs. Kaul was a very able woman and worked hard herself, along with the workers on her land. She controlled the running of the estate, the cultivation and sale of the produce, and the management of the rambling house of twenty-six rooms, where friends and relations were entertained periodically with appropriate formality. Yet no opportunity was given Kamala to make friends with girls she might meet in case they should subvert her mother-in-law's domination over her or make her long for a life of her own.

Using her advanced age as an excuse, Mrs. Kaul arranged that Kamala should sleep by her side, work with her during the day, and get no chance to exchange even a word with the young man to whom she was married. However, knowing Kamala's love for reading, her husband clandestinely passed on to her books in English. She read with avid pleasure Shakespeare, Longfellow, Wordsworth, Tennyson during the time the old lady rested and the household work was over. She had a remarkably retentive memory and memorized pages and pages of poetry that she loved. Even now, Kamala at the age of ninety is able to recite hundreds of lines of different well-known poets that she learned by heart in those days long ago.

In a terrible repetition of my mother's early life, the fact that Kamala became such an important and diligent member of the household made Mrs. Kaul most unwilling to let her visit her maternal home, where Kamala's heart really lay. She was deeply attached to our mother, and the younger sisters and brothers whom she had mothered even at her early age, and she yearned to see those who had been born after she left home. It was a great sorrow to my mother also that years went by and Kamala was growing from childhood to womanhood, and her family, whom she sadly missed, were not allowed to bring her home for visits in spite of their repeated invitations. It was five years later that she did, at last, return to Hubli for a holiday with all of us, and her joy was unbounded. She marveled at the changes that had taken place all around her and saw for the first time the two youngest brothers, who at that time were four and two years old. Five years in the life of a child is a long time and one incident in particular, both funny and sad, of Kamala's first visit home remains vividly in my memory.

Filled with excitement and high spirits we went in full numbers to the railway station to meet the train. My elder sister

Kishan, who had grown tall at fourteen, suddenly decided to pretend to be a lady doctor attached to the Railway Service, to take the temperature of all those arriving from long distances. She bustled into the compartment and peremptorily asked to examine Kamala's pulse and temperature, for which Kamala submissively held out her wrist. She simply did not recognize Kishan until the whole crowd of us burst into laughter at the success of Kishan's brilliantly clever joke. Only Kamala, for a moment, looked unaccountably lonely and left out.

Kamala stayed with us for about six months, and then her mother-in-law summoned her back to Gujrat. This time when she returned to her home the usual *gawna,* or second marriage ceremony, was arranged there, and she was allowed to live a married life with her husband. However, the old rules still applied, and the young couple, as in my mother's generation, were not allowed to talk to each other in their elders' presence and had to wait till after the day was over and the family had retired to find the privacy they longed for. If during the day my sister wished to say something to her husband, it was always said to the mother-in-law, who conveyed it to her son, and the same procedure was followed if the son wished to speak to his wife. For the next few years, again, there was no chance for Kamala to visit all of us.

Meanwhile, my parents were worrying about the marriages of the next two daughters of the family, Bishan and Kishan, aged sixteen and fourteen. Both of them were doing extremely well at school and loved their work. My mother was in favor of their continuing with their studies, and with the urgent encouragement of the principal of the school, Father d'Souza, she was more and more tempted to allow them to sit for the matriculation examination that would entitle them to enter college. But on the other hand, as in Kamala's case, relatives and friends were pressing her to fix marriages for her girls before they were too old or too hopelessly corrupted to be eligible. My mother remembered unhappily that Kamala, who had shown promise of being a scholar, had been deprived of an academic career. But could she take the risk and allow the two younger daughters to postpone marriage and go on with their studies? What fortitude it must have taken to make her decision! Bishan and Kishan stayed on in school, and in the next two years both the girls passed the matriculation examination with credit, which delighted my mother and made her proud of their intellectual achievement, but left her extremely anxious, for it was now even more difficult to arrange suitable marriages for them. Bishan, the elder, was seventeen, Kishan, the next, was fifteen, and most eligible young men were already married or engaged to be married.

She began to spend sleepless nights. Living as far away as she did from the Kashmiri community, she could not meet the right people or allow the elders of families with eligible sons to meet her daughters to prove to them that the education she had given them had not made them unfit for the duties and responsibilities of Kashmiri homes and society. She, as usual, was facing all the problems alone, for my father was still away from home most of the time on duties that required constant traveling.

At that time another painful and humiliating problem arose for my mother. In the course of his journeys in the Goa area my father had met an attractive young woman in whom he had begun to take a great interest. The affair between them had apparently been going on for some time when in the classic, commonplace way, a letter arrived for my father when he was away from home on one of his trips. It was written in Marathi, which has the same script as Hindi though the language is different.

Growing suspicious, my mother opened the letter and struggled through the message. She could not understand the letter word for word, but she got the gist of it. The young woman was thanking my father for his gift of gold bangles—a gift particularly hurtful to my mother; gold bangles are always given to a girl at her wedding. My mother had never suspected that my father could be unfaithful to her. Not unnaturally, she was furious and when he returned home there was the most unholy row, which we children overheard without fully grasping the reason for it. Clearly our father had done something frightful and was pleading for forgiveness and promising to make amends.

Although she was sure that with her as the pivotal force in the family, his interest in the young woman could only be of short duration, still the sense of betrayal lingered. Even if the incident had not occurred, in a home where the family is large and the responsibilities of the parents many, problems are certain to arise that seem insoluble at the time and cause distress and even despair. On one such troubled occasion, when my father was out of town and my mother was pregnant with her twelfth child, she was so depressed that she left the children and her worries and went for a walk to calm her mind and think out her situation quietly and alone. She walked to a deep pond and sat by the edge of it, wondering if it would not almost be easier to end it all in the water by which she sat.

Suddenly she looked up and there before her stood a tall, elderly, bald-headed man wearing a loincloth and a cotton shawl. There was, she felt, a radiance about him, and automatically she stood up and spontaneously bent to touch his feet. She did not or could not say a word, but he turned gentle eyes on her and said, "Go home. Your children need you." Somehow this cleared her troubled mind and she came back calm and resolute and ready to face all the difficulties with which she was burdened.

After that encounter she, and all our family too, became devotees of this holy man and traveled three miles every Sunday to touch his feet and ask for his blessing. When my mother met him, Shri Sidh Arur Swami had just returned from the jungle, where he had lived the life of an ascetic for years, meditating and gaining spiritual experience. Having attained enlightenment himself, he returned to the nearest town, Hubli, and was living in the hut he had built near the pond where my mother had gone to think out her dark mood. By then he was ready to teach those seeking help and extend his blessings and comfort to those in trouble. Every Sunday he expounded Vedantic philosophy to those who came to him, and during the following years more and more devotees sought him out for his wisdom and his philosophic discourse. In time they built an ashram to accommodate the thousands of his followers.

To her dying day my mother's faith in his teaching never flagged, and whenever she faced trouble she prayed to him for help, even after his death at a great age. His biography, written in Marathi by one of his disciples, mentions my mother and her devotion to the saint and the spiritual uplift she derived from her weekly visits to his ashram.

Throughout this trying period in my mother's life, she was plagued by yet another nagging worry, one she could not help feeling she had brought upon herself. After both my sisters had successfully passed the matriculation examination, both were understandably eager to go on to college. The nearest college to Hubli was in Poona, a twenty-four-hour train journey from Hubli. If Bishan and Kishan were to go to college they would have to live in a women's hostel. Sadly, my parents balked at the idea of sending two young girls so far away from home, probably ruining their reputations (who could know how carefully they would be chaperoned?). Besides, there was the prohibitively high cost of college education and hostel living to be considered. The only alternative course my parents could think of was marriage, and negotiations were begun with friends and relatives to find suitable matches.

They were by this time eighteen and sixteen and considered old to be brides. Fortunately, young men were gradually beginning to delay their marriages, some even till they had completed their college education and were either newly employed or looking for jobs. In time my sisters got engaged and were married at a double ceremony in Kanpur in North India to men they had never met.

Although according to our custom girls are married in their parental homes, for my sisters an exception had to be made. We lived too far away for North Indian bridegrooms, their relatives and friends, or even our own relatives and friends, to attend in the proper way. Besides, we couldn't arrange the correct festivities and dinners when there was no Kashmiri community in the South, apart from our own family, to attend the celebrations. My mother had a cousin in the North who offered to find suitable accommodation for my parents and their relatives and arrange for the parties of the two bridegrooms in his own home town of Kanpur. My parents traveled with our whole large family, as we were all entitled to free passes on the railway. Bishan married Dwarkanath Razdan, employed by the North Western Railway, and Kishan married Chandramohan Nath Sharga, a district officer in the Government.

CHAPTER 7

WHEN WE RETURNED to Hubli from the weddings, I was fourteen years old, the only daughter in our home, for my youngest sister had died at the age of eight. I had five brothers, all of us were at school, and my mother still cooked for all the family and called upon me to help with housework after school hours. I still remember that most of my evenings were spent darning my brothers' socks and stockings, which were always in need of repair because of their violent enthusiasm for the sports they played.

This was the period when, after school and during holidays, I spent so much time alone with my mother and learned so much about her life and thinking. She did not encourage friends and visitors to our home. Language and the difference in her ways made a barrier she found insurmountable. The close association of those years created a bond between us, and her readiness to share her thoughts and discuss problems, both domestic and social, filled me with deep affection and respect for her views and general approach to life. I know she loved me with a great warmth though she never made a fuss over me or applauded any success I may have had either in school or at home.

From the age of four I had been expected to take life seriously and was no longer considered a baby. All the same, when my mother had decided that I was old enough to be entered formally as a pupil in the school, I had been filled with fear. I had once been taken to visit my elder sisters' classes and had seen a long cane on the teacher's table and a flat ruler which was used to strike children on the knuckles for naughtiness or mistakes they made in their lessons. On that first day of school I remember crying copiously and resisting strenuously all efforts to keep me in my classroom when my sisters left me to join their own classes. It took me a long time to realize the menacing long cane was not used indiscriminately as part of school work, and I gradually began to look on it with less apprehension.

English was the medium of instruction, and as my eldest sisters and my brother had already acquired some fluency in the foreign language, it did not take me long to pick it up in school, and as I grew older I developed, like Kamala, a love of reading. Education at that time was based on the system devised in the days of Lord Macaulay, who had played an important part in framing the educational policy for India in 1835, when it was generally believed by those in authority that the whole of India with her teeming millions would one day abandon all the languages indigenous to the various states of the country in favor of the English language. There was also, we always thought, the hope among the British that, with the spread of education, conversion to Christianity was bound to follow. Under this educational policy, even the textbooks for primary and secondary schools were the same as those used in England. Rows of brown-skinned, dark-haired children sat in classes all over the South learning to read with an alphabet book which began, "A is for Apple," and wondering what on earth an apple might be.

Nothing that we learned in school was related directly to India and the Indian scene in which we lived. Even our history books allotted only the first twenty or thirty pages to describe the long and tumultuous centuries of Indian history. The rest were devoted to a detailed account of happenings in England from A.D. 1066. We learned, as we got older to recite the names of the dynasties that ruled over England; we could name the wives of Henry VIII; we read with horror of Bloody Mary, the strife between Catholics and Protestants; we marveled at the glorious deeds in the reign of Elizabeth I; we studied the succession of English monarchs, right down to the reign of Queen Victoria. We were barely acquainted with King Ashoka, the Mogul Empire, Akbar the Great, or the world-shaking events during the early years of our own history, centuries before 1066. We were taught the literary works of English poets, dramatists, and prose writers from the days of Chaucer, but not a word did we learn of Indian authors, ancient or modern. Laboriously we memorized the names of English flowers—the daffodil, the tulip, the crocus, the lavender—flowers we never expected to see, but we knew nothing of the flowers that grew in our back garden and were unable to name any of our great variety of trees, except perhaps the great banyan because of Buddha's association with it, and the mango on account of its annual delectable fruit. Whatever we learned of our own country was through educated elders, who had no power to change the curriculum prescribed for schools, but could supplement our education with whatever they knew of Indian history, Indian traditions, Indian culture, and might create in us a desire to seek information that was not to be found in our schoolbooks.

It seems strange to me, now, that as we progressed in school we never gave a thought to the anomaly of an English education against the background of our strongly traditional Indian family and the learning we absorbed there. We kept the two forms of knowledge we gained in our ordinary daily routine in separate compartments. The subjects I was taught in school were English, French (thanks to our good French teacher, Father d'Souza, who had been brought up in Mauritius), mathematics, history, geography and astronomy. I learned my multiplication tables standing in line with my classmates in two rows with the teacher walking up and down between the rows and all of us chanting in a singsong, "Twice one are two, twice two are four," and so on, learning by heart until we reached "twelve times twelve." Progressive education was, of course, unheard of in the early years of this century.

Since reading was important to me and there were no Hindi libraries in South India, I devoured every English book I could lay my hands on. Inevitably, English gradually become more important to me than Hindi, for there was so much more to explore through the English language. The school had a very limited library and the Railway Institute, a sort of social center to which all railway officials belonged, had a small lending library. They provided me with countless hours of pleasure and excitement. A totally undiscriminating reader at first, I devoured quantities of poetry—Tennyson, Wordsworth, Keats, Shelley, Shakespeare—memorizing long passages that I found especially moving and beautiful. Whatever novels were available—Jane Austen, Charles Dickens, William Thackeray, George Eliot, the Brontës—I read with the same uncritical absorption. It never occurred to me that all the time I was learning many aspects of Western culture, I was putting together a picture of the English countryside, of the ways and manners of the people who lived in that far-off land, of what they valued and what they hoped for and what they feared. I never identified myself with either the authors or their characters. Their whole way of living, their expressions of feeling, sometimes embarrassingly frank, sometimes inexplicably reticent, were too remote for any intimate involvement. If anything, all my reading made me more emphatically Indian, though I came to love the English language and its literature.

At that time I had never heard English spoken by Englishmen and women. All our teachers in school were Indian, and the few Englishmen who were the top officials of the railway were too high and mighty to have any contact with the families of the Indians who worked for them. As for the English women, they were even more distant from the "natives" than their menfolk. The English people in India seemed to have no relationship with the English writers and their fictional characters who so enthralled me. I saw nothing unusual in the curious triple existence I led, conforming to certain Western standards required in school, plunging back into an Indian atmosphere the moment I came home, shedding my shoes, stockings, and Western frock, and all the time the world of my imagination was peopled by Elizabeth Bennet and Darcy, Romeo and Juliet, Silas Marner and Little Eppie. The strange thing was that there seemed to be no clash or psychological repercussions from accepting all these standards simultaneously.

My only other contact with the Western world came at Christmastime. Father d'Souza never failed to invite us to the big party he held on the 25th of December and easily persuaded each of us to carry away some of the cakes, sweets, and fruit that Christian members of his congregation had presented to him. Another great Christmas party was given by the railway officials at the Railway Institute—a party to which all the railway officials contributed. There a tree was set up in the conventional British way and hung with shining baubles and tinsel, with an angel as the topmost decoration. The drab hall looked festive—beautiful, to our eyes—and there was always a present for each of us under the tree. The party was the highlight of the year, and we looked forward to it for months beforehand. These were the only two occasions in the year when we joined our schoolmates in a party spirit, feasted and played games together, admired the baby Jesus in his crib, and sang Christmas carols with the rest.

I did well at school and, like my sisters, won many prizes at our annual school functions. At fifteen I appeared for the matriculation examination in Bombay, a twenty-four-hour journey from Hubli, but our nearest center for university examinations. I had traveled by train before to weddings and sometimes during school holidays, when my father had work in Goa and took a few of us with him for company. I loved the sights of the seaside town, the rocky coastline, the ships in the harbor, the fishermen busy with their nets on the beach, and, most of all, the open ocean and the waves crashing upon the shore. Once we even dared to look for a hidden cove where, fully dressed, we dipped into the surf, exclaiming about the nasty taste of the salt water.

But Bombay was altogether a different experience. The capital of Bombay Province and the first large city I had ever seen, it filled me with awe and admiration. Between the wonderful old Victorian buildings the roads were all surfaced and jammed with traffic—the one-horse hackneys that we called "victorias," the more dignified broughams, a few cars, the rackety trams, the bullock carts, handcarts, and, of course, thousands and thousands of pedestrians.

My examination was held in the Bombay University Hall, one of the most imposing buildings, and lasted a week. Every morning my father accompanied me to the hall, bought me a sandwich and some fruit for lunch, and fetched me again at five in the evening. We were staying with friends of his family, and he made a point of driving me home by the beautiful new road that had been built along the curve of Bombay's back bay. I thought it more sophisticated though not, perhaps, as romantic as the seafront in Goa. As a treat he sometimes stopped to buy me an ice cream, a most exotic and delicious new taste. I returned to Hubli feeling immensely important, with all the new experiences I had acquired.

Even before my examination results were announced my father was informed that he was to be transferred to Madras. The Southern Mahratta Railway for which he worked had bought the Madras Railway, and since Madras had larger offices and was a far more important city on the southeastern coast of India, the main administrative offices were shifted there. It was a great upheaval. My parents had lived in Hubli for nearly twenty-seven years and, not surprisingly, my mother was rather daunted by packing for the large family, reorganizing the education of the children, and starting all over again to make a home in a city she had never even visited.

As a college student, age 17

CHAPTER 8

V ERY SOON AFTER our arrival, someone told us that Madras was known to have only two seasons—hot and hotter. It was easy to believe. After Hubli's dry and temperate climate, we thought we would never get used to the unvarying humid heat of Madras. In those early days of our life there, all of us were struck by the differences we noticed everywhere in dress, looks, language, manners, habits, food, transport—just about everything. I had never, for instance, seen a ricksha pulled by a coolie, and I was horrified that human beings could be used in such a manner and that people riding in rickshas could be so matter of fact about the whole arrangement.

Like many North Indians, our first impression of Madrasis was that they were uncouth and immodest in their dress and ways. Women walked about the streets unchaperoned, wearing bright-colored saris with nothing, not even the ends of their saris, to cover their heads, and no sandals on their feet. The working women often went about without a *choli,* the tight little blouse we always wore under our saris. They simply tucked their saris tightly around their bodies to cover their breasts but left their backs exposed. The men's appearance shocked us almost as much. Instead of the shirt, *dhoti,* and turban that we were used to seeing in Hubli, most Madrasis wore *lungis,* like waist-to-ankle sarongs, with a towel flung over one shoulder—bare-bodied, bareheaded, and barefooted.

Often as I stood watching the workmen and women carrying great loads or drawing handcarts that were heavily piled with bricks or bamboo or bulging sacks, I was astonished to see their lean bodies, shining black skins wet with perspiration, and marveled at the stamina of people who could carry such burdens under a burning-hot sun. So much near-nakedness was never seen in Hubli, nor were the working classes, as far as I can remember, able or required to perform such feats of strength.

The city itself, however, made up in elegance and beauty for all the surprising and often unpleasant sights that first caught our attention. Madras Presidency, at that time, included the present states of Tamil Nadu and Andhra Pradesh, a very large section of British India, and its capital was the third-largest city in India. Madras, the oldest of the "modern" cities, had grown from a collection of fishing villages into a valuable port for the trade of the East India Company before the military conquest of India by the British. Remnants of its importance as a garrison town in the days of Clive are still vividly evoked in the museums, the old church, and the houses of Fort St. George, built to command the harbor. More recent and more magnificent are the Victorian Gothic extravagances of Madras's High Court buildings, Government House, the residence of the state Governor, and the many colleges of Madras University stretching along the city's extraordinary and beautiful seafront. Miles and miles of gleaming white sands extend north and south of the city, and in the evening all of Madras seems to pour out onto the beach to stroll in the brief coolness of evening.

Immediately after we arrived in Madras, my parents looked for accommodations in the suburb of Perambur, where the railway offices were placed. My father found a comfortable house with a reasonable rent opposite a large coconut grove. Although I was disappointed that we were far from the sea, we were all charmed with the house and its surroundings. I had never seen a coconut grove, and I found it delightful to wander under the tall, graceful trees laden with fruit and watch the men climb the smooth trunks either to collect the coconuts or to attach earthen pots to the sprouts to collect the toddy. The men were small, lithe, and agile and, using two woven loops to grip the trunk, one for the feet and one around the shoulders, with a belt holding a large clay toddy pot, they climbed tree after tree to dizzying heights in what seemed to me a most perilous undertaking.

Another strong memory of the coconut grove is my first sight of the full moon gilding the tops of the coconut leaves and the gentle clicking of the fronds in the night breeze when all the day noises were stilled. Our house had an open terrace where we used to sleep under the sky on mattresses we carried up each night. This was a common practice in the summer months in the North India of our parents' youth, but I and my brothers had never slept in the open, as the climate of Hubli did not allow it. I came to love these very ordinary pleasures that were part of our new life.

The great excitement of that time, as I remember, was watching Halley's comet, faint, as small as a hand when it first appeared, growing in size night after night till it swept across the sky, thrilling and beautiful in its grandeur. Its bright glory lives with me still, after all these years.

It was holiday time when we moved to Madras, and my brothers Bali, Ram, Hari, Shri, and Gopi were all at home. As I was the closest in age to my eldest brother, Bali, we had much in common, though I always looked up to him as wiser, more experienced and more sophisticated than I ever expected to be. He was always protective of me, determined that I should continue with my studies and not be maneuvered into an early marriage. He promised me that he would persuade our mother to allow him to change his university from Bombay to Madras so that he could act as my guardian, protect my interests, and bolster up my courage if it showed signs of failing. When the results of the matriculation examination were published, we were not too surprised that I had passed, but, astonishingly, I had won the Parmanand Mahadev prize for standing first in English in the whole province. Naturally my ambition for a university education soared.

Immediately my father and Bali approached the Madras University authorities to allow him to transfer from Bombay University and for recognition of the Bombay matriculation exam for my admission to one of the Madras colleges. It took some time to sort this out, as the standards of the various universities in India differed and the courses required were not uniform. With some difficulty and much argument the recognition was granted and Bali and I were both admitted to the Presidency College in Madras.

While these negotiations were in progress, a great event had been arranged to take place in Madras. The National Congress, the organization for political and social reform which met every year in a great convention in a different city of the country, was to be held in Madras. The papers were full of the importance of the occasion, and my father managed to get tickets for my brother and me to attend the Congress session. It was my first contact with public affairs and my first view of men and women in public life. I was thrilled beyond measure that so much fire was brought to the dialogues between Indian politicians and the representatives of the British Government and by the discovery that demands for political reforms and for India's right to home rule had been going on for years while we, living in Hubli, were ignorant of this whole crucial area of national activity.

Bali and I went to the crowded meetings and picked out the leaders we recognized—Sarendra Nath Bannerji, Rash Behari Ghosh, G. K. Gokhale, and a number of others—but most important to me at that time was Sarojini Naidu. A slim, small, vivid figure, beautiful and intensely alive, she was known as the "Nightingale of India" for her exquisite poetry. She sat at the back of the platform until she rose to speak, and as she came forward I trembled to think that it was her turn to address the huge audience and compete with the elderly, self-assured men who had preceded her. But as soon as she began I was filled with admiration for her poise, her effortless eloquence, her low and dramatic voice, which carried to the last seats of the vast hall. I was proud that so young a woman could command such respect from her older and more experienced colleagues and could stir her audience to resounding applause.

This Congress session was my first introduction to the problems, both political and social, of my country. To me, the most astounding and personal new vision came with the realization that I was not one of the first generation of Indian women to aspire to higher education. Women older than I had already taken professional degrees and were working as doctors, lawyers, and teachers. Though they were only few in numbers and communications in India were difficult and slow, still we heard something about the social changes that were making an impact, however limited, on orthodox society in different provinces of the nation.

As I became more confident in the big-city currents of life in Madras, I was determined to learn as much as I could about these pioneers and their work in the emancipation of women, and I date from that time and the incentive their courage provided my own drive to work in social welfare and the women's movement. The first step for me was to get a higher education. How easy that sounds nowadays! If my parents had not moved to Madras, I, like my sisters, would have had to give up the hope of a university education, since it would have required my living in a hostel in a distant town. Even in Madras University there were no women's colleges, and the women students in the only colleges that accepted them at all were greatly outnumbered by the men.

In 1909, the year I entered the Presidency College, there were only two other women students in my class. The total number of women was eleven among six or seven hundred men. It was quite hazardous for young women to stay the course for a university degree because they were behaving so contrary to the usual social pattern that even young men students resented their presence in classes. Many of the boys enjoyed harassing women students, although the professors, both European and Indian, made special provision for women by allowing them separate

65

seating accommodation in the lecture rooms and providing other facilities to protect them. My parents, in spite of the stories they heard, still wanted me to have a university education. Theirs was a brave decision to make in those days, for the reputation of a girl had to be guarded in every way. One false step, however innocent, could make her the subject of scandal. No woman student would walk the corridors of the college alone, even on an errand as blameless as getting a book from the library. She would have to be accompanied by another woman student lest she become the target for gossip amongst the men: Was she going to an assignation? Why else was she by herself?

The year before I entered college, a senior woman student was subjected to so much annoyance by her men fellow students that she complained to the principal, who reprimanded them. In retaliation a group of the men immediately formed a "K" (the woman in question) persecution society and made life miserable for her, not by molesting her directly, but by following her every time she appeared, waiting at her house till she left in the morning, cycling along beside her conveyance to college and back to her home after classes. Her life became a nightmare for the rest of her career in college. Very similar behavior was accorded me, for I was the only Indian girl in my class. The two others were both Anglo-Indians, who did not attract so much notice from Indian men students. With my brother Bali accompanying me to college and back to our home, I was more protected than poor "K" and did not suffer quite so much unwanted attention. All the same, I never dared sit on the gallery benches with the men students or enter a classroom until the professor had arrived and one of the college servants had provided chairs next to the professor's platform for us.

In the early days of my college career, Bali and I had a shattering experience that nearly caused my parents to withdraw me from college. I received a letter from a classmate who lived in the Presidency College hostel expressing great admiration for me. He was lyrical about my good looks and said he craved an appointment as soon as I could manage it. This letter scared me and I immediately showed it to my brother. He never mentioned

66

it to anyone. A few days later I received another letter, even more ardent and poetical. I did not know the young man, even by sight, though his name was regularly called out when the professor took the roll call. I handed this letter also to Bali. He was greatly annoyed and cycled off to the college hostel to confront the student and ask if he had really written those letters. The young man admitted it and added, "I have fallen in love with your sister and my intentions are perfectly honorable." At this brazen attitude Bali struck him and told him not to harass me in the future.

This caused an incredible furor in the college hostel, some students supporting the young man, but the majority on my brother's side because the other student had transgressed a recognized social code. My brother was threatened with a court case for assault, which upset my father because my name would be dragged in if the case came to a hearing. My mother was ready to withdraw me from college, and my brother wondered how big a fine he would be required to pay. He could not deny that he was definitely guilty of assault. We were all much relieved when we heard that the young man had decided to withdraw the case. There were other incidents of like nature, but I prudently ignored them and never reported them to any member of my family.

Even so, there were times when my mother wondered if she was wise in letting me take the risk of scandal that might injure my future. But I ached to go on with my education, and she, with what misgivings I can only imagine, encouraged me and helped me whenever I got despondent about the false gossip that was reported back, in spite of all our precautions. Luckily, my family came from the North, and, since we did not fit into any caste group in Madras and had no close social contacts with the families of my friends at college, the talk about me was not quite so damaging. Yet it was not very long before members of the Kashmiri community in the North heard stories of a young Kashmiri girl mixing closely with other young women of several different castes and working with men students. Friends deplored the fact that my parents were not arranging a marriage for me when I was already sixteen. Was it possible that I meant to continue my education for several years, till my college career was over, before a match could be found for me?

My mother's desire that her daughters have an education equal to that of her sons was so great that when the talk reached her it did not influence her. In this her views were far more advanced than those of most women her age, and her regret was only that her three married daughters had not had my opportunity for higher education.

I had started college with my mind filled with thoughts of what would be most useful in helping my contemporaries to carry on work for changes in our social system. I decided that a science course would be of the greatest practical value, and elected to take physics, chemistry, biology, zoology, and physiology, besides English and French, intending to enter the Medical College.

Before I qualified, however, my mother discovered that there was no women's medical college in Madras, and the women students in the men's Medical College had an even more difficult time than we did in the Presidency College. She heard that indecent and vulgar practical jokes were played on them, and this was enough to induce my parents to decide that I should give up all hope of becoming a doctor. I was bitterly disappointed, but realized that my parents' liberal approach to my education had already been stretched as far as I could reasonably expect. Besides, Bali, my ally and protector, had completed his B.A. degree and was soon to go abroad to study medicine at Edinburgh University. Therefore, for my second year I enrolled in the English honors course, based on the Cambridge University degree courses. This meant the study of Anglo-Saxon, Gothic, Old English, Middle English, Philology, and Modern Literature, specializing in the Elizabethan period.

Before going to Europe Bali traveled north to see his three married sisters. He knew that he would be away for years and wanted to bid them more than a casual farewell by letter. Bali had a sharp, unsentimental eye and during his visits to his sisters observed and fixed in his memory the difficulties that they faced in their homes. Our eldest sister, Kamala, although she did not live in a conventional joint family with a host of relatives, still followed her mother-in-law's very strict discipline. She spent all her time looking after their estate, while her husband was building up his law practice. She had no friends and no entertainment in the small town of Gujrat where they lived. He was reckoned to be a very good lawyer but depended entirely on Kamala for much of the writing and copying necessary for his work because, he said, he could trust her accuracy ahead of any clerk's. This meant that, besides the work of her household and the affairs of the estate they owned, she had to write pages and pages of legal briefs and notes for her husband. It was exceedingly tedious work, and she never developed any real interest in legal matters.

Bali next went to our second sister Bishan's home in Lahore. She and her husband were living in a large joint family where his eldest brother, much older than her husband, was the head of the household. The family had to conform to his ways, and though there were no open clashes, Bali was acutely aware of the irritating restrictions on their freedom, the maddening demands on Bishan's time, and her unflagging efforts to curb her independence of spirit for the sake of harmony in the large family to which she belonged.

Last, he visited our third sister, Kishan, whose husband was a giant of a man over six feet in height, with a black, volcanic temperament. He was a cruel man to whom physical violence seemed a perfectly acceptable part of married life. He criticized everything his wife did, insisting that the women of his own family could always do it better. He was a Government district officer in the United Provinces, traveling and living in the small towns within his jurisdiction. He imposed purdah on Kishan, a custom, adopted from the Muslims, of keeping women in seclusion, veiled from the sight of all men except their blood relatives and husbands, and he confined her to the house, where she was expected to cook and clean and prepare new and fancy dishes for him, for he claimed to be a gourmet. He genuinely believed that she was only dutifully carrying out her responsibilities and deriving happiness from the service she gave him. Kishan was a clever girl, grasped ideas quickly and enthusiastically, loved to read, and longed to improve her mind, but this ambition was derided and ridiculed by her husband. She was, however, inescapably married to him, and duty demanded that she make no complaints. Bali watched this wretched relationship with greater and greater despair.

He returned to Madras after these visits greatly disturbed and determined that I, his youngest sister, should be safeguarded from such a situation. He made my mother promise not to arrange a marriage for me till he came home. He wanted a voice in the matter, and he assured her that he would choose a husband for me himself after his return from Europe, for he wanted me to marry a man who would have a wider vision and a more modern outlook on life than he had found in his sisters' homes. After his departure, I went on with my college work, returning home each evening to help my mother care for my four younger brothers, who were all at school.

CHAPTER 9

SOON AFTER I STARTED college I entered a much larger social circle than the circumscribed group among whom we moved in Hubli. Apart from the young women students in the Presidency College, now thirty-three in all (among approximately a thousand men students), I met other women who shared my interest in social-welfare work, and I greatly admired those few who had already acquired the qualifications for professions in both the medical and educational fields. Once a year the British Governor of Madras Presidency and his wife invited important officials to celebrate the King Emperor's birthday at a large garden party, very much on the lines of the annual reception at Buckingham Palace. To this party not only the Government officials but also a large number of the elite of the town received invitations, as did the prominent figures of trade and industry. These were formal, stiff occasions, with ADC's introducing long queues of guests to their excellencies, who were almost as surrounded by ceremony as their majesties the King Emperor and Queen Empress of England.

My parents, Bali, and I had attended these parties, and at first their chief interest was that they provided our only direct contact

The full roster of women students at the Presidency College, Madras, in 1909. There were 700 men students enrolled at the time.

with those mysterious people, the British. Not long after Bali left, a new Governor was appointed to Madras. Lord and Lady Willingdon brought a refreshingly new approach to the people they had to govern. They were dismayed to find that there was so little social exchange between the Indian and the British communities. The British had a very conservative and restricted society, with most of their leisure-time activities centering on clubs to which no Indians were admitted. Indian men, in turn, had formed their own clubs, where they met every day for relaxation, conversation, and sports. Indian women were left out completely. Apart from a few groups engaged in social-welfare work, Indian women had no clubs and no idea what club life for recreation meant.

Lady Willingdon soon sized up this situation and recognized the need of educated Indian women for a place to meet each other as well as the British women who had always kept their distance from us. She established a Ladies' Club, became its chief patron, and, unlike all other governors' wives, invited Indian and British women to take tea with her at the club.

Because Lady Willingdon was the Governor's wife, the British women, however scandalized, couldn't refuse her invitations, and the Indian women, from curiosity if nothing else, didn't refuse. Even more extraordinary, she frankly suggested that Indians return her invitation. In such an unusual and liberal atmosphere the Ladies' Club quickly flourished. The sponsorship of the club was so indisputably respectable and its purpose so properly progressive that my mother allowed me to go there once a week. She always came with me even though she still could not speak English or Tamil, the language of Madras. She had met a couple of Muslim ladies who could speak Hindi and would sit chatting with them while she watched me playing badminton or ping-pong or talking to the other members.

It was at the club that I met a young, fashionable woman (by "fashionable" we only meant "Westernized"). She was about my own age and the wife of a leading lawyer in the Madras High Court. I admired her greatly for her vivacity and cheerful self-confidence, and we became friendly. One day she invited me to a dinner party at her home. I was longing to go, but my mother had many reservations. An afternoon safely chaperoned at the Ladies Club was one thing, but for a girl to go out alone after dark was quite different. It took a great deal of persuasion before my mother gave me her consent, provided I would take our woman servant with me in our carriage and let her wait till the party was over, to accompany me home.

Only when I arrived did I discover that the party included several British and Indian High Court judges, lawyers, and their wives, and that the table had been arranged in the European style, with different knives, forks, and spoons and glasses of all descriptions. Never having been a guest at a formal European meal before and not knowing the correct use of Western crockery and cutlery, I felt very nervous because the guests were important people and all used to European ways. I happened to sit next to a judge of the High Court who would certainly know how to manage all these baffling implements, so I thought that the best thing to do would be to follow him carefully and copy him exactly. I found eating in that way most difficult, trying to serve myself and cut my food with my left hand, and wondered why it was not considered easier to use one's fingers as we always did at home. Toward the end of the meal, to my acute embarrassment, I discovered that the gentlemen I was imitating was left-handed. I had been doing everything wrong at the table, and only the courtesy of my fellow guests kept my humiliation from becoming a hilarious joke. I have never forgotten the misery I suffered, though now we laugh about it. When the party was over and all the guests were leaving, there was my woman servant waiting on the veranda to accompany me home, although the carriage belonged to us and the coachman was an old, trusted man who had worked for us for some years.

In 1913 my second brother, Ram, a very promising student, went to Edinburgh University to join Bali, although Ram would be studying law. Our family now consisted of my parents, me, the eldest, and three younger brothers all at school. In 1916 my sister Kishan, who had two children, a boy of three and a half and a girl eighteen months old, died of a miscarriage. She had

74

never complained of the cruelties she had endured during the years of her marriage. She knew my parents could do nothing to help her, and except for Bali's disturbing report after his brief visit to her, none of us had any reason to think that her marriage was exceptionally thorny. Certainly she would never have thought of separating from her husband permanently. A broken marriage in those days was a social stigma that would affect not only her but her whole parental family, who would be held responsible for such rebelliousness, self-indulgence, and inability to shoulder her proper burdens. On one occasion she had managed to get away from her husband for a few months. In a freakish moment of generosity he had consented to her going to Benares to teach at a new boarding school where she was allowed to have both her young children with her. This was a happy time for her, living in a normal, busy atmosphere, among educated women, and with the sympathetic and intelligent company of Padmabai, the principal of the school. Padmabai became a great friend and the only person in whom she could confide some part of the sufferings that had driven her from her home. In this matter even Padmabai couldn't help her—a sadness she was to describe to me many years later.

When the long school vacation approached, Kishan wrote to my mother, asking if she could visit us in Madras. My mother, unaware of her trials in her husband's home, chided her and replied, "You have spent a whole term away from your husband. How can you now ask if you may come to us in Madras? Your duty, my dear child, is to go back to your husband." Kishan did go back and soon after became pregnant again, had a miscarriage—we never knew why—developed septicemia, and died. My eldest sister, Kamala, from Gujrat, rushed to her bedside, and during the last few days of her life Kishan related the hardships she had had to bear. This tragedy was a life-long sorrow to my mother. She blamed herself for refusing Kishan the visit to Madras she had suggested. If only my mother had known the whole story, Kishan's death would never have happened.

Our only comfort was that both Kishan's children were sent to live with us. Their father could not care for them. They needed constant attention, his duties as district officer required him to travel a great deal, and they were too young to be left with the servants. So both Makhan and Sheila soon became part of our family, and we received them with much love. I knew that the major role in caring for them would fall to me because my mother's domestic preoccupations left her little free time. They clung to me with an agonizing intensity because I resembled my elder sister closely, but they loved my mother as well and fought for her affection with my youngest brother, who had been the spoiled baby of the family until they arrived. So once more there were little ones to look after and, as the only girl in the family, once more I spent all my leisure hours sewing and mending for them, darning socks for the older boys and repairing and mending the clothes that did not need a tailor.

Of course college work had to come first during the term. We could never go for holidays; we were too big a family to travel to any resort. The expense of such a holiday would have been prohibitive, and it was exhausting even to think about the complicated arrangements that would have had to be made. Instead, during the long summer vacation, when my friends were all making holiday plans, I was occupied with figuring out how I could help my mother provide the family with all the clothes for the year. I was the only one who knew how to use a sewing machine. During term time she bought bolts of white muslin and cotton, muslin for *kurtas* for all of us and cotton for pajamas for my father and the boys and now for Makhan and Sheila. Her experience had taught her that the requirement of each boy and my father was six pajamas and ten *kurtas* for the year; six petticoats for me, six saris for college wear, and six for home wear, six for herself, and six frocks for Sheila.

Gradually, month by month, she made the necessary purchases, cut out the garments and folded and stored them in one large box in her room. As soon as the holidays started, I knew I had three months to complete the family sewing, and I settled down to my machine and worked long hours through the hot summer months. Meanwhile, my mother continued her usual chores, and when she found a few free moments she helped me sew on buttons, make buttonholes, and give the finishing touches that had to be done by hand. When we stopped work in the evenings, she read to me the beautiful poems and sayings written by her favorite Hindi authors. I could no longer do this for myself because my Hindi was inadequate, having been badly neglected because of the concentration on English required for my school and college studies. Sometimes I did read for my own pleasure, and sometimes I read to my younger brothers and my nephew and niece.

When I try to describe those days now, they seem like a sadly dreary way to spend a summer vacation. At the time I never found them so. I always finished the year's sewing with great satisfaction and a sense of pleasurable achievement. I looked forward with interest to hearing about the holiday experiences and pleasures of my friends at college but never once regretted being tied down to a sewing machine and a couple of small children during the long summer months.

Years went by; I did my M.A. Hons. in 1917. My brother Bali in Edinburgh had done his M.B.B.S. and become an intern, hoping to get home the following year. He had had a successful academic career, and was, besides, an excellent tennis player, having won the Dundee Cup in tennis in Edinburgh before the end of his studies there. My second brother, Ram, had graduated from Edinburgh University and had joined the Inns of Court in London.

My husband and I shortly after our wedding in 1919

CHAPTER 10

THE FIRST WORLD WAR broke out in 1914, but we in India were not immediately affected in any marked way. To begin with, we noticed it chiefly because of the long delays in receiving letters from my brothers abroad. In England a large number of doctors were sent to the front, and Bali, though inexperienced, was recruited for work in the Lodge Moor Hospital in Sheffield the year before he was due to return to India. My parents insisted that he wait till it was safer to make the voyage. The seas were mined, and the only way to travel from England to India in those days was by boat. People who were obliged to travel did so in convoys, though even then it was dangerous.

In 1917 I considered my college career had come to a close. I had graduated with an honors degree and had received the award of the Griggs Gold Medal in English. Now I was expected to mark time till my brothers returned from England, when a marriage would be arranged for me. This was an irksome prospect, and I persuaded my parents to let me attend the Teachers College in Saidapet, Madras, to save myself from boredom and to keep up some sort of intellectual exchange with young women of my own age who were students there. My mother saw my point and, as usual, her agreement was the deciding factor. Thus I began to attend college once more.

Two years before I graduated from the Presidency College, the University of Madras had opened the first women's college, Queen Mary's College, and that same year the Women's Christian College in Madras was also established. Three months after I entered the Teachers College I had an offer from the government women's college of an assistant Professorship in Queen Mary's College. The university authorities had decided that it was time to appoint two Indian women graduates as assistant professors; so far both women's colleges were staffed only by British women. This offer seemed like a great honor, and we discussed it in the family circle. My father raised his hands in horror, for to him it seemed unworthy, almost insulting, that a daughter of his should consider taking a paid job when she had her father and five brothers to care for her. Back and forth the argument went, he insisting that it would be a humiliation for a girl from a good family to earn a living, and I pleading that though I loved him and my brothers dearly and would always accept help from them should I need it, it would give me great satisfaction to be independent financially. After great thought my mother gave her verdict. Her view was that there was no dishonor in working for a living, and so long as one observed the rules and regulations of decent society, paid work could not demean one. Triumph! My brother Bali applauded the decision by mail, and I accepted the job.

Queen Mary's College is situated on the Marine Drive in Madras, not far from the Presidency College and the men's hostel of that college. At that time it was housed in three separate buildings. Queen Mary's is a residential college, and the staff members were required to live in staff rooms, situated at each end of the ground floor of the three buildings. Between these rooms were lecture halls and classrooms, which were, naturally, empty after working hours. The students' rooms were all upstairs. The Anglo-Indian women students dined in the main dining room, where a special table was set aside for the staff

80

members. All of them ate European or semi-European food, using European crockery and cutlery.

In my first interview with Miss de la Hay, the principal, I made a couple of conditions before taking up the appointment. I would not occupy the staff room on the ground floor reserved for me, I said, as I was afraid of the pranks of the hostel students of the Presidency College next door, having already had such embarrassing and such recent experience with the jokes and torments of the students. I had never lived away from my own home and I was nervous about not being within easy reach of the staff member at the other end of the building I was to occupy. Miss de la Hay was clearly amused, but she readily complied with my request and assigned to me two rooms on the floor above—a bedroom and a sitting room which had originally been meant for four students.

The second condition I made was that I would not eat in the main dining room with the other staff members, for I was used to Indian food in my home, and (remembering with agony my first attempt) did not know the use of European crockery and cutlery. Miss de la Hay simply could not believe me. Did I *really* like Indian food better? Did I know I would have to sit on a low stool in the large Indian mess hall and eat from a *thali,* a big brass plate? Did I know I would have to enter the mess hall barefooted lest it become polluted? Did I know I would have to eat with my fingers? It sounded undignified to her. But I had my way and became a member of the "Indian mess," sat at the head of two rows of low stools, and ate with my students. This gave me the chance to get to know them better and break down the usual reserve between professor and pupil. Soon after I established this pattern, Miss Joseph, a Syrian Christian and the second Indian appointed assistant professor, broke away from the formal staff table and joined the kitchen that served the other Indian Christian students in like manner.

Queen Mary's had a hundred and fifty women students, ninety of them Hindu, who were under my immediate care and supervision, and we had a very happy time together. Early on in my teaching life, Miss de la Hay told me that it was part of my duty to watch out for unnatural relations between the students under my authority. After my very protected upbringing it is hardly surprising that I had no idea what she meant and asked her to explain. She stumbled through a little speech about how some girls established relations with each other that exceeded the bounds of ordinary friendship. I should try to discourage any relationship that seemed abnormal. Her explanation was so oblique that it left me more puzzled than ever, and it was only years later that I realized Miss de la Hay must have been talking about lesbianism.

I much enjoyed living with the students next door, and they were free to come into my sitting room at any time. Our talks were wide-ranging and interesting, though I never saw nor heard of "unnatural relationships." I went home for weekends, except when I was on duty. The professors, in turn, had to keep a register of the students' comings and goings, where they had gone, what time they went out, and when they returned. My own movements were almost equally scrutinized and supervised. My mother, who was always obsessed with the idea that baseless scandals would vitiate the liberty she wanted me to have, placed certain restrictions on my movements for the protection of my reputation. I was not allowed to leave the college premises except to go home to my parents. Invitations from my friends or students were always refused unless my mother or one of my brothers could accompany me to the function. I often resented these barriers and boundaries and argued with her. I was not a child; I held a responsible position in the college and was in charge of grownup girls. Surely no one could accuse me of frivolity or unconventional behavior? I knew that the society we lived in was ready to condemn any departure from strict decorum and I was not likely to flout its rules.

My resentment was always assuaged by the argument that my parents desired progress for women. While we lived in a narrow society, was it not worth maintaining the greater ideal of education and work, even if it meant renouncing the lesser one of a pleasurable hour or two which might be misconstrued? I cannot really say that I felt confined. I was free to take an interest in matters that at that time were just breaking the surface of orthodox Indian life. Many of these new social concepts were connected with that small segment of educated women who were examining intelligently the reforms necessary for the progress of society generally, and women in particular.

Those of us who had had the privilege of education felt it was our duty to talk to small groups of women about child welfare, the breaking down of the caste system and the evils of secluding women in purdah. Reforms in these areas had already been advocated by great leaders who lived before our time. But India is so large a country and communication in those days was so limited that the voices of those pioneers of the emancipation of women reached only small groups in their own provinces. Raja Ram Mohan Roy in Bengal, Justice Ranade in Bombay, Pandita Ramabai, and Maharishi Karve in Poona had already become known for their efforts to break outmoded social taboos and encourage women to emerge from their seclusion and shake off the shackles of superstition and restrictive customs.

The first hostel for Hindu child widows was opened while I was still in college, and soon after I was privileged to receive the first of these orthodox Brahmin women who had gained admission to Queen Mary's College and were put under my care in the Hindu hostel of the college.

Since child marriage existed in all parts of India to a greater or lesser extent, it was not unusual for a girl, married as a child, to lose her husband, as Birjo had, before she attained puberty and was ceremonially allowed to live with him. Even if the second ceremony had not been performed and she was still young, once her husband had died she was considered a widow without having been a wife, which had been the wretched fate of my aunt. She was not allowed to marry again, nor was she permitted to train for a job. Only domestic work under the strict supervision of her elders was her lot, no matter how gifted, intelligent, or beautiful she might be. No amusements were provided and no young companionship allowed for fear of some forbidden emotional entanglement. In some parts of India these young

Brahmin widows were made to shave their heads, wear their saris over their heads, and dress always in white, the color of mourning, or red, ironically the color for a bride. No jewelry or adornment was allowed them.

All this seems a very long time ago, but even then, by the time the widows' home in Madras was opened, social reformers had already spread new ideas and asked for fairer treatment for these young widows. Education, job opportunities, and even remarriage were advocated, and it was as a result of such propaganda that the widows' home was opened in 1917. Some progressive parents had begun to educate their unfortunate daughters privately, recognizing that young widows should not be deprived of the opportunity of higher education and perhaps professional training to give them a place in society. They would never have gone to a men's college, of course, but when the women's college was established, those who had passed the matriculation examination were enrolled in Queen Mary's College, going to the widows' home for holidays and weekends. It was my pleasure and my duty to support, encourage, and help them as much as I could. I made many lifelong friends among them.

In 1918, the year after I had joined the staff of Queen Mary's College, a great tragedy befell my family. As I have said, my elder brother, Bali, had been working in Sheffield. The terrible influenza epidemic of 1918 was raging all over the world, and hundreds of soldiers were stricken and sent to different hospitals in England from the various war theaters. One contingent was sent to the Lodge Moor Hospital, where my brother was in charge of these new patients. Bali fell a victim to this scourge and died within a week. News of his sudden death shattered my parents and broke my spirit. He was very dear to me, a great support for all my ambitions for the future. I was always sure he would help and guide me, support me in even my most unconventional projects. What would happen to all my bright dreams now? This calamity befell us in October, a month before the war came to an end.

My mother was ill with grief at my brother's death, increased

84

by anxiety on my account. My father's work still took him out of town frequently. I was obliged to live in the college, and my younger brothers were either at college or at school. My mother, as always, had no friends. Loneliness and grief, unrelieved by the solace of companions and relatives, left her defenseless against the danger of brooding too much on her bereavement. If her thoughts turned from her sorrow at all, she was filled with anxiety about the problem of finding a suitable husband for me, the task Bali had promised to undertake as soon as he returned from abroad. She had not even looked around to find out who the eligible young men of the community were, so much had she depended on my brother's judgment.

Once my father retired, in another year, they would have to move to North India, where the language would be familiar and where they would live among relations and friends in their old age. They would choose a university town because the education of the younger children must be considered, and at last a permanent home would be made where the family members could visit them periodically. Which was the best university in the North? Could my parents be within reasonably easy reach of their relations, who were spread all over the North from Lahore to Allahabad? The most worrying problem, however, was what they were to do about me. My mother couldn't dream of letting me continue to work in Madras, even though I had already established myself and was making good progress. How could I live without my parents and family at least in the same city? How could they face the criticism of my upbringing and activities? I was already twenty-five years old and had been working for over a year and a half. Could I find a similar job in North India? Would scandalmongers within the Kashmiri community cause me distress? All these questions plagued my mother, and she spent sleepless nights and sorrowful days.

We were still reeling under the shock of Bali's sudden death when my second brother, Ram, wrote my parents an astounding letter. Ram had completed his studies at the Inns of Court and been called to the bar. Now he had taken a job as a junior editor with Butterworth, the law publishing firm in London, and had decided to marry a young Belgian girl, who, with her mother, had come to London as a refugee when Belgium was overrun during the war by the German armies. We gathered, from photographs and Ram's explanations, that Marguerite was a lovely girl, not quite eighteen years old. Ram was a handsome twenty-two-year-old barrister with bright prospects ahead of him. Marguerite, an only child and the apple of her mother's eye, could not, at that stage, dream of leaving her mother, Europe, and the cultural background to which she had been born to venture out to a new country so different from her own, and where her mother would not be able to accompany her. Ram, in turn, was not prepared to return to India alone, establish himself and make a home suitable for a young foreign bride. They were both very much in love and anxious to get married. Not unnaturally, he accepted the first job offered to him and decided to marry and settle in London.

This decision was a shock of a different kind to my parents: they felt that their second son too was lost to them and the family. He would never be able to take his place in their home nor would his wife, a foreigner, ever be able to help them or take care of them in their old age. In a country like India such considerations matter a great deal. They still had three younger sons to provide for and settle in life.

Just at this time a curious conjunction of circumstances was to change my whole future immeasurably. My father was a member of the Saraswath Club in Madras. The Saraswaths are a Brahmin community with two branches, one belonging to the South and one to Kashmir. The men's club of the Saraswath Brahmin community had many members from all over the South and one or two, like my father, from the North. One evening at the club my father happened to meet and talk with a fellow member, Dr. Raghavendra Rao. Dr. Rao was much concerned about his son, who had passed with distinction into the Indian Civil Service from Cambridge and was posted in one of the country districts of Madras Province as a junior civil servant. However, this curious son, Rama Rau, a most eligible young man, good-looking, intelligent, and hard-working, with an excellent record and outstanding ability, refused to consider any of the marriage proposals received by his elders.

Rama Rau, his father reported, argued that marriages should take place between members of different communities. That was the only way in which orthodox beliefs, rites, rituals, and customs peculiar to each community could be wiped out. Then, very delicately and rather indirectly, Dr. Rao reminded my father that he had an eligible daughter. Shouldn't the unconventional son and the unusual daughter be given an opportunity to meet?

As my father related this conversation to my mother, it struck them both that remarkable progress had already been made in much of Indian society since my childhood. Not that they thought that this possibility of a match for me was an opportunity for further reform in the Kashmiri community; rather they discussed with open-minded interest the idea of an intercommunity marriage. Progressive as my mother already was, she set about making further inquiries about Dr. Raghavendra Rao's son from relations in North India. It turned out that Rama Rau's older brother, Sanjiva Rao—they continued to spell their last name differently when it was transliterated into English—was a professor at the Hindu University in Benares, and his wife, Padmabai, had worked with my late sister Kishan and become her good friend in the last happy period of her short, sad life. All reports were favorable, so very delicately, again through friends, it was suggested that a meeting be arranged between Rama Rau and me before any commitment was made by our elders—in itself an extraordinary break with custom.

Early in January 1919 Rama Rau traveled to Madras from his up-country station for a weekend with his family. We met in my parents' home for lunch, looked each other over although we conversed only with our elders, and after the meeting were asked separately by our parents for our approval of the engagement they proposed. I knew that this marriage would solve all the anxieties my mother was going through on my behalf. I had no opportunities to meet young men, and the only way in which I could be married was through an arrangement made by my elders. My acceptance would relieve them of the problem that my prolonged spinsterhood presented and would give me a chance to make a home with an honorable man whose relations would not interfere with our lives. It all sounds very cold blooded when I write about it now, but at the time I had no other basis for a decision and I was vividly aware that I was taking the biggest, most irrevocable step of my life.

At the time we met, Rama Rau was thirty years old and had a promising career ahead of him, and although we did not fall in love with each other at first sight, I felt that a marriage between us would work out, allowing for all the give-and-take that every marriage requires. Certainly it would be better than an arranged marriage to a Kashmiri with all the old-fashioned manners and customs that would be imposed on me. Belonging to different communities, Rama Rau and I could form our own patterns of living, unhampered by traditional habits. I was nearly twenty-six years old and conscious of my unwillingness to sink back into orthodoxy, too old and too independent to be molded by a dominating mother-in-law in a joint family.

Although at that first meeting we didn't speak to each other directly, I was internally agitated. From external appearances I saw that he was presentable to look at, reserved in manner, somewhat embarrassed and rather unsure of himself—and this I felt was natural in the circumstances in which we were meeting. He was not brash or boastful; his manners were impeccable: the right deference to my parents, though he could not converse with my mother as he could speak no Hindi and she knew no Konkani (his language) or English. He talked to my father and brothers and I spoke to Padmabai, his sister-in-law, my sister Kishan's friend from Benares. I suppose he listened, as I did, unobtrusively and carefully. I knew I had the advantage over him because I was in my own home and more relaxed with my parents and brothers around me. I felt I should not judge him too severely. However, I understandably had a sleepless night after that first meeting, revolving in my mind the pros and cons of the step I must take. I knew that some day I would have to submit to an arranged marriage and that to an unknown partner. It was then that I came to the conclusion, after deep thought, that mine would have to be a registered marriage, for that alone would give me the right to a divorce should I find it impossible to make the adjustments that would be asked for. It would be the first Kashmiri marriage by registration, and I would have to broach the subject of this determination to my parents with plausible reasons for my decision and then to the man who had done me the honor of offering me a place in his home and, I hoped, later on in his heart.

The following day Padmabai and Rama Rau's elder brother, Sanjiva Rao, invited me to tea. My mother would not let me go alone, so my younger brother, my niece Sheila, and my nephew Makhan accompanied me. Again we had no chance, and in any case were too shy, to talk to each other but, naturally, watched each other with interest. On the third day Rama Rau came to our house again, made a formal proposal, was formally accepted, and that same day returned to his work in the up-country town of Masulipatam. Our wedding was fixed for the 3rd of May, as my father was retiring in June and would be leaving Madras for good soon afterward with my mother, my three brothers, and my niece and nephew.

As soon as my engagement was announced by my parents, a great hue and cry was raised by the Kashmiri community in the North. Even my realistic mother had not imagined such ferocious denunciation. Relations, friends, and even strangers wrote to my parents to say that it would be better to drown their daughter rather than let her marry a non-Kashmiri. They were called vicious to agree to such a marriage and were warned that they would regret it all their lives. A cousin wrote to me to say that a Kashmiri gentleman was willing to marry me on the same day as had been fixed for my wedding to save me from the pollution of a "mixed" marriage. My parents took all this opposition with considerable stoicism, but not without some apprehension. They had put the alternatives before me when they first considered my fiancé's proposal, and now they asked me again if I was absolutely certain about my decision. I told them I was, repeated Rama Rau's objections to marrying within his community, said I agreed with him entirely on this point, and added briskly that an extra advantage to this marriage was that I would never have to face the Kashmiris' stupid fury. My parents began to be less perturbed by the fuss their people in the North were making.

I did not know my fiancé at all. His likes, dislikes, temperament, and interests were all equally obscure to me. I did not even know how I should behave toward him or how to address him on paper. We corresponded during our engagement in brief, formal letters with nothing personal in them, only descriptions of the work we were doing in our respective fields.

The one serious topic I broached was the form our marriage should take. I was not a child; I knew that marriage could be unhappy for many and varied reasons. If it should prove so in our case, it would be wrong to be tied together for life. Hinduism did not at that time recognize divorce, and polygamy had not yet been abolished by law. I told him I would like to be married in a civil ceremony by the registrar at a registry office. The difficulty was that registered marriages in those days required a declaration by both the bride and the groom that they belonged to none of the recognized religions of India. I was prepared to make such a declaration, as I believed in all religions and generally called myself a "theist," one who believes in God but not particularly a Hindu. Would my fiancé agree to do the same? Rama Rau had joined the Theosophical Society, a powerful group under the presidency of a great woman, Dr. Annie Besant, who preached the unity of religions. Theosophy was considered a new religion and was not listed among the recognized religions of India. "Yes," came my fiancé's answer, "I can make such a declaration with a clear conscience if you wish to have a registered marriage." All the same, my parents felt it desirable to have our own Kashmiri family guru from Delhi come all the way to Madras to perform a religious ceremony, and my parents-in-law also brought their guru from their home town of Mangalore on the southwest coast for his part of the ceremony. I resigned from my post at Queen Mary's College with great regret, cherishing the affectionate farewells of my students

90

and the staff members at the great party they gave me.

It was a quiet wedding, as we were still in mourning for my brother. None of my relatives from the North except my second sister, Bishan Razdan, and her husband, Dwarkanath, with their young son attended the wedding. The others refused the invitation because I was marrying a non-Kashmiri.

We had hired beds for Bishan and her family, and in setting one of them up I dropped the iron frame for the mattress on my big toe, crushing the nail. I suppressed my agony as best I could. I did not want to make a fuss over this mishap on my wedding eve. All the beds were arranged in the usual way in a row on the veranda upstairs and we all went to sleep early to be ready for the ceremonies the next morning. My toe, however, swelled up, and excruciating twinges kept me awake until I could no longer bear the pain and a groan escaped me. Dwarkanath, my brother-in-law, a light sleeper, jumped up and came to my bed to find out what the matter was. I burst into tears and showed him the great blue bruise on my toe and explained why I was in such distress. He immediately roused the household, ordered hot water and compresses, and sat down himself to foment my foot, which gave me great relief.

The next day I struggled through the preliminary ceremonies, grateful that I was supposed to be barefoot, and limped along till the evening, when the wedding proper was to take place. The gurus had set the auspicious time for the beginning of the Hindu ceremony at midnight of the 2nd of May, and since it was performed in Sanskrit, I understood very little of it. However, when I was told that it began with the *kanya daan,* the giving away of the girl to her husband, I bristled in defense of my newfound independence. I resented anyone, even parents, claiming the right of "giving away" a daughter, especially when she was a willing partner to a marriage. Another part of the ceremony further angered me. Traditionally, the guru takes the bride out at dawn to point out the north star. He recites Sanskrit verses which mean, "Be thou as pure, as constant, and as chaste as the north star is in the universe." This injunction applies only to the bride. My toe hurt more bitterly than ever.

After all the religious rites were over, Rama Rau and I signed the big book recording civil marriages, which the registrar had brought to the house, and took the vows that we felt were really binding. Later we went to my parents-in-law's home and were received with the appropriate ceremonies that welcome a bride, the garlands, the prayers and the *arti*. As usual, the tray containing auspicious things—a coconut, the red powder for the *tika* on the forehead, sweets, and a silver vessel of oil with a lighted wick —was carried around us to keep off evil before we entered the house. My mother-in-law, as is the practice in all Hindu marriages, gave me a new name, Sita, to mark my entry as a bride into my new home. Sita is the legendary devoted, unswervingly loyal, unquestioningly obedient wife of Rama, the perfect counterpart for the hero of the *Ramayana*. I never used the name. My own family and friends and even my husband's people were already too familiar with Dhan to be able to change.

Two days later we left to spend a month in Ootacamund, a delightful hill resort, or "hill station" as we used to say, in the great southern mountain range called the Nilgiris. To my great discomfort, my foot swelled up alarmingly, and there seemed nothing to do except keep it propped up, soak it from time to time, and wait for it to get better. We stayed at a small family hotel, and our landlady kindly offered to serve all our meals in our room. My husband either ate with me or went out into the dining room alone, but made no friends. He went for long walks though he did not encourage me to limp out of my room or meet any of our fellow guests in the hotel. I did not know him well enough to ask questions, but got the impression that he was rather shy about having a wife, particularly of being seen helping me to move about in public. A fortnight later, when I could put on my shoes with comfort, I did enjoy walks with him, for Ootacamund is beautiful and I had never before been in the mountains, though I had heard a great deal about such holiday places.

CHAPTER 11

WHILE WE WERE away in Ootacamund, my parents had decided on their own future plans. They were going to settle in Allahabad, a city set at the meeting place of the Yamuna River with the great Ganges in the northern province now called Uttar Pradesh. It still has a good university and is the home town of two prominent Kashmiri Brahmin families, the Nehrus and Saprus, among whom my mother had many relatives.

My husband had been promoted to be joint magistrate in Masulipatam, a district center in what is now Andhra State. We spent a few days with my family in Madras while they were in the last stages of packing up all the accumulation of the last ten years of living. Then he went ahead to Masulipatam while I followed later with my family. Our journey north followed the same route for part of the way.

At the big junction station of Bezwada, where the train stops for nearly an hour, my husband met us to take me to the branch line for Masulipatam while the rest of the party went on to Calcutta, where they would have to change trains again to go to Allahabad. At Bezwada my young niece, Sheila, who had been asleep, woke up and, seeing my husband there, sensed that I would be leaving with him. She clung to me and screamed and wept and refused to let me go. The stationmaster and several railway officials rushed to see what was happening. My parents pushed us out of the train sooner than we need have left, for only then could they pacify Sheila and calm her down. I heard afterward that she fretted and missed me for many days. For me too it was a miserable parting and it almost broke my heart to leave her. She was like my own child and I could not bear her distress.

We reached Masulipatam the following morning, and I was able to get a first glimpse of my new home. Masulipatam is an important eastern coast town, on the Bay of Bengal, with the River Krishna flowing through it. The whole area around it is intersected with canals and was known in those days as the granary of the Madras Presidency. The land is fertile and rich harvests are reaped except, of course, when the monsoon fails. The climate is hot, and as my first experience of the weather was in the month of June, the hottest of the hot summer, I wondered how I would be able to bear it. The temperature the day we arrived was 116 degrees, with not a breath of air.

Our house was large, single-storied, whitewashed, and roofed in red tile, with a deep veranda running all along the front and the semblance of a garden surrounding it. Inside was a very large sitting room sparsely furnished with tawdry government furniture. This opened into a dining room, which led to the back veranda. On either side of the sitting room were bedrooms, dressing rooms, and bathrooms, one set for the official occupying the house and the other set for guests or fellow officials who might be visiting the city. We had an army of servants, but most important was my husband's personal major domo, Francis, who ruled the household. The two individuals who did not welcome me were Francis and Punch, my husband's fox terrier, which he had acquired as a young puppy. Punch learned to tolerate me in time, though he followed my husband to the gate of the house every morning when he left for the office and howled for at least a quarter of an hour before coming back to me in a sullen mood.

Francis was a more difficult problem. He was a very efficient servant, who had run my husband's ménage and personal affairs for several years. I was his natural implacable adversary, and we never did come to a workable truce.

It was when I came to Masulipatam that I realized how little I knew of the Western ways adopted by those Indians in British official circles to which my husband now belonged. The house was run on models set by the British. The butler—in this case Francis—was in charge of all the other servants, and there seemed hundreds when I first met them. The cook did the daily shopping and cooking, the cook's mate did the washing, cleaning, preparing of vegetables and the scrubbing of cooking vessels. A woman servant did the sweeping and washing of the kitchen itself and the grinding of *masalas,* the mixture of spices and seasonings necessary for all Indian food, which was ground fresh every day. That comprised the kitchen staff. Two boys did the sweeping and dusting of the house twice a day and carried dishes from the kitchen to the pantry. They also, by turns, walked Punch every morning and afternoon, bathed him once a week, and brushed him every day.

Francis supervised the household, hired and fired any one of the servants who was not satisfactory, served at table, took orders for all the servants, arranged for parties, gave out and received the laundry, looked after my husband's clothes. He was, in fact, the only link between my husband and me and the rest of the staff. He received the household money from my husband and rendered accounts to him. He continued to do this even after my arrival, as I had yet to learn how to run this kind of a household, how to order meals of a European pattern, and how to entertain non-Indians in the formal way required of us. Out on our veranda were two uniformed *chaprassies,* government employees for whose position or job there is no adequate English equivalent. They ran errands and dusted and arranged my husband's office room in our bungalow, for he often worked in the house. They carried files for him from the house to the office and back, posted letters, bought stamps and other such items that meant waiting in line. Often they sat for hours on the veranda just gossiping, which worried me; it seemed such a waste of time.

At first I kept very much in the background, as I was afraid of making mistakes and upsetting the smart running of the household. But soon I began to feel like a guest rather than the mistress of the house. I was still too shy to ask my husband to let me cope with the household accounts and to direct Francis to take orders from me. The truth was that I did not know what orders to give or what sort of food my husband liked. Certainly I did not know anything about English cooking and could not differentiate between a roast, a baked, and a grilled dish, and as for desserts, I had never heard of baked custard, cabinet pudding, Swiss roll, or any of the other common desserts popular at the time. I was afraid to show Francis my ignorance of Western ways and Western food, about which he knew much more than I did. My husband knew that I came from a completely Indian home, and he kindly continued to order his Western household to save me the embarrassment of having to admit my ignorance.

Gradually I learned more about the way our life was run and summoned the courage to suggest to my husband that I should take over the household accounts. He agreed immediately, arranged with his bank to open a joint account and send me a checkbook of my own. Francis was upset. When I began to deal directly with the many servants who were under his direction, I discovered that they had to pay a tribute to Francis each month from their salaries. Naturally he resented this loss of income and began to show his discontent by complaining about the work of the servants over whom he no longer had authority. Matters came to a head when my husband, with his own work to think of and bored by "servant trouble," suggested I should let Francis go back to handling the staff. He was sure things would run more smoothly and I would be saved the effort of looking into servants' squabbles.

I was furious. Our first quarrel was over Francis. I told my husband that Francis would have to go, that I wished to deal with

96

those who worked for us myself, and my authority could not be gainsaid. My husband was very unhappy, for Francis had served him well, but there seemed no way out of this impasse. Francis went, but for months after that my husband fretted for his efficient servant and never failed to point out the great sacrifice he had had to make.

After settling my household in Masulipatam I began to look around for some interest or occupation I might pursue, some kind of congenial life I might make for myself. Slowly I realized that I would become just as lonely as my mother had been in Hubli, and for some of the same reasons. My husband's work began at 9:30 A.M. and did not end till 6 P.M. The language in Masulipatam was Telegu. I could understand some Tamil, for I had lived many years in Madras, but Telegu was completely different and completely strange to me. The men my husband met at his office spoke English. Besides, he had studied Telegu and did a lot of his magistrate's work in the language of the people of the area. But Indian women in the district towns did not go out with their husbands, and I found I had no one to talk to, or to exchange any thoughts with. The only place I could meet people was the club for the officers of the Civil Service, where most of the members were British, such as the magistrate and collector, or regional chief officer, the district judge and other high officials, or the European missionaries running local schools and dispensaries.

Every evening we went to the club. My husband played tennis and sometimes bridge, but I did not play cards, nor had I ever handled a tennis racket. I did not drink the customary sundowners. All I could do was sit by and watch the games or read and reread the two- or three-week-old English papers, an essential part of even the remotest English club in India. For my husband, going to the club was, in a way, part of his duties. He had to keep in touch with his colleagues and could always talk shop with them. I had no subject of conversation I could hope to introduce successfully. My interests had always centered on social-welfare work and women's education, and no one seemed interested in those. I could not get to know the Indian social group because

97

of the language difficulty. In the end, my time was spent with the books in my husband's limited library.

Even gardening was an impractical hobby. Our bungalow had extensive grounds, too big to be converted into a garden, as it would require an army of gardeners to keep the area in order. A small part in front of the house was cared for by a gardener, though the climate made it very difficult to grow any flowers except the usual hardy hibiscus and bougainvillaea and a hedge to keep the cattle from grazing at our front door, and in that heat the prospect of amateur attempts at gardening were far from inviting.

Even indoors it was almost impossible to keep cool, though we had the old device of *punkhas,* wood-and-cloth ceiling fans pulled by a coolie on the veranda outside—the same arrangement that my grandmother had had years before in her Delhi house. We had no electricity, but used kerosene lamps. In those large rooms it was difficult to brighten the gloom in the far corners even at midday. All day the *punkha* coolie followed me from room to room, ready to create his warm breeze wherever I might decide to sit. In the evening, the night coolie took over and pulled the *punkha* rope while we slept. I always felt sorry for the poor man, who worked all night, sometimes tying the rope to his toe and lying down, still pulling the rope back and forth with his leg. He often fell asleep, and we would wake up in almost a bath of perspiration. Then my husband would shout from within, *"Punkha lagao"* ("Pull the *punkha"*), which woke the man to begin the tiresome task again. We tried sleeping in a tent which we had pitched in our garden, but the mosquitoes and the garden insects gave us no peace, so back we went to our stuffy hot bedroom.

One day, while tidying up some bookshelves, I told the servant to put the books out in the sun, valuable ones that my husband had been awarded when he got his degree from King's College in Cambridge. Among them was a complete set of Meredith's works with the Cambridge University stamp on each book. A couple of hours later I went out onto the veranda and to my horror found that the cows grazing in the grounds had been eating the books as well as the scanty grass. It was the first time in my life that I had come across such a sight. I never again tried to air books without more careful supervision.

One part of my husband's work as magistrate provided me with the most lively interest, pleasure, and sense of participation. Every two or three months we toured his district in a houseboat on the canals of the Krishna River, which laced across the area. The houseboat had an open deck and a large room with two bunks that could be hooked up during the day, a central table, and four chairs. Off this room were a bathroom and lavatory, and beyond was the kitchen. Servants always traveled with us on these tours, in a separate boat tethered to ours and drawn by it. It was a true joy to glide smoothly and silently through lovely wooded stretches, among villages, paddy fields, and pastures, with only the rippling of the water below us and the haunting, soft singing of the boatmen, commandeered at each village to tow our houseboat to the next village, night after night. At each stop, under shady trees, the houseboat was tied to the canal bank, and an office was set up, on board or on the grassy shore, where my husband listened to the grievances the villagers brought to the magistrate in charge. Mostly, he settled their disputes over land, crops, and water, and then traveled over the cultivated area to assess the taxes to be paid, but all this work was in Telegu and I could not really enter into the people's problems.

The sylvan scene enchanted me. The villagers were all farmers, bare-bodied men with the usual loincloths and turbans, and women with their colorful home-woven saris drawn well above their knees for the work they did in the fields with their husbands. They showed signs of interest in and friendliness to me, but we had no language in which we could communicate. Our pet fox terrier ran wild when he was allowed on the shore, daring the monkeys in the trees above us.

We traveled for a month or so in this manner, returned to headquarters for a spell, and then set out on a similar journey in another direction. It was the periods in Masulipatam that dismayed me. I was completely removed from the active life I had led before my marriage and the welfare work my friends and I had been doing with such enthusiasm, and it filled me with surprise that the English men and women I met were not interested in the human problems either of their own country or those of the country they were living in, except, of course, from the strictly official or governmental angle. When I first talked at the club about the wonderful campaign for equal votes for women that had been exciting England for years and filling us in India with sympathetic interest, I was treated with the patronizing indulgence one might show a precocious but unmannerly child. When I praised the bravery and courage with which the suffragettes had protested their injustices and unequal treatment by the Government, facing jail sentences and going on hunger strikes, the response was colder and more formidable. I was young and easily intimidated; the fire in me died, leaving me helpless, frustrated, and embarrassed.

Very little entertaining was done in Masulipatam. Since everyone of the acceptable "official" circle met every evening at the club, it was hardly worthwhile inviting the same familiar faces to dinner in our homes. There were not many members, in any case, and of those, several would always be touring the district at different times as their special jobs required, just as my husband and I did. A couple of times we dined at the homes of my husband's fellow officers and, of course, such invitations had to be returned. These occasions were always very formal in what I now know to be a rather provincial way. Too much elaborate food, too much absurd etiquette—fish knives and forks, finger-bowls, the ladies retiring from the table after dessert—and not a word of interesting talk. I soon learned how to entertain in a Western manner. It wasn't very difficult, but it was extremely boring.

My chief regret was that we could not make friends with the educated Indian men in Masulipatam whom I was really eager to meet. They were all, in one way or another, connected with politics, and as junior officials we were supposed to eschew the company of anyone "politically minded" or in any way "controversial."

As for the missionaries, they seemed to me far less progressive than Father d'Souza of Hubli. Their activities were limited to the teaching of kindergarten children, church work, and helping out in a few medical clinics. Possibly I was prejudiced against them because at the club they always talked so patronizingly of the children in their classes and gave the impression that the Indian families they met lived in utter darkness—a darkness they worked so hard to dispel in order to lead them from primitive paganism to the enlightened Christian life.

I'm afraid I took little interest in them. Years later I heard a story of just such missionaries in Bengal. A peculiarity of the Bengali language and the Bengali pronunciation of any other language is that every "s" sound becomes "sh." The missionary preachers in the story used to insist that all the schoolchildren begin the day by singing "God Save the King." This, of course, came out as "God Shave the King." To the foreigners, this was merely an amusing story. But what of the children who had no grasp of the meaning of the British national anthem? I can only wonder what went through their minds, what visions they had of primitive rites in which the deity was expected to shave a monarch. Like so much else about the British presence in India at that time, behind the political struggles and the clash of economic realities between ruler and ruled lay a far more profound misunderstanding of culture, custom, religion, values—all the basic threads in the fabric of the Indian way of life.

During this time, another, more personal theme greatly occupied my thoughts. I had been married to a complete stranger, with whom I had exchanged only a few words before my wedding day. This was not unusual, but although my own family was not orthodox, there were some habits my mother could not break, and probably saw no reason for breaking. One was that there should be an absolute taboo on any discussion of, or open information about, sex or marital relations. Any emotional awakening or physical change in an adolescent was covered up, or referred to in the most indirect way. For instance, when I was thirteen and first began to menstruate, I knew nothing about the process or the changes in my body. If my mother had not noticed it first, I'm sure I would have been terrified. She did see that I needed some instruction, but she merely made a gesture to one of my elder sisters, who took me aside and explained that this was a natural development and told me how one should cope with the situation. The only explanation given to me was that I had now grown to womanhood, and I should expect menstruation to occur each month. Nothing further was said, but after that I noticed that my mother exercised greater vigilance over my appearance and activities, and soon after told me to start wearing saris and discard my frocks. She was particular about my covering the front of my body and head whenever I went out or when visitors came to the house. Indirectly it was suggested to me that modesty required such observances, and I accepted the convention without question. I wasn't given and didn't ask for detailed explanations. It was a subject I was too inhibited to discuss. And so was my mother.

I had heard stories from her about the correct behavior of young married women. They were not, for instance, allowed to talk to their husbands in front of their elders. They were expected to meet their husbands only after the household had retired, and emerge from their rooms at the crack of dawn to keep up the pretense that the family would not notice that they had spent the night with their husbands. All of us had been amused by the story my mother told of a young bride whose husband had been rushing off to work one morning and called up from the street to his mother to drop him a handkerchief he had forgotten in his room. She, in turn, had asked her daughter-in-law to fetch the handkerchief and drop it to her son waiting downstairs. In doing so, the bride saw for the first time, in full daylight, the face of her husband. Later she excitedly told her friends that she had had no idea how handsome he was, with his fair skin and gray eyes (not unusual among Kashmiris). They had been married many months.

Another story my mother told me concerned a young bride who, observing the usual modest behavior required of her, had to accompany her husband on a train journey. Etiquette required that she keep her head bowed and her eyes on the ground while she walked a few steps behind her husband. Disembarking from the train and walking with head bowed, she followed her husband's shoes. They got mixed up in a crowd, but she disentangled herself and again found the shoes to follow. When they got to the ticket collector, the shoes she had been following passed through the exit without a backward glance, to her great consternation, leaving her behind. A few minutes later her husband, who wore a pair of shoes similar to the ones she had been following, caught up with her and rescued her.

Incidents of this kind used to entertain us enormously, for we believed that we had outgrown such customs and inhibitions. Certainly I did not realize till I got married that those vestiges of an old social order could persist directly or indirectly in both my husband and myself from our ineradicable childhood training, however broad-minded and emancipated we might consider ourselves. Manifestations of such inhibitions appeared early in my married life. In my relationship with my husband, I was often irked and unhappy at what I believed was a lack of communication between us. The repressions he had been subjected to in his early years colored his maturity and kept him from any emotional demonstration, no matter how deep his feelings were. It was just Not Done to express by word or gesture a feeling that would betray an involvement with a woman, especially if it related in any way to sex.

I had a great respect for my husband. He was a man of unshakable integrity and intelligence and I never knew him to do or think a dishonorable thing. He was dutiful, generous, and concerned about our new relationship, wanting to create in himself and in me a depth of feeling that would take the place of emotional attachment, or what my children and grandchildren would call "being in love." He was, however, reserved and undemonstrative by nature. Yet, even during the most frustrating times, I realized that it was his strict upbringing that had fashioned his armor against giving or receiving love in an open, uncomplicated way.

His upbringing had indeed been strict. He and his three brothers had been brought up in the old-fashioned way. Their father laid down the law and all the children obeyed. Their mother, a sweet, gentle lady, served her demanding husband most dutifully. Their home was in Mangalore in South Kanara, where all four sons were educated till they passed the matriculation examination and were ready to go to college. There was no college in Mangalore at that time nor was there one in Salem, the district town where my father-in-law was a surgeon. The boys, as they qualified for college, traveled to Madras to stay with their mother's brother, who was professor of mathematics at one of the Madras colleges.

This uncle of theirs was a strict disciplinarian, a brilliant man himself, and expected each of his four wards to win similar success in their college careers. Like my father-in-law, he brooked no argument from the boys, and if they disagreed with him they learned to keep quiet about it. All the boys did outstandingly well in college, and that was all that mattered. Nobody gave a thought, in those days, to what the emotional price of such training might be. My husband graduated with distinction from Presidency College in Madras, went on to King's College, Cambridge, and, after he took his degree, entered the Indian Civil Service.

Later, I used to be astonished when I saw any of the brothers together at how little they had to say to each other. I came from a large, vocal, argumentative, frank family, free to express our most outrageous opinions to our parents or to demonstrate our fondness for each other—though we might be quarreling the next minute. It was years before I could speak as frankly with my own husband and years more before he was able to respond in the same way. When my husband's family met, they spoke only about intellectual subjects in the most impersonal manner—if they talked at all. And I never knew people who needed to talk less, or were able or willing to show affection less. I discovered this in my husband early and worried about it, but as time went on I realized that such characteristics cannot be changed.

A few months after I was married, while we were still in Masulipatam, I discovered that I was pregnant and, as there were neither good hospitals nor nursing homes where we were stationed, we decided that I should go to my parents in Allahabad for my first confinement. I was traveling by train, and knowing that a demonstration of affection in public between husband and wife would not be considered in good taste, I offered to shake hands with him formally to wish him good-bye as my train was ready to leave. He blushed and turned away. Even that small gesture would be a betrayal of unseemly sentiment. I was his wife, yes, but no outsider should ever guess that there could be a sentimental involvement between us, and the station platform was crowded with strangers.

More than a year later, after we were transferred to the Madras Secretariat and my baby was a year old, I often used to go to his office, a distance of five miles, to pick him up at six o'clock, the end of his working day, and drive along the beautiful Madras seafront before returning home. The first time I took our baby and waited for my husband, Premila, who was just beginning to babble, shouted with excitement as soon as her father appeared, "Da-da, Da-da," loud enough for those who were leaving the office with him to hear. This so abashed him that he actually suggested that I should not bring the child to the office when I came to meet him. This upset me beyond measure, for I was so proud of my lovely, happy child. I made a fuss about it and insisted that she could always call for her father with me, or with our driver.

It took me some time to realize that, deep down, his objection to having his child shout her recognition had something to do with the fact that our baby was the result of sex relations, that he found it unseemly to acknowledge her publicly. It took time, but I got used to the attitude and accepted it, for in all other ways he was kind, dutiful and loving—and inordinately proud of Premila himself. In truth, he could never deny his children anything they wanted. He loved them dearly and deeply, even though he could not spontaneously demonstrate affection toward them except in private. So deeply ingrained was this bashfulness that it was not till they were grown to young womanhood that, out of their own affection for him, they forced him into public demonstrations by putting their arms around him and

My first child, Premila, in 1921

kissing him on their arrival or departure. Even so, he remained somewhat embarrassed by such behavior. Yet he always spent many of his leisure hours with the children, especially during their school holidays. In fact, he was never interested in much besides his work and his family. He played games with Premila and Santha and taught them with great patience the principles of bridge when they were quite young. He, I, and the two girls made up the foursome, and the children grasped the fine points of the game sooner than I did. Today, whenever we settle down to a game of bridge, my daughters laugh at the mistakes I make, while both of them are quite expert—the result of their father's teaching.

One incident that stands out in my memory as proof of his quiet care and concern for them occurred when, in 1930, after the work of the Simon Commission in London was completed and before my husband's new assignment was announced, we left for India in December, and stayed a few days in Paris. Neither he nor I had thought particularly about Christmas until, on the 24th, Santha began to make preparations for Santa Claus's visit. I had no gifts for the children and explained to them that Santa Claus would not visit our hotel as he would not know where we were, and therefore they should not expect any Christmas presents. The children said nothing and we said no more about it. They had their supper and went to bed as usual. We dined later and, before turning in, we looked in on the children in the adjoining room. There I noticed that they had both carefully hung up beside the fireplace not their stockings but two pillowcases, in anticipation of Santa Claus's visit. This distressed me, but I thought we would have to give them further explanations the next morning and promise them some compensations for the disappointment they would feel.

Not so my husband. He could not bear the thought and forced me, late as it was, to get into my overcoat and accompany him to the shops, which were open on Christmas Eve. It was cold. I was tired. I suggested he should go alone. But, no. I had to choose the gifts because I knew better what the girls would like. Very reluctantly, I accompanied him and we came back with an armload of presents, filled the pillowcases and woke early the next morning to watch the children's reaction. They burst into our room, shouting, "Daddy, daddy! Mummy said that Santa Claus would not find out where we were, and look what he has left for us—such lovely presents." The happy glint in his eyes —he feigned surprise—his real pleasure in their excitement made me feel churlish for having resented going out on that nighttime expedition.

He denied the children nothing and rejoiced in bringing them happiness, although other children did not interest him—not his sisters' nor those of my brothers or sister. In fact, his indulgence sometimes annoyed me because I felt he was spoiling our daughters. I remember the many holidays in Europe, when the children had their summer vacations and he got his month's holiday leave. Whether in Knocke in Belgium, Paramé in Brittany or Interlaken in Switzerland, the time was always spent with the children in mind. No grown-up entertainment—a visit to the casino, a concert, a play which the children could not enjoy— was even thought of, so complete was the concentration on them and their pleasures. Later on, when the grandchildren arrived, even his daughters began to take a back seat in favor of the younger generation. Jai, Santha's son, on his rare visits, considered my husband the authority in the house and pompously called him "Grandfather," while Premi's children, who were constantly in and out of the house, called him "Pop-Pop." They all made impossible demands on him.

In all respects, he was a man of strict self-discipline, regular hours, punctuality to the minute. It was not often that the routine of his life could be broken, and nothing as frivolous as, say, a beautiful moonlit night could delay our evening meal, nor could friends who outstayed their visiting hours be tolerated with patience, however congenial or interesting they might be.

He never called me by my name, in deference to an outmoded Indian custom forbidding a husband and wife to use given names as too intimate and lacking in decorum and respect. Of course, I never thought of calling him by his name. We said, "Listen," when either of us wished to attract the other's attention, although in talking about each other to a third person we freely used personal names. He had little time for friends, only for official colleagues, and he resented my eager gregariousness and the readiness with which I responded to people who had nothing to do with the official circle in which we moved.

He watched me closely in public places, because subconsciously he was afraid I was going to override some of the conventions, the manners and behavior to which we had both been brought up. I was inclined to be affable and friendly on short acquaintance and enter more easily into a party spirit, which he considered undignified. He was especially disapproving if I was paid a compliment by a man, something which I took gaily and lightheartedly, giving it no special consideration. When, years later, I gave up wearing my sari over my head, as I had done in my younger days, he objected to my discarding a North Indian convention, although women in the South and in his own community always went with their heads uncovered. His argument was that I was born in a society where such a custom denoted modesty and I should maintain it no matter how irksome and uncomfortable it might be. Later still, when I went with him to England and adopted some of the ways of my English friends, such as smoking cigarettes or using lipstick, he felt I was rapidly going to the dogs, behaving in a more and more unseemly manner.

He did not much approve of my public activities, either, no matter how serious and well intentioned they were. For all his education, for all his liberal views about marriage and the sort of woman he wanted as a wife, deep down in him lay the old-fashioned conviction, though unexpressed, that a woman's place was in her home, and her husband and children should be her main preoccupation. This must, however, have been a mixed feeling. There were times when he could not bring himself to express open approval of some project I was working on, yet he did not actively oppose it. Soon I learned to assume, without anything being said, that while he wasn't exactly on my side, as long as he wasn't clearly against me I could go ahead. Finally, I gained enough confidence to assert myself by pursuing what

I thought were purposeful outlets for my interests and activities in public affairs, always taking care that I did not neglect my duties and responsibilities to my home, my husband and children and did not compromise my husband's position or career.

CHAPTER 12

AFTER MY MARRIAGE and after my parents had left Madras and had settled in Allahabad with my three younger brothers, Hari entered the Medical College in Lucknow, only four hours away by train. Shri entered Allahabad University, and Gopi was still at school. My nephew Makhan and niece Sheila, who had been with my parents since my sister Kishan's death, remained with them when they arrived in Allahabad. But, soon after, their father, Chandramohan Nath Sharga, arrived at my parents' home, quarreled with them because they had allowed my marriage to a non-Kashmiri, and accused them of being unfit to look after his children. My parents' ideas and actions were too advanced, in his opinion; his children could not be allowed to live under their influence. Much to my mother's distress, he took them away to Benares and put them in the Vasant Ashram boarding school, where my sister had worked for a term some years ago. This separation caused my parents much agony, but, of course, they could not gainsay the right of the children's father. They had to submit to the wrenching, heartbreaking farewells and accept the idea that their large family had now dwindled to just Shri and Gopi except when I and my sisters

My parents in 1925

visited them. My brother Ram had now married Marguerite and was happily settled in London, and his mother-in-law had come to live with them, a sweet, gentle person who gave Ram all the loving care of a mother and fostered a deep attachment among all three of them. Ram was rising in his career and would soon be the managing editor of the *English and Empire Digest.*

When I went north to my parents in Allahabad for medical care during my pregnancy and at the time of my confinement, my elder sister Bishan was visiting them and so was my grandmother, in her seventies. This was my father's mother, whom I had not seen since I was a child. I was naturally curious about her, for I remembered all the stories I had heard about how hardhearted she had been when my parents left home to make a life for themselves. All her dire warnings of disaster if my parents rejected her guidance had proved false. My grandfather, her husband, had died. It had been years since my father had left his home, got well established in his work, and began his intermittent correspondence with her. Yet she insisted that she was still his mother, she expected him to be a dutiful son and my mother to give her respect and service as a daughter-in-law should. This was my mother's one vulnerable spot. She still felt that she owed every subservience to her family elders. She still respected her mother-in-law in spite of the past and immediately complied with whatever demands were made. My grandmother remained a dominating woman, still good looking, still expecting her growing family to wait on her, for that was her due.

My parents were living in a house they had built on the outskirts of the city, with a large garden and mango and guava orchards. Inside, the main room was arranged in the correct North Indian style, with all the appurtenances of a decent North Indian home that they both remembered from their childhoods —the *takth,* the low wooden platform; the *chandni,* the white sheet covering the padded platform; the *gao takias,* large bolster cushions; the *paan daan,* the betel box containing areca nuts, chunam, catechu, cloves, cardamoms, and scented eating tobacco—with the spittoon and the hookah for the menfolk. There were no private rooms for individuals. We slept two and three in a room, men on one side of the house and women on the other side. Our doors were always open except in cases where a young couple needed a separate room and privacy. This was always respected by the other members of the family. Our night clothes were the same as our day clothes except that we changed into light cotton saris for the night if we had been wearing silk or embroidered saris for some occasion during the day.

As the weather got hotter and hotter, our light *charpoys,* wooden beds, were moved out of the rooms in the house into the courtyard, where we all slept in rows under the open sky. My grandmother would move the light mattress from her bed into one corner, and just before she lay down to sleep she would call, *"Bahurani* [daughter-in-law], I want my feet washed." My mother, much to my annoyance, would bring a bucket of water and wash her mother-in-law's feet before rearranging her bedding for her comfort. My mother never resented such demands. She said that these services were the right of elders. I did not have so charitable a view of the old lady. To me she seemed critical and demanding and made shameless use of my mother.

My daughter Premila was born on the 3rd of May, my first wedding anniversary, in my parents' home in Allahabad. It was a very auspicious day according to the Indian calendar, for it was the day of Buddha's birth and the day on which he achieved enlightenment. It was a full-moon night and there was an eclipse of the moon, when orthodox Indians believe that the moon has been swallowed by a demon and they must fast and wait and pray for the eclipse to be over before they rejoice, bathe, and eat. The eclipse ended at 7 P.M. and Premila was born at 7:10, when the drums were being beaten and the rejoicing was at its height. Superstition says it is inauspicious for a child to be born during an eclipse, and although I do not really believe in such folklore, still I was pleased that my first child was born to the sound of rejoicing. God bless her. She has been a wonderful daughter to me. My husband came up to Allahabad to see her but could only stay a week, and my elder sister Bishan was my chief support at this time because my mother was still fully occupied with her household duties and would have found it hard to deal with the added work created by a new, inexperienced mother and a tiny baby. I could not travel back for a month, and then my father accompanied me as far as Calcutta, an eighteen-hour journey, and my husband sent an ayah to meet me there for the long journey back to Masulipatam.

I now had a new interest to keep me occupied, and my husband was thrilled to be the father of the first child in his family. None of his older brothers had children. This was a happy time. The baby was healthy, good-natured, and well contented, for I was able to breast-feed her, and although I had an ayah, I loved doing everything for her. The only discontented member of the family was our dog, Punch. He bitterly resented this new pet in our home. He tried a hunger strike, a threatening growl whenever he saw her, an occasional yap when she cried, but failed to make us give him the priority he sought. It took us time and tact to make him accept Premila as part of the household, but, once he did, he became her most faithful attendant and protector, even ignoring my husband and me when she was around.

In a very short time my husband was transferred from Masulipatam to the Secretariat in the Madras Government and, to my great joy, we had to move back to the city that I loved, that I connected with my college days, and working days, and where I had a large number of friends with whom I could renew contacts. Just as important, my interest in social work could be revived, and I could rejoin the women's organizations with which I had been connected before my marriage. By that time there was also a well-organized Women's Club, which I joined and where I could learn to play tennis and badminton on free afternoons. The austere life in the district was over at last and a vista of purposeful activity opened before me.

I still had many things to learn when I returned to Madras as the wife of an official of the Imperial Service. Before my marriage I had had virtually no contact with officialdom, but now I had to observe the formalities required by my husband's service. Perhaps the thing that most struck me for its utter absurdity was the matter of clothes. My husband had to order a new wardrobe, for he now had to wear a heavy flannel morning coat and striped trousers to all formal and official daytime occasions. He needed a close imitation of a British tweed suit with padded shoulders for everyday wear, a dinner jacket and black tie for informal parties, and tails and white tie with pumps for invitations to Government House, formal dinner parties, and other evening functions. All this in the climate of Madras—hot and hotter.

Again I realized how ignorant I was, for I did not know the difference between a trilby and a bowler, ordinary smart shoes and evening pumps, soft and stiff shirts. My husband painstakingly taught me these lessons in dress and etiquette, though I remained appalled at the weight of the woolen clothes and the thought that any sane person could subject himself to such discomfort. I felt deeply sorry for my husband and all his fellow officials dripping with perspiration, wretchedly ill at ease at formal receptions. The other wives and I suffered less. We were supposed to wear stockings and high-heeled shoes, but we were allowed to wear our nice, loose, comfortable, flowing saris.

(Some years later, when my husband was transferred to the Imperial Secretariat in New Delhi, he had to equip himself with court dress—gold-embroidered tailcoat, white breeches, long white silk stockings, pumps, and a sword. I still have a picture of him arrayed in this regalia. You would never guess from his calm expression and the characteristic half-smile on his face how miserable he felt.)

Ridiculously enough, great store was set on the wearing of the correct dress for the correct occasion. The prestige of the Imperial Government required it in those days. Indian men who dared to wear their own costume at grand receptions were called *"baboos"* or "natives," both terms of contempt for the crudeness that such departure from English trappings indicated. We used to be told the familiar story about the English officer who traveled in Indian village areas and stayed at Dak bungalows—government rest houses provided in those remote areas to accommodate touring administrators. Even there, hundreds of miles from his nearest British colleague, he would still change into his

117

dinner jacket before he sat down to his meal in case his servant might think he was not a true sahib and would no longer respect him.

I daresay the story is true. Which doesn't make it any less idiotic. All the same, Indian Civil Service officers who had risen to the same status as Englishmen in the service had to follow the same traditions, however inappropriate they might seem. As newcomers to the Madras Secretariat we had certain social duties to perform. We ordered engraved calling cards, one batch with both my husband's name and mine, and one with my name only. Then I started on a long series of formal calls, visiting the wives of all the officers in the Secretariat senior in rank to my husband. Since Indians had only very recently acquired the right to enter the Indian Civil Service and share in the government of their country, practically all the senior officials were British.

Calling hours were usually in the afternoon, and I made my rounds, clutching my cards, ready to leave one of each kind if the lady of the house was "not at home," or to be ushered in if she was willing to receive callers. On those occasions the butler would lead me to the drawing room, where my hostess would offer me what I came to recognize as the standard "English tea" —sliced bread and butter, hot scones, and a slice of cake. Any social exchange between the Europeans and the Indians was still severely restricted, and no English man or woman would call freely on an Indian. Thus, the carefully regulated calling system gave the senior English official's wife the chance to look over the Indian newcomer over a cup of tea and get an impression of how much she knew of Western ways and to what extent she observed them in her own home. If the Indian lady knew how to serve an English meal and could speak the language fluently, her call was returned, and she and her husband might be invited to lunch or dinner as a gesture. If, however, she lived in the Indian style, ate with her fingers, served Indian food at her table, her call was discreetly not returned, and no further hospitality was extended to her and her husband.

I found this system intensely tiresome and intensely tedious, but by that time I had learned to serve Western food and could use European crockery and cutlery without fumbling, so I paid my calls with no qualms about the return visits. Twice a year we were invited formally to a meal and twice a year we repaid hospitality, and when that was over, I took no further interest in the social circle to which we officially were supposed to belong. On those stiff and dreary occasions we served and were served, *de rigueur,* seven-course meals, an appetizer or hors d'oeuvres, soup, fish, an entrée, game or chicken, dessert, and a savory, with wines to go with each dish. My husband managed the ordering of the wines and the liquor for cocktails and after-dinner drinks. I had never tasted liquor before my marriage and even now I can't tell the difference between one wine and another.

Strangely enough, the British women I met were not even faintly curious to know anything about our Indian homes, our ways and manners, how we lived when we were not conforming to their social codes, our family relationships, or what made Indian society tick. They spent their time in their own Western groups, at European clubs to which Indians were denied admission. They played tennis, golf, bridge, rode their horses, even arranged hunting parties in some places. Every summer the women went to hill stations to avoid the heat of the plains, though work prevented their husbands from accompanying them. Most of those who had children sent them to schools in England well before adolescence because the tropics "thinned the blood," or made the girls "mature too early." Their time was their own, they had plenty of servants, they needed only half an hour in the morning to give the household orders for the day.

Watching them from a distance, my Indian friends and I deplored the empty lives they seemed to lead and felt our own lives were more purposeful. We did not envy them the luxury in which they lived. We were very conscious of our domestic and public duties, and could find nothing in common with our European counterparts. But we resented hotly the superiority complex from which the majority of them suffered. We were galled by an attitude that betrayed their feelings toward Indians generally, treating us all as inferior, referring to us as "natives," an innocuous word which acquired a derogatory meaning when the British used it slightingly to refer to Indians even when they had been formally introduced. On more than one occasion when I was traveling by train, British officials' wives refused to occupy a compartment with a "native" and insisted that the stationmaster attach another compartment to the train or persuade me to move.

Only once, some years later, did I have the satisfaction of teaching an army officer's wife a lesson. I was traveling with my two small children, Premila six and Santha three years old, from Ootacamund to Madras. Coming down from a hill station, one had to travel on the hill railway to the junction on the plains where the regular broad-gauge railway functioned. The hill railway compartments are small and usually very crowded. At one of the stops, an army officer's wife got into my compartment with two adorable Pekinese pups for which there was no room on the seat of the compartment. The floor was cold and the puppies looked for some warm place on the seat. They were scrambling up on their owner's lap, but she was a stout woman and could not accommodate them. My children longed to caress them, and we would have helped her but for the fact that she turned on me most rudely and said, "You have paid half fare for your children. I have paid full fare for my dogs. Hold one of your children in your lap and make room for my dogs."

I laughed in her face and said, "Are you comparing my children to your dogs?"

"Yes," she said, "my dogs are very costly."

The dogs in the meantime were scrambling up and Santha was longing to make room for them. But I pushed the little creatures aside and said, "No, you certainly don't."

Seeing that I was prepared to stand up to her, she grumbled, but made no further move. When we came to the junction, I knew she and I would be traveling in the only first-class ladies' compartment all the way to Madras, an overnight journey. I was still fuming inwardly and hurried to the stationmaster to make sure of the booking of our seats, rushed to the compartment with my children, settled them down, and then stood at the door of the carriage. I knew there was a rule of the railway that dogs could travel with a passenger only with the consent of other passengers in the compartment.

As soon as I saw the woman approaching the carriage with several military officers—she seemed to be an important man's wife—and her two puppies, I hailed a station official and said loudly to him, "I am traveling with two small children and I object to having dogs in the compartment with me." I enjoyed the consternation on her face.

She sent word through the guard that she would keep her dogs under control, for they could not travel in the dog box of the train as they were very precious.

"Sorry," I replied, ignoring my children's agonized pleading, "I cannot have dogs in my compartment."

She bustled around furiously and then asked the authorities to find her another compartment, leaving me in sole possession. I felt mean about this and my children kept on begging me to let the puppies in, but I was determined to teach this English woman that she could not always override an Indian, as she expected she could.

Sometimes the incidents which all Indians experienced in one form or another were both comic and outrageous. Once a dinner for the officers of the Indian Civil Service was arranged at the English Club in Madras. Beforehand, incredibly enough and with no thought that anyone might be offended, the club secretary told the Indian members of the service that they would have to enter the club building by the back entrance since the club rules refused any Indian admission by the front door. Naturally, the Indians refused to attend the dinner. Not so naturally, the British officials found nothing odd—or even embarrassing—in the situation, saw no reason to complain to the club authorities and seemed quite unaware of the insult to their Indian colleagues.

Such incidents seem small and insignificant now, but someone once told me that bad manners would break up the British Empire long before bad government, and, in an important way, that insight was accurate. I, when I was young, grew red with indignation when I came across such coarse discourtesies and was ready to fight with any weapon to assert my rights. Not my political rights—I had not thought so far ahead at that time—simply my social rights for dignity as a human being. Still, in any serious sense, these pinpricks worried me only superficially. I had become deeply involved with my old friends from my college and post-college teaching days and with the work we were doing and planning for the great awakening we hoped for among Indian women, help for the underprivileged, and the reform of our social system. I could not waste too much time on our misunderstandings with the British.

CHAPTER 13

WITH MY HUSBAND'S TRANSFER to Madras in 1920, I had an opportunity to get better acquainted with the members of his family. So far, I had had only a nodding acquaintance with some of them, and others I had not met at all. Soon after we were settled in a comfortable house in a residential area not far from the center of Madras, my parents-in-law came to visit us and to meet Premila, their new and only granddaughter. My father-in-law, Dr. Raghavendra Rao, had just retired and was visiting various relatives before settling down to a quiet life in Mangalore, his home town on the southwest coast, where he had a wide circle of friends and relations. He was a slim, tall, handsome man, stern and exacting where his own family was concerned, but affable and charming to friends; deeply concerned about social-welfare work, especially work to promote education and enlightenment for women in Mangalore. He had made regular financial contributions to welfare agencies, and demanded that his sons, especially my husband and my brother-in-law, Narsing Rau, who was also in the Indian Civil Service, contribute handsomely to his social work even though at that stage in my husband's career we could ill afford to do so. But of course neither of his sons dared to disobey or even to object.

He and I became good friends. He felt he could relax with me as he could not with my husband, and Premila, then a year old, with her chubby good looks, filled him with pride and affection. Our conversation ranged far and wide but usually returned to our common interest in social welfare, and I found his views both refreshing and progressive.

My mother-in-law, a tiny woman not quite five feet in height, was gentle and affectionate and never contradicted her husband or her sons. She was orthodox, believed in the value of caste, and followed its restrictions. She was a strict vegetarian and would not eat food cooked by a non-Brahmin. She did not mind if her husband, sons, or other relations did not adhere to her codes, so long as she personally was not forced to accept their standards. As soon as I realized that she believed in the importance of these practices, I arranged a separate kitchen for her, stocked it with the grains, condiments, and other kitchen requirements she would use and found a Brahmin cook, whom I engaged to help her. In spite of that she spent her mornings in the kitchen—not preparing elaborate meals for herself but cooking delicious Mangalorean dishes for all of us, which were sent to our table at mealtimes. She always ate separately but usually sat with us to watch our reactions to her efforts and rejoiced in our enjoyment of her cooking. Fortunately for me, she spoke Hindi fluently, having lived in Benares with her eldest son, Sanjiva Rao, for some time. She and I therefore could carry on long talks in Hindi, a language which my husband could understand but in which he could not easily express himself. His mother tongue was Konkani, which I did not know. The only language we could communicate in was English.

I came to admire the sons of my parents-in-law greatly, for although they had been brought up so strictly each had branched out in his own way as soon as he had grown to manhood, with very definite and independent views of his own. For example, the only son who had conformed to a conventional marriage was Sanjiva Rao, who had been married at eighteen, just before he went to Cambridge University for further studies.

At the time, Padmabai, his bride, was eleven years old. By the time he returned to India he had made up his mind to devote his life to selfless work for the country with the Theosophical Society under Dr. Annie Besant's guidance, much to the distress of his parents, who had visualized a bright career for him, with financial rewards as well as other satisfactions. He persuaded Padmabai to do the same, and my parents-in-law had to accept the situation.

Their second son, Narsing Rau, had fallen in love with an English girl, Daisy Palmer, when he was still a student at Cambridge. As soon as he got into the Indian Civil Service and returned to India in 1911, he informed his parents that he intended to marry Daisy. My father-in-law was greatly upset, tried to dissuade him, but failed, and therefore refused to attend the wedding the following year, when Daisy came to India.

My husband chose a Kashmiri, but since that marriage came about to a good extent because of my parents-in-law, they minded it less, though they were still quite aware of its unconventionality.

There was yet another shock in store when, some years later, their youngest son, Shiva Rao, married a Viennese girl who had come to India for a Theosophical Society convention. In spite of their strict upbringing, all the sons had acted independently of their father's wishes. In his old age he accepted these events more gracefully, for he too had outgrown the narrow prejudices that had acted on him when his sons were minors.

In any case, by the time I got sufficiently acquainted with both my parents-in-law there was complete harmony in the family, no rancor about the way of life each son had chosen, and a desire to integrate all of us into a family group. I enjoyed knowing my parents-in-law, and I respected them and appreciated the difficulties they had faced as members of an older generation adjusting to the needs and ways of ours.

The first time I met my brother-in-law Narsing Rau was when he came to visit us in Madras. He had been abroad at the time of our marriage and later had been stationed in Bengal, a long way from us. I had heard of his brilliant career in school, where he had come in first in every examination, gone to Cambridge on a major scholarship, and continued his record of achievement in Trinity College. The only thing I knew about his personal life was based on rumor. Daisy and he had separated because, according to gossip, she had contracted a bad form of malaria in the up-country Bengal districts where Narsing Rau was working. The doctors had advised her never to return to India to avoid further injury to her health. But all this had happened some years before I was married. The family never spoke about the breakup of his marriage and I never mentioned it either. I was not sure of the true reasons for the separation.

Narsing Rau was reserved, retiring, and self-conscious. His extraordinary qualities of mind and heart did not reveal themselves until he somehow felt free and emotionally comfortable. Then it was a joy to discover the elegant brilliance of his intellect and the progressive, fair-minded, balanced, and learned nature of his approach to life. He was a brilliant bridge player, an excellent tennis player, an outstanding golfer, and, in fact, excelled in all outdoor and indoor sports without becoming an addict, and, oddly, without a driving sense of competition. He spent hours alone, solving mathematical problems (higher mathematics had been his subject in college, in both Madras and Cambridge), solving difficult crossword puzzles or any other brainteasers that came his way. Perhaps it is not too surprising that he was at his best and most relaxed with children. My daughters adored him and he kept them amused for hours with funny stories, limericks, tongue twisters, and simple puzzles, of which he seemed to have an endless store.

He was painfully shy about personal matters. He always came out of his room in the morning correctly dressed, shaved, and with socks and slippers on. One morning we were chatting on our terrace veranda when Premila took it into her head to examine her uncle's feet. She noticed that he always wore socks, unlike the rest of us, who went about in sandals and bare feet. Suddenly she sat down on the floor next to him, looking very solemn, and said, "Narsing Uncle, I have never seen your toes and I would like to see them."

126

He blushed to the roots of his hair and tried to distract her attention, but she persisted, pulled off his slippers and his socks, and had a good look at his feet. Satisfied at last, whatever her initial concern had been, she said, "Now you may put them on again." Over the years, watching how beautifully in tune he was with my children, I too came to know and respect him, in spite of the lack of personal communication. But that was not peculiar to him. It was shared by almost all the members of the family into which I had married.

The only exception was Shiva Rao, my husband's youngest brother, who lived several miles outside Madras but made the tedious journeys by bus just to spend a little time with Premila. He was warm, affectionate, talkative, unlike his brothers, and ready to play games with Premila and her friends, however childish they were. Although his attention was riveted more and more on politics as the campaign for Indian rights grew stronger, he always found time to get away from public affairs and visit us, bringing us news of the happenings in a sphere from which we in our official world were far separated. He was the most outgoing of the brothers, but even he, in the company of his father and his brothers, felt all the inhibitions of his early childhood days.

He and I were good friends from the first, for we could gossip cozily, especially when we were by ourselves. He was also more demonstrative with my mother-in-law than the others were; he would tease her and make demands on her for a favorite sweet or a special pickle. She loved it, but the others would hesitate to talk to her like that or put her to any extra trouble. He also had a wide circle of friends from different walks of life and had no reservations about associating with anyone he found interesting. My daughter Premila and later Santha, and later still my grandchildren, loved him dearly. Thinking back on it all now, I can see how one might have considered my children hopelessly spoiled—the only children among all my husband's brothers, indulged, made much of, loved. But I do not really think that a child is ruined by too much affection. It seems to me a healthy climate in which to grow.

127

It was much later that I had the opportunity to get to know my eldest brother-in-law, Sanjiva Rao, and his wife, Padmabai. They lived in Benares, a long way from Madras, and did not often visit us. As I have said, he had returned from St. John's College, Cambridge, fired with a desire to serve his country. Dr. Annie Besant, head of the Theosophical Society, had adopted India as her home and was trying to build educational institutions for boys and girls in Benares where the medium of instruction would be Hindi and the whole curriculum would concern itself primarily with Indian life, history, ancient languages, and literature. It was a revolutionary idea in education for India, and few people thought it could succeed. All other schools, even as small and obscure as Father d'Souza's St. Mary's in Hubli, were run along British lines, and any boy hoping to get a job in Government or any related service had to have an "English" education to qualify. Even more discouraging, Dr. Besant had to find dedicated workers to serve for very nominal salaries.

Padmabai was greatly influenced by her husband. She carried on with her own education after Sanjiva Rao returned from Cambridge and qualified to take up work in the new Vasant Ashram School for Girls in Benares, while he joined the staff of the Central Hindu College for boys. His work took him to Allahabad, then to a post as principal of a college in Jaffna, Ceylon, from there to Madras, and ultimately back to Benares, where he was appointed principal of Queen's College. His finest achievement, however, was the establishment of an educational center at Rajghat Fort, just outside Benares, on the bank of the River Ganges. He worked almost single-handed to create this center, which comprised a boys' school, a girls' school, a women's college, an agricultural school-cum-farm, and a hospital for the benefit of the villagers in the neighborhood. He succeeded remarkably well in making all his idealistic plans into a practical, functioning project, which even today is considered one of the best in India.

While all the sons of this distinguished family had begun the important public roles they would play in their various spheres of activity, the only daughter, Leela, had married young and conformed to all the old orthodox practices of her mother's period. She was the only member of the family whom I never truly got to know. She probably thought me unfeminine, even immodest; I found her good-hearted but dull and limited. Leela could not cope with the giant strides made by her brothers, but they all loved her as the baby of the family, and I soon fell into the same indulgent attitude toward her myself.

I have left to the last an account of my husband, Rama Rau, the third son of the family, as his life became linked with mine when he was on the threshold of his career. That career was outstanding, like those of his brothers, and I and my children and grandchildren continue to be proud of it. He graduated from the Presidency College the year I started there and went on to Cambridge with a scholarship to King's. After three years he took his degree and entered the Indian Civil Service. He returned to India in 1913 and was posted to the Madras Civil Service as a district officer till he rose to be joint magistrate in Masulipatam, now in Andhra State. It was at that time that the question of marriage was broached by his father.

CHAPTER 14

During the four years, 1920–1924, that my husband worked with the Government Secretariat in Madras we had to move house every six months. All the government offices moved up to the beautiful hill station of Ootacamund, where we had spent our honeymoon. It was seven thousand feet above sea level, and from April to October we all lived and worked there to avoid the heat of Madras. A similar procedure was followed by every state government as well as by the Central Government in Delhi. Each secretariat, all officials and staff and their families, moved to the closest and most convenient hill stations. It was an expensive routine, but there is no doubt that we did escape the worst of the hot weather in the plains and greeted with delight the first scent of the eucalyptus trees carried on the air miles before we arrived. Beautiful picnic spots are within easy reach from anywhere in Ootacamund, winding shady walks, and the gentle green downs that reminded all Englishmen of Sussex. More practically, a government hostel was available for those junior officers who could not find or afford suitable housing accommodation for six months only.

We returned to Madras in October, back into the heat, but I

didn't mind because I was excited at getting back to my social work again. In 1923 my second daughter, Vasanthi, known for short as Santha, was born. "Alas, another daughter!" said my orthodox relations, but to me she was as precious as my elder child and as welcome. All my life I have taken undiminished joy in my children. My parents-in-law came to live with us at that time, and a number of their relatives were also in Madras.

I knew my mother-in-law was superstitious about some things. But I'm not sure why she chose this particular time to remark on one point in my usual habits. As was the custom among women in the North, I used to wear white cotton saris with colored borders in the house, as day wear. In the South, white was usually worn by widows—miserably inauspicious for a young mother. My mother-in-law asked me one day, very gently, why I did not wear colored saris always, as they suited me so well. At once I realized that this suggestion had an underlying meaning and immediately decided to have my white saris dyed. After that I never wore a plain white sari in her presence. I was greatly touched by the tactful way she had approached the subject.

In 1924 my husband was due for a transfer. Usually an officer's term in the Secretariat was four years, but it often happened that he was transferred from one department to another, and sometimes his term was extended although there were no fixed rules about these transfers. My husband had been working in the Finance Department of the Madras Secretariat and he felt he needed further training, so he applied for six months' leave to attend a course at the British Treasury in England. He was eager that our two daughters and I should accompany him. I had never left the shores of my own country, and although I had traveled within India from north to south, and felt I knew my country fairly well, England was an altogether more alarming prospect. I knew something of England through my education in school and college and even had a sentimental feeling for it from the literature that I had read and studied. But the thought of living in a country where *everyone* behaved as did the small number of Britishers in India was far from attractive.

As it happened, I discovered that I was pregnant again. I simply hadn't the stamina to face traveling such a long way with two small children, ignorant of the living conditions I would encounter, worried about the climate (I had heard a great deal, none of it favorable, about the notorious English climate), and with a new pregnancy to consider.

My husband agreed that I should spend the six months he would be away with my mother in Allahabad and face the hot summer months there under her protection. So we traveled north with the children, a long journey, three days and three nights of constant traveling from Madras. I arrived exhausted. My husband accompanied me, stayed for two days, and went off to Bombay to catch his boat for England.

The strain of making all the arrangements for storing our furniture, packing our carpets, disposing of unwanted articles— all the countless details of dismantling an established household —and then the long journey with the children, who depended on me rather than on their father for their small wants, all in the oppressive heat of May, made me limp with fatigue when we reached Allahabad. The day my husband sailed for London from Bombay I had a miscarriage. I could not inform him till after he arrived in England, and by that time I had recovered, although I still did not feel strong enough to undertake the voyage to England with the children.

I decided to get my daughters out of the summer heat of Allahabad and to accept my sister Bishan's pressing invitation to spend some time with her and her family in Quetta, where the climate was delightful and the town itself interesting and beautiful, almost on the frontier of North India. On the train the heat was devastating, especially when we had to cross the Sibi desert. For hours the fine dust seeped in through the closed windows of the compartment, powdering everything— our hair, eyebrows, clothes, the seats and luggage with a soft, relentless invasion I could never have believed possible. The temperature was about 115 degrees and the breeze from the fans in the compartment hit us like furnace blasts. Of course, there was no air-conditioning in those days. I was torn with anxiety about putting my children through this ordeal.

However, that nightmare journey came to an end at last, and we caught sight of the treeless mountains surrounding Quetta and rejoiced in the cooler air. We were met at Quetta by my brother-in-law Dwarkanath Razdan and my sister Bishan. I could hardly take in the coolness and the beauty surrounding us, the fruit orchards, the natural springs bubbling with icy cold, fresh, clear water, and the wild flowers everywhere.

My sister had three children, the eldest a boy, and two girls very close to the ages of my two daughters. They became companions at once and we settled down for nearly three months in their hospitable home. The orchards were laden with fruit—peaches, plums, apricots, grapes—unbelievable for someone who had never seen the glory of such an abundant and varied harvest growing fresh, ripe, and succulent. The bazaars were a joy to behold, for fruit of all varieties was piled with a marvelous artistry and sense of color. My brother-in-law had a number of friends who owned orchards, and they offered to lend these shady spots for picnics. To the children's delight, we were given permission to eat as much of the fruit off the trees as we wanted, so laden were they.

By the end of August the weather in the plains had cooled somewhat and I felt it was time to leave Quetta. I had promised to spend some time with my eldest sister, Kamala, who lived in Gujrat and whose home I had never visited. Kamala had had a sad life. After her mother-in-law's death she had had a short spell of happiness, but then her husband, a lawyer with a good practice, had suffered a paralytic stroke. He had recovered fairly well except that he never regained the use of his right hand, and he continued to depend on his wife for all the writing necessary for the preparation of his cases. She thus entered on an extended form of drudgery. She worked very hard supervising the workers on her estate, she was responsible for all the housework indoors, and she had the tiresome duties connected with her husband's career. He died in 1920 after a second stroke, when she was only thirty-five years old.

At that time she was still very good looking and extremely

capable. When her husband died, her brother-in-law claimed her property on the ground that, as a widow with no son to inherit the property, she was entitled only to food and lodging, under the Hindu law. At the insistence of her husband's lawyer friends, she went to court to press her claim that the estate had been willed to her husband, was no longer "ancestral property" and therefore under the law, could be willed by him to his wife. Her husband's friends stood by her and fought the case till the judgment was made in her favor. But, even after that, she could not live alone for fear of gossip, and she had consequently invited our maternal grandmother, whose home was in Kashmir, to come to live with her. Our grandmother willingly accepted the invitation, for as she got older she found it difficult to bear the severity of the cold weather in Kashmir. She made one condition, however. She would continue to receive her own allowance from her son. In those days it was considered humiliating for a woman to accept the hospitality of her daughter's daughter, whereas she had a right to demand shelter and support from her son or in her son's son's home. My sister agreed to this arrangement, and for several years my grandmother lived in two rooms of my sister's large house, cooked her own food separately, and spent the day with my sister as her main chaperone.

Our grandmother at that time was in her late sixties. She was deaf, owing to having been burned in an accident in her youth. She felt old and was considered old. She was orthodox, deeply religious, kindly, and gentle, devoted to my sister and all of us who were the children of her only living daughter. When I went to Gujrat, she was delighted to have me stay and to meet my two small daughters. Every morning she would sit with us and tell us stories from the ancient religious books of India, taking quite seriously and literally the impossible mythological tales. Did the sister of the demon King of Lanka actually fly through the air? Yes, of course she did. Did the army of monkeys really fling great rocks and tree trunks from the mountains to make a bridge to Lanka? Naturally, look at the causeway from Rameswaram to Ceylon.

134

My sister's house was large; she always had some relatives visiting her, and so we all had company. She grew cotton, sugar cane, oranges (the blood oranges famous in the Punjab), and wheat on her land, and the villagers living in the surrounding area knew her well and were available for any work on her farm whenever their services were required. The headman of the village, who was also the man in charge of her farm, was an old Muslim, Shahji, gray-bearded, tall, and stately, who had worked for my sister's mother-in-law since she had first settled in Gujrat, when her son was only a schoolboy. Shahji was now considered an elder of the family, with the authority to reprimand my sister if she did anything unconventional. He was treated with great respect by everyone, not only in Kamala's household but also by all the villagers who lived around her property. Though he was a Muslim by religion, he acted as arbiter in the domestic quarrels of both the Hindu and Muslim young men and women, for his age and his reputation for honesty and fair-mindedness gave him the status of a judge.

There is a charming tradition that the farmers under Shahji's authority observed. When it came time for sowing wheat, after all the preparatory work on the land was done, they waited until the full moon to start this crucial activity. At that time it was the duty of the mistress of the house—in the old days it was my sister's mother-in-law, but after her death it was Kamala—to scatter the first seeds. It was considered auspicious for a good harvest that the mistress of the house ceremonially start the sowing.

There was no particular plan to the house. Rooms had been built in all directions around a central hall where visitors were entertained. The kitchen was a separate building outside the main house. It opened onto a courtyard shaded by an enormous banyan tree—as old as the hills, everyone said—around which a wide parapet had been built. In late August and September it was cooler out of doors, and we often ate our food under the tree, sitting on the carpets that were spread out on the parapet. The children, Premila, four years old, and Santha, one and a half, loved being in the open, picking the balls of snow-white cotton and following Shahji about the grounds to see how the oranges were getting on and choosing the thickest and most luscious sugar cane for after lunch. As soon as lunch was over the cry was carried loud and clear by the children: *"Shahji, gannu lao"* ("Shahji, bring in the sugar cane"). This was sweet and tender and cut in small pieces; we as well as the children would strip them with our teeth and bite off juicy bits to chew and enjoy.

All the cotton harvested was heaped in a corner of another room, and the village women brought the rollers they used to prepare and open the pods and remove the cotton seeds. Then the cotton was spun and made ready for weaving on small looms, which were set up in the grounds, and the weaving would begin in all its different patterns.

One story about our grandmother in those days still haunts me. Although she was so deaf that she could only hear when one shouted into her ear, she continued to lock the door of her room at night. She kept her small belongings there, under her bed. One night we were awakened by an earthquake, which shook the floor and rattled the windows and frightened us all beyond measure. We ran out of the house, carrying the children, and my sister rushed to our grandmother's room to wake her and get her out too. She knocked and knocked and then I knocked and rattled the door, but we could get no answer. By that time the earthquake seemed to have subsided and we felt it was safe to go back, but Kamala and I still worried about my grandmother.

The next morning when she emerged, all washed and dressed in her clean white sari, we asked her if she hadn't been frightened. "No," she said. "What was the matter?" We told her about the earthquake and realized that she had slept peacefully through it. I teasingly asked her what treasures she had in her room that she felt had to be locked in so securely every night.

"Yes, my dear," she replied, "I have my treasure under my bed and will show it to you, if you like."

"Oh yes, please, Grandmother. I long to see what you value so highly."

She took me into her room and pulled out a tin trunk from

under her bed. In it was everything she would require for her funeral—a shroud, the sacred ashes that must be smeared on the forehead of a widow at her death, a bottle of water from the Ganges, the holy river of Hindus, several religious scripts, and a small bundle of rupee notes that would pay for her cremation. "You see, my child," she said, "I may die any day, so I have made all my preparations so that my granddaughter Kamala may find everything she will require for my cremation. My son will not be able to reach here in time since he lives a long way away in Kashmir, and my granddaughter must not be put to any expense on my account when the inevitable happens."

I was greatly impressed by this revelation of the stoic and philosophical attitude my grandmother had reached at her time of life. After all the sorrows she had suffered when she was left a widow in her young life, after her children had died, leaving only her son in Kashmir and my mother in Allahabad, somehow she had come to terms—even easy terms—with the realities of life and death. I admired her courage and the deep religious faith that had sustained her and prepared her for her own end whenever she should be called, and I wondered if I should ever acquire the tranquillity within myself for so overwhelming an acceptance.

The two months in Gujrat sped quickly and I soon found that I ought to be making preparations to get back to Allahabad to await the return of my husband from abroad. I had been interested in and in many ways grateful for what life had brought my elder sisters—Bishan, happy with her husband and her children and released at last from the confines of the joint family; Kamala, now, after many years, her own person, using her excellent abilities, having the satisfaction of a well-run estate even if she had to bear a measure of personal loneliness, no hope of marrying again, and no children to give her life fullness and meaning.

My husband returned by the end of October and was immediately posted to Bangalore in Mysore State, where he was to be the secretary to the Government of India Taxation Enquiry Committee, known as the Todhunter Committee. We moved to that delightful garden city 2,500 feet above sea level, with its cool and pleasant climate. It was an important city in Mysore, an independent state under the rule of an exceedingly enlightened Maharaja, who was a scholar, a patron of Indian and Western music, and devoted to the welfare of his people. Unlike some of the rulers of other independent Indian states at that time, he was much loved by the people of Mysore. He had made his state one of the most progressive in India, providing electricity even in village areas, helping and encouraging all progressive programs, especially the education of women. He believed that it was through such education that old patterns of social practices could be eradicated and the enlightenment of all society established. The Women's College in Mysore had an Indian woman principal, and he had established many girls' schools in Bangalore and throughout Mysore.

In Bangalore we had a comfortable bungalow, entered Premila in a good school—pleased that more and more girls were seeking a formal education—and we made a number of new friends. My husband seldom discussed his official work with me, and I had learned to accept his unexpressed conviction that I would not be able to understand or even be much interested in the problems with which a civil servant had to cope. Perhaps this was true, though it was never tested. In any case, I maintained my separate concern with matters that did not particularly involve him. I soon went back to work on behalf of women in programs which were well established there by that time.

One of the most admirable of the new friends I made was Dr. Marchant, the superintendent of the Maternity Hospital. We often discussed the tragedy of some of the pregnant women, still almost children themselves, in the maternity wards. One day she asked me if I would like to meet one of her patients, whose case worried her greatly. She was a girl of twelve, a young child in appearance, who was expecting her baby very soon. It would have to be a caesarean birth, for the girl was too small to bear a child naturally.

"Yes, of course, I would," I said at once. Some of my friends and I were studying the question of banning child marriages by law.

On the day this girl began labor, Dr. Marchant sent word to me and allowed me to watch the delivery. It broke my heart to see this child, barely showing signs of maturity herself, operated upon and delivered of a tiny live baby. When everything was tidied up and the nurse brought the baby to her, she pushed it aside and burst into tears.

This event left a great impression on my mind. I was stirred to work harder to make such tragedies impossible. Motherhood in a case like that was incontrovertibly a tragedy. I believed ardently that childbirth should always be the radiant culmination of married life and the child a supremely welcome gift to the parents. I think that I date from that moment, from those miserable, despairing tears of the child mother, my determination to dedicate all my energies to the banishing of such evils in Hindu society. This became, years later, a determination to spread information about planned parenthood, about how it was possible to be sure that every child was wanted, received with love and with the hope of proper care, a decent upbringing, and a reasonable chance of a happy future.

Premila and Santha in Simla in 1927

CHAPTER 15

THE TAXATION COMMITTEE completed its report in 1925 and my husband was again posted as Deputy Secretary in the Finance Department of the Madras Secretariat. We found a suitable house in Madras, settled down, and a couple of months later once more moved with the rest of the Government to Ootacamund for the summer. Soon, however, my husband was transferred to the Government of India Secretariat as Deputy Secretary to the Finance Ministry, which meant that our headquarters would be New Delhi, with the summer hill station of Simla. We packed our possessions in Ootacamund, returned to Madras to collect the belongings we had left there, closed our new home and in June, the hottest month of the year, traveled from the cool hill climate of Ooty, as we called it, through the whole length of India.

It was a journey of five days and five nights to Simla, and I had to cope alone with the children because the ayah from Madras refused to move to such distant places as Simla and Delhi. No government house had been allotted to us and we stayed in a hotel, where both children promptly came down with measles. They seemed too young to be left in the care of strangers, so I spent all day in the Infectious Diseases Hospital in Simla for nearly three weeks till they were both well again. A few days after we returned to the hotel, even before I could look around and assess my new surroundings, back I had to go to the hospital with Santha, who had contracted a severe case of dysentery. I spent a fortnight of great anxiety, for she was very ill indeed. Meanwhile Premi was left in the hotel in the care of her father, a new ayah, and the kind neighbors in the hotel, with whom I had scarcely become acquainted.

Simla was hot and dusty at that time of year, compared with Ootacamund. The only transport allowed was the rickshas drawn by four coolies because no cars or carriages could negotiate the steep roads. The one pleasing sight was the view of the snow-clad mountains in the distance, at which I stared with wonder. Our southern hill stations, high as they were, never had snow on them.

When both children had fully recovered, I had time to meet the people who would be my new associates. I found them to be "fashionable" or Westernized women of northern India. They wore georgette and ninon saris of the prettiest pastel shades, vied with each other in aping European ways in their homes, and entertained lavishly the large British, mostly official, population of the seat of the Indian Government. It was an artificial society. The Indian women had little to do besides entertain each other during the day and join their menfolk in club life, games, and parties during the evenings.

I felt very much like a fish out of water, a crude country cousin. In the South I had moved in a wide, non-official circle of Indian friends and co-workers, and I was still uneasy with the Western ways of Indian official society in the North. Our relations with British officialdom in the South had been stiff and formal.

I had always loved and worn the South Indian saris of heavy handwoven silk, in brilliant primary colors with contrasting borders. My reds, yellows, blues, and some shot silks with unusual color combinations, made me conspicuous in any group of North Indian women. Many of them thought I lacked refinement, for I gloried in things that belonged to the true Indian

142

culture of the South. Also I was annoyed by the disparaging remarks made by North Indians about Madras and the South generally, and their harsh and ignorant judgment of so many beautiful things in that area. I resented their surprise that I, a northerner by birth, could adopt so much of the South in my dress and manners and feel so closely linked with the life of Madras. However, I reminded myself of my own first impressions of Madras and I eventually found that we could become friends in spite of these differences of opinion.

When we moved down from Simla to New Delhi, my husband was allotted a very nice house with a garden. The plan that Sir Edwin Lutyens had made for New Delhi was most impressive, but the city was still undeveloped. This was to be the nucleus of the great Imperial Capital of India, the most populous dominion of the British Empire, the brightest jewel in the British crown. The designs were on an appropriately grand scale, and some of the important buildings were already finished. The great circular Parliament House, the houses for secretaries, deputy secretaries and the staff were already occupied, and the Viceroy's house, which today is Rashtrapati Bhavan, the residence of the President of India, was well on the way to completion. The wide, shady roads were ready, their roundabouts planted with the grass and flowers so characteristic of the new city, and the vistas promised great beauty when the city was entirely built.

The trees bordering the avenues had not, in 1926–1928, grown to their full height. And there were other complaints, too. New Delhi was all too official, too new, and too unfinished. There were transport and shopping difficulties that made day-to-day living almost impossible for those who were not part of the government machinery. Old Delhi, the true, established capital of the Mogul emperors, was miles away, a real city teeming with people, crowded houses, business of all kinds, shops and bazaars, the marks of a flourishing metropolis. Much as I admired some parts of New Delhi, I was not thrilled to be living there, for I could not find among the young people any who took an interest in the Indian problems which had so deeply concerned me in Madras. Society was made up of officialdom and

143

concerned primarily with government interests. Social functions occupied them fully: bridge parties, dinner and luncheon parties, and, of course, the latest fashions of the day, in which I had very little interest.

However, I soon discovered that exciting and serious events were taking place in the country and I could feel closer to them and understand them better by attending the meetings of the Central Legislature. There politicians from all over India met in parliamentary session to discuss the burning issues of the day.

I have not so far mentioned political problems because we, as officials of the British Government in India, could take no active part in the drive for further and further political reform for India. Interested as we were in the awakening of the general Indian public to the demands of our leading politicians and the issues raised at the annual National Congress meetings, we could express neither an opinion nor our sympathy with the work being done by the nationalists. All the same, I found it wonderfully exciting to attend the Legislative Assembly meetings and listen to some of India's greatest political leaders, who sat on the opposition benches. They had a fine gift of oratory, and were eloquent in presenting convincing arguments on important issues: Pandit Motilal Nehru, the father of Jawaharlal Nehru, Pandit Madan Mohan Malviya, Mr. Goswami, Mr. Chamanlal, Mr. Jayakar and Mr. Satyamurti of Madras, and Mr. Mohammed Ali Jinnah, later the founder and first President of Pakistan, who at that time was an ardent Indian Nationalist. It was a wonderful opportunity for me to learn from and meet these great men.

I was particularly impressed by Pandit Motilal Nehru, of whom I had heard glowing reports when I was a young student in college. He was an elder of my own Kashmiri community, the leader of the bar in the High Court in Allahabad, where my parents lived, and stories about him and the elegance of the way he lived sounded like fairy tales to us. Under the influence of his son Jawaharlal Nehru, who, after a completely British education at Harrow and Cambridge, had become converted to Mahatma Gandhi's political campaign, Motilal gradually began to align

144

himself with the Indian Nationalist cause. I had met him several times, during my visits to my parental home in Allahabad, but on those occasions we had chatted mostly about family matters —we were, in fact, distantly related. When I saw him for the first time from the gallery in the Council Chamber, I realized the complete change that had come over him. He appeared in a flowing *dhoti* and *kurta,* with a Kashmiri shawl over his shoulders. He was short, white-haired and rather heavily built, but with a striking, dominating personality that immediately drew the attention of everyone present and forced us to recognize that here was a natural leader to whom one could give unstinted and instinctive homage.

Mohammed Ali Jinnah was equally impressive but in an entirely different way. He was tall, slim, handsome, and distinguished-looking, immaculately dressed in Western clothes. His severe, cold manner held a hint of latent cruelty and sarcasm, but he was an excellent speaker and was always listened to with respect and in pin-drop silence. He seemed, and I think he was, Indian at heart—at that time. Only later when the cry was raised for a separate Muslim country—Pakistan—did he break with his old Nationalist colleagues. Jinnah, in my opinion, was not a man with whom one could easily make friends, but Motilal Nehru was warm, human, and lovable. He received even young and unimportant people like us with genuine friendliness and a charmingly paternal attitude.

I have always been deeply affected by public speakers who can express their thoughts not only in good language but forcefully enough to hold the attention of the audience. In those days, in political circles India had a galaxy of effective speakers both inside the Legislature and outside on the platforms of political meetings. New Delhi, the site of Parliament and the seat of Government, attracted everyone—those who worked on the fringes of political life in support of the proposals and arguments of the leaders who could speak directly to Government, as well as interested bystanders like me. Thus I had the good fortune to attend meetings held by Dr. Annie Besant and to listen to her flawless flow of thought and language; to hear

Srinivasa Shastri, president of the Servants of India Society, who was known as one of the most distinguished speakers of the British Empire; to Sarojini Naidu, whom I had admired from the time, years earlier, when I had first heard her in Madras. The array of talented men and women, some emblazoned in history, some who are already forgotten, all of whom had a great influence on my life, makes me marvel at my good fortune in being in such a place at such a time: Jawaharlal Nehru, Subhas Chandra Bose, Sardar Vallabhbhai Patel, his brother Sardar Viththalbhai Patel, Maulana Mohemedali, Maulana Shaukat Ali, Dr. Rajendra Prasad, Dr. Abul Kalam Azad, and, towering above them all, Mahatma Gandhi, the leader who was responsible for the ultimate achievement of Indian independence. It was an exciting time to live in, to feel the gradual awakening of the immense population of our country to the call, so difficult to describe to the Western world, of the new message, which Mahatma Gandhi sounded: *"Satya, Satyagraha,* and *Ahimsa"* (Truth, Resistance in the Cause of Truth, and Nonviolence). With that rallying cry he won the greatest victory modern India has ever seen.

The meetings of the Central Legislative Assembly turned my attention more and more toward the demands for political reforms which the Indian members of the House were making. Until then I had had no direct connection with, and only a superficial understanding of, the many currents in the political world. In the Assembly I heard the views of the moderates as well as the extreme demands of other political parties. Most of all, Mahatma Gandhi and his philosophy began to have a clearer meaning to me.

I was thrilled when we were asked to extend our hospitality to Dr. Annie Besant, who was deeply involved with the campaign for "Home Rule" and was considered a moderate, although she was as progressive as any Indian leader at that time. She was our house guest when she attended the All Parties Conference in 1927, and Sir Tej Bahadur Sapru, a relative of mine, and also a leading lawyer and politician, visited our home frequently to discuss political issues with her. Not only was Dr. Besant the

My husband in court dress in New Delhi, 1928

president of the Theosophical Society, to which many of my husband's family belonged, and one of the leaders of the "Home Rule" movement, she had become completely integrated with the hopes and aspirations for Indian political freedom and was a preeminent figure at the All Parties Conference. (At that time the demand for complete Indian independence had not been raised nor had the "Quit India" movement—addressed to the British rulers—taken any strong hold in political circles.) She had snow-white hair, was short and rather heavy in build, but distinguished looking, and had a dominating personality. Her voice, as I still remember it, was soft and melodious, and yet, when she spoke at public meetings, it had a carrying power that made her words resound to the last rows of the large audiences she always attracted. With us she was gentle and kindly and was especially sweet to my children and to a great big dog called Tippu we had at that time—a Rampur hound—which, at meal-times, liked to stand at table with his head resting easily on the tabletop, as though ready to join in any conversation we were having. Dr. Besant always ate with our family, and when we discouraged Tippu from appearing at the table, he crouched down at her feet with his head on her lap and she surreptitiously fed him bits of *chapati.* Being a strict vegetarian she could not provide him with a crunchable bone, but he seemed to be quite content.

One day Tippu ran away from home, having been attracted, we believed, by a young female of his own species. We were anxious, upset, tried to trace him without success. Late that evening he dragged himself home, badly injured and in great pain from a broken front leg. It was nearly eleven o'clock and we tried hard to get in touch with a veterinary, but failed. Annie Besant came out of her room and began to caress him. Strangely enough, he was so soothed by her ministrations that he became entirely limp and quiet as though she had some healing in her touch. We couldn't understand it, but she sat with him into the small hours of the morning although she had an important meeting the next day, and her soothing presence at last put him to sleep. The next morning, of course, we took him to the doctor, where he had the medical attention he needed, but we continued to be greatly touched by her care and solicitude and we felt sure that she had transmitted some inexplicable and soothing communication of hand or voice that helped him through that terrible night.

We sensed that India was on the eve of a political upheaval, and I spent hours in the gallery of the House while my children were both at nursery school. I also had the good fortune to meet several of our great men socially. One party I will never forget. An eminent economist, Professor Robertson from Cambridge, had a letter of introduction to my husband from a mutual friend. My husband invited him to stay as our guest during his visit to Delhi. Professor Robertson wished to meet some of the out-standing politicians in New Delhi, and we invited Pandit Motilal Nehru; Mrs. Sarojini Naidu, the poet turned politician; Lala Lajpat Rai, a political leader from Lahore; Srinivasa Shastri from Madras; and a few others—hoping that the discussion would be serious and impressive. But Mrs. Naidu, a gifted conversational-ist and a dedicated Nationalist, was in a frivolous mood. Instead of discussing politics she kept the whole table in roars of laugh-ter with her mockery of her fellow politicians and her anecdotes and jokes that soon infected everyone else at the table. It was a very successful party as such, but nothing serious was dis-cussed, and we were greatly embarrassed that Professor Robert-son got so little of what he was looking for. We did make other opportunities for him to meet the people he was interested in who would discuss Indian economic problems with him, but I wonder whether he enjoyed those occasions nearly as much.

Besides my political education, another project interested me in 1927. In talking to some of the staff of the Finance Ministry I gathered that members of the Secretariat who had small school-age children found it a great hardship to move every six months from New Delhi to Simla. They often could not get their children admitted in the middle of the school term, and they could not afford to leave them at boarding schools in Delhi. It struck me as most unfair that nothing had been done about this very real problem.

149

This was my first essay at taking the initiative in a concrete cause, however small in scale. I whipped up the interest and enthusiasm of a few serious and interested women and then approached the wife of one of the senior, respected Executive Council members to head a committee I had formed to collect funds for a school in Simla for the children of the Secretariat staff. This school would operate from May till October—the six months that the Secretariat was obliged to be in Simla—so that the continuity of their children's education would not suffer. I took on the secretaryship of the committee, made appeals, sought contributions from the well-to-do in Delhi, including the members of the Assembly, and soon collected contributions that enabled us to try out the experiment.

I next took over the material arrangements of the project. As the secretary of this new Lady Irwin School (Lady Irwin was the wife of the Viceroy of India), I found a building in Simla, engaged a headmistress, a Mrs. Roy, who came to us highly recommended from Calcutta, and we were all ready to start work when the Government moved to Simla in April of that year. We had prepared for 100 children, a liberal figure, we thought, to start with. When we opened our doors at the new premises, we had 250 children with their mothers waiting on our doorstep and refusing to be denied.

It took a lot of hard work to extend the building, to enlist more teachers, to buy secondhand furniture, and to make provision for this entirely unexpected avalanche. As the secretary, I went every morning to the school building, about a mile away, to supervise and help with the classes and to support the new headmistress, who was bewildered by having to face a much bigger and more complicated task than she had envisioned. By the following year the school was well established, much to the satisfaction of the parents and apparently of the children, too, who had now some semblance of coherence in their education. (After Independence the Lady Irwin School was shifted permanently to Delhi, when the Government exodus to Simla in the summer months was stopped. Today it still flourishes and has become one of the well-known schools of the capital.)

CHAPTER 16

A COUPLE OF YEARS earlier the Government had appointed a committee of men and women to study the question of the "age of consent." At that time, with child marriage the generally accepted convention in India, there was no real supervision on a matter as delicate as the "age of consent" for girls. When did a husband's right to marital relations constitute rape? How could a young girl, ignorant and frightened, be told that below a certain age she could legally refuse him? The committee traveled all over India taking evidence and recommended the raising of the age of consent for girls to fourteen years.

Soon after this a well-known leader interested in social reform, Mr. Har Bilas Sarda, introduced a bill in the Central Legislature recommending the abolition of child marriage. This was at the session of the Legislature in Simla where several women from other parts of the country were vacationing. Some of them were social workers, especially interested in the question of child marriage. I called a meeting of those workers whom I knew through other organizations to discuss Har Bilas Sarda's bill. It was here that the Child Marriage Abolition Society was formed, and I was elected secretary of the new association. We decided to carry on a campaign in favor of the Sarda bill, and to propagandize the necessity of supporting it in all educated circles we could reach.

Clearly, if the Age of Consent Committee was recommending fourteen as the age of consent, it was because they had learned that girls married between six and thirteen were in actual practice exposed to the danger of being molested with impunity by their husbands and could neither complain nor take legal action. In the absence of legislation such as the Sarda bill, complaint against the husband would be legally ineffective and would mean the breakup of the marriage. In orthodox communities such charges would never be made. We felt, therefore, that even though the Sarda bill did not go far enough, it was necessary to support it to help break the custom of child marriage and perhaps strengthen those who disapproved of child marriage but had not the courage to defy an ancient custom.

Armed with the figures and statistics collected by the Age of Consent Committee, which showed that 40 percent of the Hindu and Muslim girls at that time were married before they were fourteen years old, I arranged for meetings, placing the facts before audiences and pleading for support for the Sarda bill. So far, it had been introduced in Parliament but had not yet been considered. I wrote to social-welfare societies all over India, pointing out the desirability of demonstrating their support for such legislation by sending letters and telegrams to the Home Minister endorsing the proposed measures, so that a solid body of favorable opinion should influence the Government group when the bill came up for discussion. Certain doubts were being expressed in Government circles about allowing such a bill to be brought before the House. We knew that all progressive Indian societies would support the bill, but we did not know the minds of the British women whose husbands sat on the Government benches with the majority in the Legislature. Might these women persuade their husbands to defeat the measure for mysterious reactionary reasons of their own?

The only European women's group we could approach was the National Council of Women, formed by the wives of British

152

officials at the instance of Lady Aberdeen, the president of the International Council of Women. I had been a member ever since the society was formed, and in Simla Lady Birdwood, the wife of the Commander-in-Chief, was the president. I suggested to her that a meeting of the National Council of Women should be called in Simla because I thought it would be useful for all of us to talk about Har Bilas Sarda's pending bill. I hoped in this way to win them over to influence their husbands to support the bill. Lady Birdwood very kindly called a meeting at her own residence. It was a crowded one and, called on to speak, I explained in detail the ancient system of child marriage, the relationship between child marriage and the age of consent, the hardships endured by children who had been legally married, and the danger of their molestation by their legally and religiously approved husbands. I knew of cases, I said, thinking of Dr. Marchant's patient in Bangalore, of girls under fourteen who bore legitimate children because the law did not forbid child marriage. I appealed to the British women, especially the wives of Government officials, to persuade their husbands to support a bill framed and brought into the House by a progressive Indian leader and supported universally by leading educated Indian men and women, officials and non-officials.

I thought I had made a convincing case, but I was dismayed and infuriated when the wife of one senior official stood up and said that she did not think she could support such a measure, nor did she think that any of the British officials in the Legislature would be willing to support such a bill. Her argument was that the Queen's Proclamation, issued when India became part of the British Empire, stipulated that there should be no interference with the religious rites and practices of the people of the country under British rule. After all, Queen Victoria had not inherited the title of Defender of the Faith for nothing. The British were surely committed to defending the practices of *all* religious faiths under their protection.

I should have been prepared, but I wasn't. Some obstinate optimism had kept me hoping that, if not good sense, at least plain humanity would triumph. But the bill was indeed defeated in Parliament, introduced again in 1928, and once again defeated. It was ultimately passed only in 1929, when the minimum age of marriage for girls was fixed at fourteen and for boys at eighteen.

I was involved in another clash with British women soon after. I was the secretary of the Purdah Club (a women's social club in Simla—called "Purdah" because there were several Muslim women members who wore the veil and did not appear before men). We met in a conveniently large room—women of all communities, British and Indian officials' wives, the wives of members of the Legislature, and women of other social groups. We either played games or chatted around tea tables, and thus we got an opportunity to meet women who did not appear at public gatherings. One day we were advised to move to a larger room, the ballroom of a restaurant called Davico's in a new building on a hill. The subject of the change of venue for our club came up at a committee meeting. One senior British official's wife said that it would be a great expense if we accepted the move to Davico's. The hand-pulled rickshas of the members could not climb the hill, and what's more, we would have to have screens stretching all the way from the main road up the hill to Davico's ballroom, so that the Muslim members would be properly protected from the gaze of strange men. I, as the secretary, objected and said, "The ladies who are in purdah can keep their veils on. The others can climb the hill from the main road."

"Oh, no," came the objection. "This is a Purdah Club, and we must make proper arrangements for the purdah ladies."

This infuriated me. We were anxious to abolish purdah gradually and none of the other Indian members, including several Muslims, indicated any qualms. I turned to them and appealed for a decision. Fortunately it came out in my favor, but incidents of this kind made bad blood between Indian women and the British. Indignantly I felt that it was the British women who wished to perpetuate the outmoded customs we were trying to change, that they were not sympathetic to the fundamental re-examination that our society needed. Yet, apart from recording

154

our disagreements and our protests, there was little we could do.

All through this time there was an unformulated current of dissatisfaction with the content of the education our girls were receiving in the recognized girls' schools. Parents were reluctant to send their daughters to the Government schools because the curriculum prescribed for all educational institutions still followed the British model, just as it had in my years at St. Mary's in Hubli. For boys this kind of imitation English education had its uses, since they needed it for the jobs they would seek under the British Government.

Daughters were another matter. Parents felt girls should have a uniquely Indian education that would teach them about their own country, its history, languages, geography, social system, cultural patterns, domestic economy, and such subjects as would fit them for life in their own homes later yet would still give them the chance to take courses that would be appropriate should they follow professional careers. In fact, a complete re-evaluation of the educational system for women was needed, and this led, in 1927, to the first All-India Women's Conference for Educational Reform. Organized by a group of university women from several Indian provinces, it met in Poona to review the existing educational syllabus, to introduce subjects of special interest to women, and to suggest changes primarily for the purpose of making education better adapted to the needs of Indian girls. It was meant to be convened only once, to make recommendations to the educational authorities for suitable changes in the school curriculum.

It proved to be an explosive meeting. Nobody could have foreseen that it would mark the founding of the largest women's organization in the world, with branches in every province of India and an influence that would help to shape far more than educational policy alone.

So much enthusiasm was aroused in discussing educational reforms that the delegates soon took up allied topics. What about the backward, tradition-bound conditions in Indian

155

homes? How could we help the young women of Indian families to become eligible for higher studies? Customs that hampered the education of girls were chiefly, we had to admit, early marriage, the veiling of girls from the age of fourteen, and the caste system. The women at that first conference realized that their work would have to be much wider in scope. They decided that the All-India Women's Conference should be a permanent body meeting every year in different parts of India and advocating social reforms of every sort, including, of course, the educational system. Among the basic tenets of the new organization were opposition to distinctions of caste and creed and the exclusion of any involvement in party politics. Each province of India was to form a similar organization linked to the Central Committee to study subjects of interest to women, both political and nonpolitical, and to report annually on their findings.

In 1928 the All-India Women's Conference met in Delhi, where the Begum of Bhopal, the woman ruler of an independent princely state, presided. She was a very well-educated woman, and although she had observed the Muslim custom of purdah all her life, she had attended imperial conferences in England, fully veiled, and played a forceful role in their discussions. At this first meeting of the conference the much-respected Begum amazed us all with a gesture that would have been impossible even five years before. Speaking from the platform about the necessity for Indian women to move forward, to discard the shackling customs of the past, she gave them the initiative. First, she declared, we should abolish the whole system of purdah, which so demeans and constricts women, and, with a marvelously dramatic sweep of her hand, she ripped the veils from her face, exposing it in public for the first time since she was a child.

In India, in those days, travel from one province to another was long and tedious. Allowing a week for the conference and another week for travel, it was difficult for many women to leave their homes and children for the required fortnight. Also, all expenses had to be met by the delegates themselves, and they were mostly women of small means who saved all year round to be able to attend these conferences. Some had friends who offered them hospitality, but most of the women traveled, lived and ate at their own expense—and as cheaply as possible. In spite of these obstacles, the awakening was so wide and the rising excitement so great that every year the membership of the All-India Women's Conference increased.

The Indian women were quick to recognize the advantages of these meetings. They began to discover their own country. South Indians found the North very different in food, climate, and language, in problems and social practices, while North Indians similarly found themselves virtually in a foreign land when meetings were held in the South. In the camps set up for the delegates at each conference, all castes and communities lived side by side and ate the same food, except for the provisions made for vegetarians and nonvegetarians. They learned to appreciate new tastes, new methods of cooking, unfamiliar costumes. The loose trousers and tunics of the Punjab, the hand-loomed saris of Maharashtra, the heavy, bright-colored silks of Madras, the dainty ninon and georgettes of the Delhi area—all were represented in the camps and at the meetings. Most important of all, these women made friends with one another, an opportunity they would never have had if they had stayed in their own homes.

The All-India Women's Conference was starting to educate in ways it had never planned. Women were learning to travel without escorts. South Indian delegates knew they must provide for the extreme cold of the North (all conferences were held in December), and North Indians happily discarded their woolens when the venue of the conference was in the South. Their minds were opening to new situations; a breadth of vision, a tolerance and understanding unknown in the old days were gradually being created. And Indian women were ready for it. The conference must have touched some unsuspected wellspring that was suddenly flowing with tremendous force.

The work of the conferences expanded from year to year. Not only were internal social problems discussed, but international subjects, chiefly concerning women, were studied. In England women's groups were still agitating for equal suffrage, equal pay

157

for equal work, the abolition of the brothel system and the general exploitation of women, and we in India took up the study of these questions in our own country as well as problems peculiar to our society. We had not, for instance, given sufficient thought to the illiterate working women of our own country. When the British Government appointed a parliamentary commission to recommend changes in labor laws in India, one of the members was an intelligent woman whose special sphere was the predicament of unskilled or semiskilled laboring women. She enlisted the help of educated women in each state she visited to act as interpreters. This immediately aroused the interest of women who had not so far made contact with the laboring class and who came to realize more vividly that these other women, unreachable except by word of mouth, were very much our concern. We waited for the report of the Labour Commission, studied its recommendations for bettering the working conditions of women and carried on propaganda demanding that the proposals in the report be implemented by the Government. In fact, the plight of the laboring classes continued to be a serious interest of the All-India Women's Conference.

CHAPTER 17

IN 1928, WHILE my husband was still the Deputy Secretary of Finance with the Government of India, a great tragedy befell our family. A year before we had been posted to Delhi, my sister Bishan's husband, Dwarkanath Razdan, had been transferred to Delhi. Bishan and her family, with whom we had spent such a happy time in Quetta in 1924, lived not very far from us, and we had many noisy, cheerful visits with each other. Early that year, returning home from work, my brother-in-law was knocked down by a car. He was taken to the hospital immediately with a grave head injury. Before he became unconscious he gave the police our address and telephone number, having no telephone in his own home. On receiving the message my husband and I rushed to my sister's home, picked her up and took her to the hospital. Dwarkanath was able to recognize her and even to say a few words to her before he died.

The shock was unimaginably terrible. Bishan could hardly accept the fact that she was left with three young children—a boy of fourteen, a girl of twelve, and one of seven—and no great financial resources to educate and settle them. My parents traveled to Delhi from Allahabad to be with her till she decided what she should do. She could either settle in Lahore, where her husband's family would welcome her and the children, or live in Allahabad, where our parents lived. After much thought she decided against Lahore and a resumption of joint family life, which had so constrained her in the early years of her marriage. Instead she went to Allahabad, where there was a small cottage on the grounds of my father's property which she could rent, and where she could live independently, educate her children, and still be within easy reach of her parents and other relations.

Before she had firmly decided, the hot weather arrived, signaling the annual April-to-October exodus of the Government. Soon after we reached Simla a curious incident kept Bishan in my thoughts in a rather upsetting way. I had returned to my work at the Lady Irwin School, and one day the headmistress invited me to tea with her staff. In the course of our talk she told me that one of her teachers had a peculiar gift. If she sat idly with a pencil in her hand, it began to move with no control from her, writing messages of which she could make no sense at all. I had never heard of "automatic writing" at the time and was, naturally, intrigued and skeptical, and jokingly asked to watch such a demonstration.

All of us agreed excitedly that this would be interesting and gave the teacher paper and pencil. To my astonishment her hand began to move vigorously, scratching across the paper at first, and then words began to form. This young woman knew nothing about my family, or the name of my sister, or the loss we had recently endured in New Delhi. I asked questions. Who from the outer world was trying to get in touch with me? The reply came at once, clear and without hesitation, "Don't you know me, Dhan? I am Dwarkanath."

I felt stunned and shaken. But the writing continued, with one word repeated again and again: "Bishan, Bishan." I waited a little while to try to find some logic or reason for what was happening. Then I asked what Bishan should do. The answer came promptly. "Tell her to go to Allahabad. She will be better able to educate the children there."

As soon as I got home I wrote to my sister. Though she had

already made her decision, this message reassured her. We had always been told that we should not seek communication with the dead, for there was a belief among us that it caused distress to the departed soul. Certainly I had no wish to trouble Dwarkanath and never attempted to do so again. However, my sister did well to settle in Allahabad, for not long afterward my maternal grandmother died and my eldest sister, Kamala, with whom she had lived her last years, decided to sell her estate in Gujrat and move to Allahabad. There she was within easy reach of my parents and the rest of the family, who frequently visited them, and of Bishan, with whom she finally made a permanent home. Years later, we realized how wise Kamala had been to give up her home in Gujrat. The Partition of India, which accompanied Independence in 1947, placed Gujrat in Pakistan. Those Hindus who owned property in the Pakistan section of divided India suffered great financial loss, if they escaped with their lives at all.

In 1928 a Royal Commission was appointed, with Sir John Simon (later Lord Simon), an eminent lawyer, as chairman, and representatives of all the parties of the British Parliament as members, to collect evidence for further political reforms for India. Ten years had elapsed since the last such commission, and the British Government had given an undertaking that every decade the political position within India and of India within the British Empire would be reviewed. By this time political agitation had grown in the country, under the leadership of Mahatma Gandhi. The initial demand for "Home Rule" for India within the framework of the Empire had developed into a determined cry for complete independence. The slogan "Quit India" spread like wildfire throughout the country.

The Royal Commission, or the Simon Commission, as it soon came to be called, was hotly resented by India. First, the members were all British; then the majority of them had never visited India; and, worst of all, they had no previous knowledge of or connection with the demands for greater political responsibility that were being made through the All-India National Congress. Indians felt that questions of such great importance to their country should not be decided by a body with no Indian representative and that it was unrealistic and an insult to the nation to expect such a commission to make fair recommendations.

Political India led by Mahatma Gandhi raised a loud and persistent protest, "Go back, Simon." The shouts, quite literally, greeted the Simon Commission when it arrived in India and echoed and re-echoed in every province as the members began taking evidence in different parts of India. "Black flag" processions met the special train in which the commission and their staff traveled, stopping at all the major towns. Most of the important nonofficials, politicians and civic leaders refused to cooperate with the work of the commission or appear before it to give the evidence the members were collecting. But those Indians connected with the Government and thus unable to express their political opinions carried on the work of the commission without joining in the protests no matter what their private views were.

My husband was appointed financial adviser to the Simon Commission, to work directly with Sir Walter Layton, at that time the editor of the influential English journal the *Economist.* As most of the members of the commission were accompanied by their wives, I too had the opportunity of traveling with my husband in the Simon special train under the very comfortable and rather unusual arrangements made for these eminent British visitors. I was very excited to travel to areas of my country which I might never otherwise have been able to see, and I left both my daughters, aged eight and five, with my parents in Allahabad. One of the very pleasant aspects of a large Indian family is the easy coming and going and staying between relatives. There is always room for a daughter's or a sister's children, with or without the parents. There is no sense of imposition and none of indebtedness—at least that was true in our family. As easily as my mother had accepted Makhan and Sheila, so she did my daughters. They, in turn, were happy; they had both my elder sisters to take care of them and Bishan's three children and my parents to keep them company.

My husband and I joined the commission in Lahore. Immediately, we were met by a huge crowd protesting against the commission, carrying black flags and shouting slogans. We were horrified when the police charged with their *lathis*—long, dangerous bamboo batons—to break up the crowd. Some important leaders were beaten up. One of the injured leaders was a well-known politician and a member of the Central Legislature named Lala Lajpat Rai, who had become a personal friend of ours during our stay in New Delhi. We were deeply concerned and called on him to pay our respects and sympathize with him on the ruthless brutality he had suffered. I was extremely touched and angrily indignant when he removed the towel from his shoulder to show us the great blue bruises across his shoulders and chest caused by the police *lathis.*

He, however, showed no resentment and said, "Such sacrifices are necessary in a great cause and nonviolence is the path we have chosen." Turning to my husband, he said, "Your work must go on, just as our work is going on. Someday the British will see the light."

After we left Lahore we heard with deep grief of his death as a result of the *lathi* charge.

Again and again during our travels we performed the official duties required of us, but everywhere, in our free time, we made private and personal contacts with those who were demonstrating against the Simon Commission. They knew our sympathies were wholly with them, though as a Government official my husband could not openly express his feelings or neglect his work. It was an odd experience, like looking rapidly through first one end, then the other of a telescope. In the evenings, with our friends, Indian hopes and problems would seem enormous, detailed, compelling. During the day, among the teacups and civilities of the British, secluded in the special train, everything—even India itself—seemed remote, without urgency, an academic puzzle for Members of Parliament.

We went on to Peshawar in that special train, right on to the North West Frontier towns of Landi Kotal and Landikhana, where the British Government had since before Kipling's time had trouble with the fierce, nomadic, fearless Muslim tribal people of the mountains. It was a daunting and impressive land-scape—the bare hills, the small fortresses, the look of a region perpetually at war, and special arrangements had to be made for our safety as we traveled through this part of the country. The men and even the boys were armed with crude guns. The tribal laws recognized no Indian legal processes as we understood them, but followed blood feuds and patterns of revenge more binding than any edict a judge or court could impose. The one law that the tribal people rigidly observed was that no child accompanied by its mother should be shot no matter how great the enmity between their households and only unaccompanied men could be shot on sight. In Peshawar we had the rare oppor-tunity of meeting and talking through interpreters to the leaders of the various tribal groups. Very courteous, they still had the air of being as intractable, as enclosed, as they seem in the stories about them.

During this tour of the Simon Commission we covered practi-cally the whole of India from the North West Frontier to Madras in the south, from Lahore in the north to Calcutta and Assam in the east. Nearly all of this was new country to me, and I greedily absorbed impressions of the drive to Shillong in Assam through dense forest which the railway had not yet penetrated, the beauty of the countryside and of the Assamese girls of the Khasi tribe. From there we went on to Burma, which at that time was part of British India. More than anything else, I think, I was captured by the assurance and efficiency of the Burmese women in Rangoon, their neat costumes, their beautiful hair, always dressed with flowers, their prominence in the commercial world, in markets where day-to-day trade was conducted, and the clean-liness and appetizing appearance of their food stalls. All were managed by charming women who seemed more prominent in the bazaars and more efficient in trading in the markets than the Burmese men.

While the men of the Simon Commission worked hard, the women had time to enjoy these new experiences, and I had the additional opportunity of making friends with many of the women traveling with us. I had never before met such a group of English women, educated and thoughtful, who actually wanted to *learn* about India. I especially appreciated the company of Dorothy Layton, the wife of Sir Walter Layton, who was well informed, sympathetic in her approach to the more serious questions concerning India, and an advocate of the rights of women in England. It was not long before I discovered a kindred spirit in her and questioned her closely and at length about women's emancipation. I learned to count on her friendship for many years after.

CHAPTER 18

THE COMMISSION WAS due to return to England with all
the evidence collected during our travels, and my husband was
asked to accompany them and stay there for the year or so that
the work of writing the report would require. He wanted the
children and me to be with him. At that time, 1929, my elder
daughter, Premila, was nine years old, and my younger, Santha,
was a little over six. I knew nothing about England and until the
tour of the Simon Commission had hardly traveled at all. I
longed to go, but my first concern—perhaps echoing my mother
—was the children's schooling. I had no information about English schools, and I had been told that London was a difficult city
in which to find suitable schools for small children. But I
thought of my friend Lady Layton, herself the mother of six
children, and she came to my help. She advised me to put my
daughters into the Hall School at Weybridge, in Surrey, where
her own three daughters were being educated, one of whom was
only slightly older than Premila. I was grateful for her advice,
and accepted it at once. She cabled to the principal, and even
before we left for England we received a favorable reply, assuring us that the children would be admitted.

We journeyed to London by ship, a long sea voyage and the first my children and I had undertaken. For all of us it was a great adventure, but I was especially looking forward to seeing England itself. It was April, and from my childhood in Hubli I remembered the line "Oh, to be in England now that April's there." I anticipated much beauty, but sadly enough it was bitter cold that year. Nineteen twenty-nine came to be known as the Winter of the Great Frost. The days were still dull and gray and the trees still stood naked. Looking out on the London streets we saw people hurrying along the roads all dressed in somber colors, black, gray, brown heavy overcoats, with hats pulled down over their heads and umbrellas against the intermittent rain.

I knew no one except a few shipboard acquaintances and a few Simon Commission wives, all now out of reach in their own homes. I missed the sunlight, the gay colors of India, and even the heat. By the time we left India, it was already warming up for the summer, and it was hard to believe that I could already be longing for that dreaded season. Everyone seemed unfriendly and tight-lipped, so reserved that one dared not approach them or venture to open a conversation with one's next-door neighbors, the usual practice in India. My disappointment was great at the time, and I longed to get back to my own people and my own country, where, in spite of poverty and misery, we could still make human contacts. This was, of course, my first impression, but it was so vivid that somewhere in my mind, regardless of later friendships and warmth, it still colors my feelings about England.

A few days after we arrived it was time to visit the Hall School in Weybridge, where the children had been enrolled. We traveled by train, stayed at a beautiful old hotel, the Oatlands Park Hotel, and went to see the school. The Hall School was a small private institution run by a Quaker committee. The principal was Miss Gilpin, who several years later married Sir Michael Sadler, the well-known educator. Although the staff were nervous about handling my children, the first Indians to attend the school, they seemed delighted to welcome both of them, per-

167

haps because India was very much on the front pages of all the newspapers in London at the time. The furor caused by the work of the Simon Commission, with all the resentment displayed by Indians, the *lathi* attacks and mob violence, had made headlines in the British papers and had aroused great curiosity among educated English men and women, even if they had never taken any deep interest in the Indian struggle before.

My first interview with Miss Gilpin was a very pleasant one. She found the children and me normal human beings, except of course for our color. Her questions were simple and straightforward: Should she make any special arrangements for their food at school? Could they play the usual games? What about their religious instruction? Remembering my mother with Father d'Souza, my answer to all of this was that the children should conform to the normal standards of the school and have no special treatment. Since the school had been founded by Quakers it provided both church attendance and Quaker meetings and demanded only that the children make some sort of religious observance on Sundays, without holding them to a particular affiliation. I gave my daughters the option of choosing the kind of worship they preferred. Premila picked the church, and Santha decided, young as she was, to attend the Quaker meetings. I still don't know what prompted their choices. Premila was admitted immediately as a boarder, but I was doubtful about Santha. She seemed too young to be at boarding school, so for the time being she was a day student.

We stayed on at the Oatlands Park Hotel in Weybridge, and every morning I walked Santha down to school and brought her back in the evening. My husband thought that he could commute from Weybridge to London, an hour's train ride, but as soon as Santha settled into the routine of school life, she insisted on becoming a boarder. She loved the companionship, the play, the mischief, and the out-of-class activities of the children, which a day student couldn't share. She was the youngest child in the school, made much of by everyone, so we decided to try it but to stay on in Weybridge and watch her progress for a while. If she was unhappy, she could revert to being a day student. During that month she became a great favorite of the staff and the slightly older children, and seemed happy, busy, and interested. My husband and I decided to find a flat in London and visit both children every Sunday.

The problem of finding a suitable service flat presented far more complications than we had foreseen. The color prejudice in London was very strong, and it took us several weeks of answering advertisements, visiting landlords and landladies, only to be told over and over again that, yes, there were flats available, but no colored couples could be accommodated. I was both furious and humiliated, for we certainly had not come to England for our own pleasure. The British Government had assigned work to my husband that compelled him to be there. At last, after thirty-five refusals, we managed to rent a service flat in South Kensington.

We met a few Indian women, mostly wives of Indian doctors settled in London, and heard that there were educated British women, deeply interested in India, whose enthusiasm had swelled with the reports, day after day, of the progress of the Simon Commission and the growing demand for political reform for India. Just at this time an American woman, Katherine Mayo, published a book called *Mother India,* which presented a picture of the worst, and only the worst, aspects of India and Indian life. Copies of this book were presented to every member of Parliament, obviously with the purpose of prejudicing them in their discussion of the case for India in the British House of Commons when the Simon Commission report came up for debate.

While we were seething with indignation at such blatant propaganda against India, we heard that a Conference on Indian Social Evils had been called by Miss Eleanor Rathbone, Member of Parliament, an influential and much-respected leader. Along with two other Indian women, who for years had worked as members of the All-India Women's Conference and other women's organizations in India, I was naturally interested, and we called at Miss Rathbone's office to offer our assistance to the conference. Since all items on the agenda were Indian topics, we felt qualified to take part in the deliberations.

Miss Rathbone was traveling in Scotland at the time, but her secretary took down our names and said she would get in touch with us on Miss Rathbone's return. Practically all the women's organizations in London, such as the British Commonwealth League, the Women's Freedom League, the League for International Freedom, and several missionary organizations, and many members of the public had enrolled to attend or had appointed delegations to the conference. As the date of the conference approached, we were dismayed to find that no notice had been taken of our call at Miss Rathbone's office and no invitation had been issued to us. Publicity pamphlets informed us that the speakers were all British women, mostly missionaries, and the subjects for discussion were the Indian caste system, child marriage, tuberculosis in women, the purdah system, education for women, etc., etc.

Offended from the outset, we nevertheless attended the first day's meeting. Our tempers at once flared when we saw the display table, where the most prominent pamphlet offered anyone attending the conference was entitled *Has Katherine Mayo slandered Mother India?* The author of this pamphlet was Eleanor Rathbone herself, and we knew that she had never been in India. However, we took our places and listened to the first few speeches, our anger steadily soaring because of the way the topics were presented and most of all because every speech stressed the fact that the eradication of social evils in Indian society was the responsibility of the British—the White Man's Burden.

I was comparatively young, excitable when slighted, somewhat rash and certainly courageous enough to face so important a person as Eleanor Rathbone in the chair, and women in the audience like Sylvia Pankhurst and Mrs. Pethwick-Lawrence, stalwarts of the exceedingly controversial suffragette movement. I asked for permission to speak, and was graciously allowed five minutes. I did not speak on any of the subjects on the agenda, but merely disputed the right of British women to arrange a conference on Indian social evils in London, when all

170

the speakers were British and many of them had never even visited India. Not one of them had even asked if there were any Indian women's organizations that were dealing with the problems on the spot, the same problems that British women were exploring from the great and deceptive distance of fifteen thousand miles. I added that, even though we had offered to help with the conference when arrangements were being made, our offer had been ignored. I told them that educated Indian women were working in every province of their country to eradicate social evils and outmoded customs and prejudices, and we refused to accept the assertion that the removal of social evils in Indian society was the responsibility of the British. We were already assuming the responsibility ourselves, and we were sure we could be more successful than any outsiders, especially those who were ignorant of the cultural patterns of our social groups and therefore could not be as effective as our own social reformers.

I had just pointed out what seemed to me a few elementary facts when Miss Rathbone, furiously and with bad grace, told me to sit down as my five minutes were over. However, Mrs. Pethwick-Lawrence, an elderly, greatly respected suffragette, got up and very firmly said, "We would like Mrs. Rama Rau to tell us more, as we know nothing about what Indian women are doing."

Miss Rathbone turned to me and said, "You may go on for two minutes more."

I replied that I had nothing further to say except to draw the attention of the audience to the pamphlet *Has Katherine Mayo slandered Mother India?* Miss Rathbone had written it although she had never been in India and had implicitly supported the deeply prejudiced and slanderous statements made by Katherine Mayo in her book. *Mother India* had been widely publicized by some unknown agency in England interested in discrediting India while important decisions on reforms for India were awaiting parliamentary action.

My protest resulted in a demand from the delegates of various women's organizations that the chairman allow me to speak on the work Indian women were doing in their own country. Eleanor Rathbone most reluctantly agreed to give me fifteen minutes the next day.

I prepared very carefully for this talk, for I was deeply touched by the remarks of Mrs. Pethwick-Lawrence, which were seconded by Sylvia Pankhurst and supported by many other delegates. The next day, the second day of the two-day conference, I tried to explain without anger or resentment how great our task was, how carefully we were already organizing to attempt to cope with it, how far-reaching the reforms were that we were planning. I also said that, grateful as we were for any British support, all it could be was *moral* support. The practical work had to be done in India by Indians themselves. The friendship and sympathy of English women would be a great encouragement to us. But only if they did not sit in judgment on questions they could not comprehend fully. In our work, progress had to take into account ancient traditional patterns that foreigners did not know or understand fully.

The result of my talk was beyond anything I could have imagined. The conference refused to pass the resolutions that Miss Rathbone's committee had framed, and it ended rather abruptly. For me this was the beginning of my work with the British women's organizations. I immediately got invitations from several of them to join as a member and from others to work on several committees. And that is how I made my first friends in England.

The publicity about the tumultuous tour of the Simon Commission had caused more and more demand by the lay public for information about Indian problems. The British Commonwealth League, which was the organization most active in Commonwealth matters, invited me to join their committee and then begged me to tour the country and speak on India to British organizations which had never discussed the subject and knew very little of what was happening there. The Women Citizens Associations, the Townswomen's Guilds, the village institutes, the universities, and other groups invited me to speak, through the British Commonwealth League, offering to pay my fare, give me hospitality, and make a contribution to the league to help its finances.

Thus I traveled a good deal. I journeyed from Carlisle to Brighton, from Bangor in Wales to Manchester. I was away only a couple of days at a time, and found my travels and the contacts I made wonderfully interesting, while my husband was working hard on the report of the Simon Commission and my children were away at school. It amazed me to discover the ignorance of British men and women about the most elementary matters concerning India, Indian life, Indian social customs and political problems. These were not ill-educated people and I was naturally indignant that a country as large as India, fourteen times the size of England and under British rule for nearly two centuries, should be of so little interest to those who elected the Parliament which decided all India's political questions. How extraordinary that they remained unconcerned while vital political reforms were being advocated in India and agitation was spreading more vociferously every year. It infuriated me to be told at meetings, "But you are so much like us. Surely you have been educated in England."

"No" was my invariable reply, "I am like thousands of other Indians educated according to English standards, entirely in India, and by Indian teachers. Like them, I am deeply integrated with the hopes and aspirations of my own country."

However, in spite of the prickliness of a great many situations, I was fortunate enough to make real friends among the British men and women I met, and I began to respect them more and more as we began to understand each other better.

London, 1930

CHAPTER 19

THE YEAR 1929 was nearly over by the time the Simon Commission report was ready for publication and our work in London seemed to be coming to an end. But a passionate outcry against the report and a complete rejection of its recommendations burst forth in India. The opposition was so strong and the rejection of the report so total that the British Government felt unequal to imposing any of the recommendations and, in an attempt to find some kind of compromise, called a Round Table Conference in London. Indian political leaders were invited to attend this conference on equal terms with the Parliamentary leaders in order to work out a new program of reforms acceptable to Indians. The deliberations continued for several months of each year over a period of three years, and although in early 1930 we returned to India for, we thought, the rest of our lives, my husband was soon appointed secretary to the Round Table Conference and we went back to England, where his work kept us until 1934.

Just before going home, and before this new assignment brought us west again, we thought we really should take the opportunity to see something of Europe, a continent we might never have another chance to visit. We drove through France and Italy, Germany and Austria, and I don't suppose our impressions were greatly different from those of most untutored tourists seeing Europe for the first time. It was a beautiful journey through a landscape so well cultivated and rich that we found it hard to think of places that might match it in India. Besides the splendid buildings, the churches, palaces, castles, one rather ominous feeling emerged in our visit to Germany. We noticed, in insignificant places, young men being trained in military exercises, and we wondered why. Here and there we were stopped by students wanting a ride to the next town or village. Wherever we could understand something of the language we developed a sense of disquieting undercurrents, at the time no more than hints, of danger brewing somewhere in the background.

Yet, in curious contrast to this, we were struck by the depth of interest and admiration for Mahatma Gandhi we found everywhere. In every country we visited, wherever we stopped, for a meal or for the night, strangers came up to ask us about Mahatma Gandhi. They wanted to know about his life, his philosophy, about his dedication to nonviolence, his political campaigns. Even when we did not know their language they looked around for someone who could interpret for them our thoughts and feelings about his work, his character, his principles. We were always easily recognized as Indians by the saris I wore, and our transient acquaintances seemed convinced that we could provide some authentic knowledge of Mahatma Gandhi's place in India's political life. This was very flattering to us, for in England the general public did not take Mahatma Gandhi too seriously. To them he was still a figure of derision and was usually referred to as the "naked fakir," or beggar. He was even made the butt of jokes and ridicule on the London music-hall stage.

When the Second Round Table Conference opened in London Mahatma Gandhi was, of course, the most important figure there. Leaders from all political groups—the Indian Congress, the Liberal party, the Muslim League, the Scheduled Classes (that is, the Untouchables, the tribal groups, the aboriginals)—

came to place their points of view before the representatives of the British Government. Mahatma Gandhi had, some years earlier, given up wearing formal Western dress as a public gesture to identify himself with the poor of India. Like any villager, he went bare-bodied, wearing a short, coarse, handwoven, handspun loincloth and a handwoven, handspun shawl for a chilly morning or a cool evening. His rough village sandals were handmade, and he carried an unpolished stick to lean on. He had already made the "Gandhi cap" and *khadi* clothes, made from handwoven, handspun cloth, the symbols of the Congress party. His followers wore the style of dress typical of their provinces —*kurtas,* pajamas, *dhotis,* jackets and coats buttoned to the neck —but everything was made from *khadi* material. This coarse cloth worn by countless thousands of people helped the village weavers financially and the Congress party as a form of propaganda.

Wherever Mahatma Gandhi traveled in India, he lived in those enclaves in towns or villages segregated for the Untouchables. In those days, with unconscious irony, the people who lived in these festering urban and rural slums were called the "Depressed Classes." Gandhi, the first great champion of their right to full citizenship, renamed them "Harijans," the Beloved of God. With such gestures he reached to the heart of our complicated and disparate country. For them his philosophy was simple: *Satya, Satyagraha,* and *Ahimsa,* those words from our ancient books which mean: Truth, Resistance in the Cause of Truth, and Nonviolence. Even the illiterate 80 percent understood those words. They heard them in the sacred readings at religious meetings, in temples and places of worship in every town and village. They even grasped their political applications. After all, they were part of an ancient Indian tradition.

When Mahatma Gandhi attended the Round Table Conference, he made arrangements to stay in the East End, the poorest part of London, refusing the lavish hospitality provided by the British Government for conference members. He continued to wear his usual costume in London, only replacing his cotton shawl with a heavy handwoven Kashmiri shawl to ward off the cold. Following his daily practice in India, he went for an early-morning walk and made great friends with the children of the surrounding slums, who got to know him and love him in spite of his unusual appearance. He was entirely willing to appear at all meetings of the Round Table Conference as well as at private and public meetings arranged by friends or people who sincerely wanted to study and understand his teachings.

When all the members of the Round Table Conference, the high British officials as well as the odd assortment of Indians, received an invitation from their majesties, King George V and Queen Mary, to a reception at Buckingham Palace, formal dress was required for the occasion. Naturally, all of us were wondering what Mahatma Gandhi would wear. Soon the word went around that the palace staff had been equally uneasy and had appointed an emissary to approach him on this subject. "I will wear," Gandhi is supposed to have replied, "what I have worn for many years in my own country, and what I continue to wear here, while I am working at the conference." Still, we speculated about whether his compatriots and close advisors would persuade him to cover himself fully in no matter what costume, Indian or British, as long as it showed proper awareness of protocol. Would it be considered an outrage to defy the formal court etiquette about dress requirements? If so, what should be done? Mahatma Gandhi was too important a member of the Indian delegation to be left out. But, if he was adamant about any change in his costume for this special occasion, and royal etiquette was equally inflexible, perhaps he would simply decide not to attend.

The King and Queen, in their full regalia, stood at the head of the beautiful staircase at Buckingham Palace. On each step stood the red-coated guards and around us were all the pomp and panoply of a royal occasion. I hung over the balustrade to watch the drama of Mahatma Gandhi's arrival. The inner thrill and suspense turned into triumph when he walked slowly up the staircase—bald-headed, ears sticking out, dark thin legs exposed, coarse sandals, a warm shawl slipping off his bare shoulders. I could clearly hear his long staff clicking step by step as

178

he mounted to meet his rulers. He had not made any conces-
sions, but there was no air of defiance about him, only a dignity
that inspired respect and admiration. It was an occasion that I
will never forget and which fills me with pride even today.

I was too far away to hear what the King and Mahatma Gandhi
said to each other, but I was told that the King remarked, "Mr.
Gandhi, I hear you are giving us a lot of trouble in India."
Mahatma Gandhi replied very politely, "Your Majesty, I'm
afraid this is a topic I cannot discuss. With you."

Occasions such as this were really only glamorous punctua-
tions in my normal life in England. I had rejoined my former
friends and colleagues and spent most of my time working in
various branches, capacities, and causes of the women's movement. In 1932 a group of Indian women was invited for the first
time to attend a conference of an international women's organization known as the International Alliance of Women for Suffrage and Equal Citizenship. Mrs. Sarojini Naidu, two other
Indian women who happened to be in London at the time, and
I attended this conference in Berlin. Mrs. Naidu was much my
senior, and I still remembered that Congress meeting, years
ago, when I had been so nervous on her behalf, hoping she
would do Indian women proud in her speech, and how she had
so far surpassed my expectations. Still, she insisted I lead the
Indian delegation.

The subject before the conference concerned Western
women only, for India had not yet begun to play an active part
in international conferences. We were supposed to be only ob-
servers and could not introduce questions of suffrage and equal
citizens' rights that concerned India. This was the first international conference I attended, and afterward I was invited to
become a member of the board of the Alliance. Later still, I
attended two board meetings of the Alliance, one in Paris, one
in Amsterdam, and made an attempt to broach some of our
rather special Indian problems for discussion. To the women at
these international meetings our society, culture, and difficulties
were almost unimaginably remote. Unfortunately, this connection was short-lived, as my husband's various postings made it

179

impossible for me to keep usefully in touch. However, for me it was not time wasted. Those meetings gave me my first experience of dealing with international work for women's rights.

In 1934, at the end of the Round Table Conference, my husband was appointed Indian Deputy High Commissioner in London for three years. This meant that, at last, we could plan ahead for the education of the children. Premila had passed the entrance examination for St. Paul's School in London, and two years later Santha joined her there. They were both growing up, beginning to find their feet and develop their own ideas just like any other schoolgirls in England. I sometimes worried about the freedom they were enjoying and the cultural patterns they were following without even realizing it. When I returned home with them, would my own and my husband's relations disapprove of them? Then again, would the restraints and values of Indian social life be so very foreign that my children would resist them and find them unbearably irksome? But I couldn't help recognizing that under my eyes they had both become responsible human beings with standards they and I respected, and I knew I must be prepared for them to fight their battles if, indeed, there were battles to be fought, and make their own terms with the community we lived in once we returned home.

When we were settled in a new house, I again found time hanging heavy on my hands and once more looked around for work I could do. I renewed my contacts with the organizations I had already served and started a new association called the Women's Indian Association in order to keep the Indian women living in London and the British women interested in India in close touch with the progress of Indian women at home. I was still intimately connected with events in my own country and as the president of this new organization I managed to keep our Indian work and problems before the attention of English friends.

CHAPTER 20

T HE THREE YEARS passed quickly enough, my husband's term of office as Deputy High Commissioner for India was coming to an end in London, and we were making preparations to return home. Suddenly, early in 1938, my husband got orders to proceed immediately to South Africa as India's High Commissioner there.

I had made many close contacts in England with British women's organizations during my ten-year stay in London, and most intimately with our Women's Indian Association. When these associations received my resignation, I was overwhelmed and incredulous at the touching tributes and the warm affection bestowed on me. A great farewell party was given by a group of organizations, and I was presented with a flattering address which expressed thanks for my having helped to bring India closer. I was showered with gifts and souvenirs, with kindness and appreciation, all of which made me feel very humble indeed. But, most surprising of all, I was honored by the British Government with the award of the Kaiser-i-Hind gold medal. When I appeared at Buckingham Palace for the investiture by King George VI, I couldn't help thinking of the first time I had ever set foot there and had watched the small, unimpressive figure of Mahatma Gandhi walking up the grand staircase on his spindly bare legs.

My husband flew to New Delhi for detailed orders in connection with this new job, and went from there directly to South Africa. I stayed in London to make arrangements for the children before joining him. It was a worrying time with no easy solutions. I wanted their studies to continue without unnecessary disruptions. We had a fully furnished flat in London with an efficient maid who had worked for us for some time. I did not want to break up our home, for I hoped to return to London from time to time to visit the children during vacations. I also wanted to give them the opportunity of finishing their university education before I packed up our belongings to return home for good.

After talking the whole matter over with my husband and daughters, I decided to keep our home intact. We took in a young Jewish refugee, recommended by the Refugee Committee of which my friend Lady Layton was the chairman, to act as chaperone for my girls. Premila had already been admitted to Newnham College at Cambridge and was making preparations for her first year, beginning in October. Santha, who had had a very creditable school career, was still at St. Paul's, working for an Oxford scholarship exam. I felt that if they had an older companion like Lilian Ulanowsky to live with them, all would be well.

Lilian, a young Viennese music student of good family, came to our home and quickly became one of our family. She had a brother in Dachau. Her mother refused to leave Austria till he could be released, but had helped Lilian to get away because the persecution of the Jews was getting worse every day. Thousands of Jewish refugees were pouring into London, and homes and jobs had to be found for them. Lady Layton and the Refugee Committee in London had been working very hard, and, as the figures grew more and more horrendous, all of us felt we had to do whatever we could—sign affidavits, guarantee housing, offer jobs—anything to help in however small a way.

182

With Radhakrishnan in South Africa, 1938

When Lilian came to us, she spoke fairly good English, and she carried on with her own music lessons while my daughters were still at St. Paul's School. She was not required to do any domestic work, but only to act as a sort of elder sister to my daughters, to help them with any problems which might require her greater experience of life. She was the daughter of a concert musician, and her older brother was the accompanist for Lotte Lehmann, but for me the most important thing was that she quickly made friends with my children.

With a reasonably easy mind, I set sail for Cape Town to join my husband. Soon after he left England, his name had appeared on the British Honours List, but since he was already in South Africa and had assumed charge of his new office, he was not able to attend the investiture ceremony in Buckingham Palace, and his knighthood was conferred on him *in absentia.*

I left England on an unusually lovely, sunny day in June, reveling in the warmth of the sun that I had missed through the long cold winter and recalling my dismal first impression of a cold and graceless country. Now the clear sunlight gave everything an extra brilliance and I felt a pang at leaving the country I had learned to love after all. But somehow I felt that the beauty of the day was a happy augury for the new life I would enter at the end of the voyage.

My fellow passengers were pleasant and took a great interest in me, especially the South African passengers returning home from England. It was unusual for an Indian woman to be traveling to South Africa. Normally, Indians were not allowed to land there. When, in answer to their questions, I explained that my husband was the High Commissioner for India, they understood how I had the right to enter and live in the country. I had not realized until then how strong the color prejudice was or how rigid the restrictions on who might be allowed to immigrate.

My husband met me in Cape Town on a damp and chilly day, a shroud of fog hanging over Table Mountain, and I realized for the first time that the seasons in South Africa are reversed. I was in for another winter. My husband had to spend several months each year in Cape Town for the parliamentary sessions, but the

184

greatest number of Indians lived in Natal, and his work chiefly concerned their position, problems, and well-being. I caught my first glimpse of this new country from the train window as we traveled from Cape Town to Johannesburg and on to Durban in Natal, which would be our headquarters. At every stop we were met by the Indian residents of the towns through which we passed. The scenery was dramatically different from province to province. Cape Town, in its magnificent setting on the bay, was a crowded, sprawling city. Johannesburg, on high ground with its ugly yellow mounds of slag dumps piled high around the gold mines, made an astonishing contrast with the Great Karroo, miles and miles of flat, desolate scrub. Then came the gentler, more India-like atmosphere and scenery of Durban, with the familiar hibiscus, bougainvillaea, and other tropical flowers everywhere. More than anything else, there was a noticeably Indian population on the Durban streets, and I felt homesick for my own land.

I was keenly interested in this new country, the new people, and the distressing new problems that began to confront me immediately. The population of this enormous nation was comparatively small, and divided into six distinct segments: the English, the Afrikaners, the Jews, the Colored (those of mixed blood), the Indians, and the Blacks. The first three segments were considered White, and the rest as their names described them. The total population of Whites was then 2 million, the Colored were 750,000, the Indians 250,000, and the Blacks, 8 million.

Every segment had its own special grievances and difficulties. The Afrikaners distrusted the British because they believed that no one could be loyal to South Africa if he thought of England as his real home. They insisted constantly that theirs was the strongest right to citizenship, pointing out that their ancestors had given up their Dutch nationality when they imigrated, and had fought the great Boer War to establish their new homeland. (They never mentioned that, however unfairly, they had lost that war.) The Jews were considered outsiders in South Africa, accused of wanting only to exploit the country through trade and the fabulous diamond and gold mines. The Indians, my husband's special concern, had originally gone to South Africa as indentured laborers when the British first took over the vast area of South Africa and wanted a steady supply of cheap agricultural labor to develop the rich sugar cane fields of Natal. Sugar was of great importance as a paying crop to the British in South Africa before the discovery of gold.

Some of the Indians we met belonged to families which had immigrated three generations before. In the early days their grandfathers had signed on for terms of three to five years, and had been encouraged to stay permanently in South Africa, tempted by the Government's gift of small plots of land as a substitute for the return passage home which they had been promised. The idea, all too readily accepted, was that they would establish a permanent labor force in Natal. They were considered good, reliable, and hard-working compared with the indigenous black population, and they soon began to earn well.

Is it a national characteristic, I sometimes wonder, that makes the British so consistently underestimate, or at least misinterpret, the aspirations—social, national, political, or educational —of another country? Goodness knows, they have spent enough time—centuries, in some cases—governing, living with, dealing with foreigners. Is it merely fear of being overwhelmed by the dark races of the world that makes them so blind?

Whatever the answer, my observations in South Africa were clear enough and, to me, not at all surprising. When the early Indian settlers had saved a little money, improved their position a bit, of course they wanted to educate their children in India and in England. In their own country or the country of their adoption, they certainly wanted to be more than laborers on the sugar estates.

When we arrived in South Africa the Indians were a comparatively small community. After three generations, they had improved their financial position, educated their children in professions—medicine, law, business—but still suffered from all the disabilities of the laws of segregation. They were denied the elementary rights of citizens because they were Indians. No

186

matter how well educated they were, they still were known as
"coolies." Even stricter rules applied to the Colored community, the progeny of the illicit union of European men and native
women, and, of course, to that section of the Black population
who were allowed to come into the cities at all; they were subject
to curfew laws and had to show passes if they were out after dark
to prove they were legitimately employed by a White family. The
majority of the natives were confined to the kraals, or villages,
restricted areas they were not allowed to leave without that vital,
humiliating pass they were obliged to carry always.

My husband's work concerned only the 250,000 Indians settled in South Africa. The majority of them knew no other homeland. Their ancestors had left India nearly a hundred years
before and they were fighting for the right to be recognized by
the South African Government as citizens of the country. By
nonviolent agitation against the Government, Mahatma Gandhi,
born and brought up there, had drawn world attention to their
plight and to the iniquitous restrictions imposed on them. At the
time my husband was posted there, General Smuts was in
power, a liberal force as far as Indians were concerned, as the
late Mr. Hofmeyr, one of the ministers in the Government, had
been.

Just before my husband left India for South Africa, his
brother, Sir Benegal Narsing Rau, had written to him, "I hear
you are being posted to a country which, in another context,
Bishop Reginald Heber described as a place where 'every prospect pleases and only man is vile.'" How true his description
was! Even now I think of the incredible beauty of Cape Town
with its many bays of different-colored water, the thrill of standing at Cape Point, the southernmost tip of Africa, and seeing the
great Atlantic and the Indian oceans merge into each other, and
knowing there was nothing between us and the Antarctic except
the ocean before us. In the Botanical Gardens in Cape Town,
every wild flower of South Africa was planted, many unknown
to the rest of the world, and when we went to Caledon, seventy-
odd miles out of Cape Town, to see the wild-flower show we
were charmed beyond measure by the overall plan of the gar-

den, which was in full bloom only in October, the South African spring, when hundreds of people visited it. There was the brief glory of the Great Karroo, usually unattractive and barren until suddenly, when the rains broke, this wasteland blossomed into a garden of flowers of all colors.

Yet South Africa was so full of hatreds. Educated, intelligent people, all nationals of the same country, were ready to tear each other to pieces on racial questions. The feelings of animosity were palpable in every mixed gathering I happened to attend. Everywhere, on park benches, over public lavatories, in cinemas, there were signs, "For Europeans Only" or "For Non-Europeans Only." An American friend of mine, a White woman of distinction, visited South Africa and made a point of using the "non-European" facilities because she was proud of being American. She could have been arrested.

One incident affected me very closely and brought home to me the shameful inhumanity of the rigorous segregation policy. It roused me to feelings I could not express as the wife of a diplomat. My husband and I were traveling from Cape Town to Johannesburg, where a large group of Indians were waiting at the station to receive us. We were in that part of the train reserved for White people because the diplomatic representative of India and his wife were not subjected to the usual segregation on trains. We were, so to speak, honorary Whites. As the train pulled in, our compartment crossed the line marked on the platform to separate the Whites from the Colored waiting there. In their enthusiasm to greet us, the Indians rushed forward to our compartment, carrying huge bouquets and garlands, across the line on the platform. Police with batons charged them, and they were pushed back. I have never felt so humiliated and infuriated as I did while we advanced toward them to receive their greetings. I could relate hundreds of incidents of this kind, but that was the first and so remains the most vivid in my memory.

A little later, when we had begun to feel our way in this immensely complicated society, my husband felt it would be a good gesture to the Indians and an asset to all the educated people of the country to invite an Indian of real stature to visit, travel and speak in South Africa. Dr. Radhakrishnan was just such a man. An eminent philosopher of world standing, then holding the Spalding Chair of Comparative Philosophy at Oxford University, he was known to be a brilliant lecturer and an original thinker. My husband wrote to ask if he would deliver a series of lectures at the University of Cape Town and at public meetings in different cities of South Africa. He accepted and then, embarrassingly, we had to ask the Government's permission for an Indian to land in South Africa. However, permission was given and we had the honor of being hosts to Dr. Radhakrishnan during the period when he delivered lectures on Hindu and Buddhist philosophy and comparative religions of the world. Our private hope was that he might, with his eloquence, his great knowledge and scholarship, and his outstanding personality, create a better atmosphere among the educated South Africans. For Indians who could never have the opportunity of meeting the great men of India, he would be an extraordinary asset, a true Indian who could make them proud of their national heritage.

Dr. Radhakrishnan, a tall, lean South Indian with a gentle, thoughtful face often illuminated by a marvelously humorous smile, addressed crowded audiences in Cape Town, Johannesburg, and Durban, and he created quite as great an impression as we had hoped. But unfortunately it was only for a very short time. He had to return to Oxford and South Africa had to continue its own struggle, but I like to think that his visit did light at least one small candle in the dark.

One incident remains with me from that time. We had arranged a dinner party for General Smuts to meet Dr. Radhakrishnan, two great men and in very different ways two great philosophers. Naturally they got together after dinner and an animated discussion went on for a long time between the two. When I had to separate them, feeling that the other guests at the party should also have a share of the company of the two chief guests, General Smuts was saying, "But the only thing about Hinduism that attracts me is the caste system."

I raised my hands in horror and said, "But, General Smuts, educated Indians have for years been carrying on a campaign, even before Mahatma Gandhi's time, against the caste system."

He calmly patted me on the arm and said, "Young woman, you are all making a great mistake."

While my husband was immersed in his work with the Indian community, I as usual took the opportunity to organize an Indian Women's Association in South Africa in order to help the Indian women undertake new projects for their own advancement and the welfare of their children. I was particularly interested in helping to establish an Indian girls' high school in Durban, which was the first of its kind and badly needed, for Indians were not allowed to enroll in any white school or college.

It so happened that 1938 was the centenary year of the great exodus of the Dutch from the Cape Province to found a new country for themselves as a protest against the British for abolishing slavery in the Empire. A great celebration was organized by the South Africans of Dutch origin to commemorate the event. Their ancestors had depended on slaves for the work on their vast farms and, rather than obey the new law, had trekked into the hinterland with their families and possessions, with their domestic animals, sheep, and chickens in covered wagons through miles and miles of difficult and dangerous country to reach Pretoria. There they put up their flag and founded a new country, Transvaal. Later, when gold was discovered and the Boer War fought, the British absorbed the Dutch colony.

In 1938, in a most dramatic way, the Afrikaners reenacted the whole great march of the Voortrekkers. They dressed like the Dutch men and women of that period: the men wore the tight trousers and the broad-brimmed hats, the women the full, long dresses and the *keppies,* the floppy bonnets. The men grew beards and the women let their hair grow long and used no makeup. They revived the old Dutch songs and dances and faithfully staged the hardships and the happenings of a hundred years before. They also revived the old animosities against the

British. To some extent, occasionally overtly, more often sub-consciously, they were also sympathizing with the Germans who, under Hitler, were carrying out pogroms against the Jews as well as threatening Britain. Within South Africa dislike of the Jews was very strong, largely, it seemed, because they were the most powerful in the gold and diamond trade, and the British had been the Afrikaners' enemies since the Boer War.

It was at this time that the South Africans demanded a separate flag in place of the Union Jack, insisted that Afrikaans be recognized as a national language and that a South African national anthem replace "God Save the King." There were excitement and much controversy about these matters in the South African Parliament. Every day at 6 P.M. an hour-long account of the progress of the Voortrekker cavalcade was broadcast, giving details of their reception at various strategic points of their journey, replaying the old Dutch songs, and describing the old Dutch dances.

This would have been interesting in normal times, but six o'clock was the time when we used to hear news from Europe on our radios. With conditions in Europe as menacing as they appeared, we were tense with anxiety about what was happening there and resented having to wait for a whole hour before we could hear whether the latest events were pushing us toward war or if the fragile peace could be maintained. The notorious talks between Hitler and the Prime Minister of England, Mr. Neville Chamberlain, had just ended, but despite the ironic promise of "peace in our time," the situation in Europe was getting more and more critical every day. German atrocities were increasing and it seemed likely that war might break out any moment. From all accounts, official and nonofficial, England was in no position militarily to face a war. Our strongest concern was, naturally enough, that our children were in London. They had, like all London schoolchildren, been issued gas masks and their letters described the trenches being dug in Hyde Park. It drove us to distraction that every day the radio news bulletins were postponed to allow every transmitter to broadcast a detailed account of the progress of the Voortrekker march.

But local problems still interested us as we observed the high tempers raised by the insistence that all parliamentary proceedings be carried on in Afrikaans and every English speech be translated even though virtually every Afrikaner understood English. In addition, anti-Jewish propaganda was growing as Hitler's murderous anti-Semitism in Germany intensified.

Once at a pleasant social gathering a charming South African lady, who had talked on many subjects with much intelligence, suddenly said to me, "You must hate the British. They have been responsible for so much repression and such atrocities against the Indian people."

"Yes," I said, "it's true that political unrest is always met with severe and violent measures. I can hate the British Government, but I have lived too long in England to hate the British people."

She replied, "We suffered during the Boer War. Our houses were burnt, our farms destroyed, our people persecuted. It may have been a long time ago, but we still hate the British for the suffering they imposed on us."

In 1939 our children came to us for the long summer vacation, leaving Lilian and her brother Peter, recently released from Dachau, to take care of our flat. Premila was all excited at the prospect of going to Newnham College in October. Santha was working steadily, even during the holidays, hoping to be able to take her scholarship exam for Oxford. We were delighted to have them with us, to travel over the whole of South Africa and show them a little of a continent they had never been able to visit. Part of this education was to see, for the first time, skyscrapers in Johannesburg, gold and diamond mines, the magnificent game reserves. Another part was something we had never planned.

One day our girls decided to go to a cinema. They telephoned their father at his office to ask if he could get away a little early to join them for the five-o'clock show. Rather guardedly, he asked them which film they wanted to see and at what theater it was playing, and finished by saying noncommittally that he would try to be there. What he really wanted to do, since he knew he couldn't leave his office early, was to have time to

192

inform the management of the theater that his daughters would be arriving for this particular show, that they would probably be in Indian dress but, as children of a diplomat, they should be properly seated and not turned out of the theater by the ushers.

At once it became a ceremonial occasion, a recognition of our diplomatic status, tiresome and, in a backhanded way, insulting. The same procedure was followed everywhere, at restaurants, hotels, or any other public meeting place. We were treated with respect once it was realized we were not local Indians, but we soon stopped going out except to the houses of friends.

The summer holidays were nearly over and my daughters were preparing to return to London. The week before they were due to sail, war broke out in Europe. Of course we canceled their passages. They were distressed at having to give up their studies, but all we could pray for was that it would be a short war and not too disastrous. "Over by Christmas," people used to say to encourage themselves. As time went on and the news grew worse and worse, we had to abandon all thought of letting the children return to England.

We toyed with the idea of sending them to Cape Town University or the Witwatersrand in Johannesburg, both reputable institutions, but no Indians were allowed in the regular schools or colleges. We were told that special arrangements could be made for their admission if they did not live on campus. The thought of their having to be labeled as the daughters of the Indian High Commissioner lest they be subjected to insult during their educational careers was too obnoxious, and we decided against asking for such a concession. We also realized that our daughters could not continue to lead the restricted lives forced on them in South Africa. We decided that, instead, I should show them as much of this country as possible, for they would never have the chance of seeing South Africa once our official duties there ended, and then take them back to India and await events.

We traveled to Bulawayo in Rhodesia and on to the Victoria Falls, over five hundred miles of sparsely populated country, stopping only at towns where stray families of Indians were settled and where we gladly accepted their hospitality, uncertain that inns in these remote areas would accept us. When we arrived at the falls toward evening and went straight to our hotel, we were puzzled by the loud boom-boom that resounded around us. Of course it was the thunder of the water cascading over the cliffs. The next morning we saw the full glory of the falls, incredibly beautiful, pouring into the ravine. All around us was the rain forest, the great trees dripping gently and constantly from the spray flung up from the boiling chasm at the bottom of the falls.

After a few days' rest in Johannesburg, we went to Kruger National Park, a new experience for all of us. Even though India abounds in big and small game, we had never seen wild animals in their natural habitat. My husband accompanied us for three days, and we slept at night in rondavels, the characteristic round thatched African huts, which seemed frail and unsafe considering we were surrounded by wild animals. We heard the lions roar all night, sounding close enough to be just outside our windows. The days were filled with excitement as we drove through the park seeing herds of springbok, wild boars, zebras, warthogs, all at startlingly close quarters. Most thrilling of all was our sudden encounter with a pride of lions. One enormous maned male was apparently keeping guard over three lionesses lying around him relaxed and asleep. We stopped to watch this superb picture, and in a few moments the lion, evidently bored, gave a warning to his mates, who woke up one by one and very slowly and deliberately walked into the bushes. Then the lion himself rose, looked all around, yawned a great yawn, and majestically stalked off after them.

After this spectacular tour we returned to Durban and made arrangements to get back to India by the end of the year, leaving my husband to complete his assignment as High Commissioner.

CHAPTER 21

WHEN AT LAST we arrived in Bombay, we had no home of our own to go to; we had lived abroad for twelve years. But, as usual in India, the homes of relatives were open to us. My parents, much to my grief, had died during our stay in England. My brothers were all working in different parts of India and in England, and though my sisters, Kamala and Bishan, were living in the family house in Allahabad, I didn't want to burden them, especially with my two daughters, whose only wish was to get back as fast as possible to their school and college life in England. The children and I, once we returned to India, were not entitled to government accommodation while my husband held a job abroad, and his term of office in South Africa still had a year and a half to run. Moreover, we did not know where else he might be sent when that assignment ended. We therefore stayed for some time in Bombay with my sister-in-law Leela and her husband, Dr. Savur, the head of the Meteorological Department. My parents-in-law were also staying in their lovely, spacious house and made us very welcome. My father-in-law was tall, dignified, and handsome as ever, and they were thrilled and proud to see their grandchildren grown almost to womanhood, for they had last seen them as young children.

My daughters, I am sorry to say, were less than delighted by our return to India. I remember thinking of that old verse that moved me so much in my youth:

> Breathes there the man, with soul so dead,
> Who never to himself hath said,
> This is my own, my native land!

The answer, I now saw, was, yes indeed, there are people who don't respond immediately to their native land. And two of them are my daughters! They were frustrated, anxious about their future studies, cut adrift at one stroke from all their friends, their hopes, their ambitions, and the interests they had developed during their long stay in England. India would have been more exciting if they had returned at a different moment in their lives, after the completion of their education, when they would, perhaps, have felt how wonderful it was to get to know their own land, their relatives, the manners and customs of their people, so alien, by now, from their own.

But everything was different for them—and not very appealing. They had more or less forgotten Hindi, their relatives were strangers, they could not conform to the manners and customs. They were uncomfortable in the climate, the heat of the southern summer and the cold of a North India winter. But, external conditions aside, their main problem was that they were both at a difficult adolescent age. On whom could they vent their spleen, their disappointment, their bewilderment that their lives were not working out exactly as they wished and had planned? Their mother, of course. I tried to smooth over the abrupt change in their circumstances and worked hard to reconcile them to the impossibility of returning to their English education in the immediate future.

We spent a month or so with our relatives in Bombay and then went to New Delhi, where my two brothers-in-law Sir Benegal Narsing Rau and B. Shiva Rao and his wife had their homes. Narsing Rau was a highly placed official in the Indian Civil Service, and Shiva Rao was an influential journalist. They welcomed us and my daughters began to feel much freer and more at home than they had in Bombay in the circumscribed regime of my parents-in-law. They found more to interest them in the surroundings, the political and social activities, and the young people they met when we arrived. Most of all, they were delighted to be with their two favorite uncles.

Both uncles were, by then, well embarked on careers that brought them special distinctions of very different sorts. Only a few years later, in 1946, Narsing Rau would receive his most important assignment. He would be asked to serve as the constitutional adviser to frame the first draft of free India's constitution to present to the Constituent Assembly. In collaboration with Burma's constitutional adviser, he also drafted the constitution of Burma at the invitation of President U Aung San. To carry out such important tasks he traveled in America, England, and the Irish Free State to consult experts, winning rich encomiums everywhere from eminent jurists. Justice Frankfurter, of the Supreme Court of the United States, commented, "If the President of the United States of America were to ask me to recommend a judge for our Supreme Court on the strength of his knowledge of the history and working of the American Constitution, B. N. Rau would be the first on my list." When he was serving on the International Law Commission the Brazilian delegate described him as "a man of angelic appearance, extremely sweet in manner, a full idealist, but capable of dealing with reality and coldness from the right angles and not in a dreamy way. Sir B. N. Rau is a man possessing the gift to surprise us when we least expect it."

When he was elected Judge of the International Court of Justice in 1952 by the United Nations General Assembly, Justice Frankfurter wrote to him again: "You are one of the few people I have ever encountered who had a deep instinctive sense of justice. I begrudged the years you gave, I am sure conscientiously, to diplomacy and rejoiced when you took your rightful place on the Court."

My husband's youngest brother, Shiva Rao, was closest to me in both age and personality. When he was a young man, he was regarded as the black sheep of the family, perhaps because he did not win the sort of honors in his student days that the other brothers did. However, he rose to eminence in his own way. He had in him a deep strain of religious philosophy and, because of his eldest brother, came in contact with Dr. Annie Besant, who inspired him as she had done Sanjiva Rao. Mrs. Besant was working in the political field as well as the educational and religious. She had started the campaign for Home Rule so that India might obtain equal status with the other British dominions in the reconstruction of the British Empire at the end of the First World War, and she published a paper, *The New India,* in Madras. Shiva Rao offered his services to her as sub-editor. Through this work he became involved with nationwide politics and the political personalities who were campaigning for Indian political reform.

Even earlier, he had worked to organize the first trade unions in the country, concentrating on the vital problems of the workers—housing, indebtedness, lack of education and of medical services. Inevitably he became a writer, and of the many books which later accrued to his credit perhaps the most pioneering was his study *The Industrial Worker in India.*

Shiva Rao, after his early years of work with Mrs. Besant, the Home Rule movement and the trade unions, had become the New Delhi correspondent of South India's most influential newspaper, *The Hindu* of Madras, and of the Manchester *Guardian* of England. This gave him an added incentive—if he needed it—to keep in touch with the important political currents, national and international, that touched not only India but also England and America. He helped to organize the Indian Council of World Affairs, attended the inauguration of the United Nations in San Francisco in 1945, was a delegate to the UN General Assembly for five years, from 1947, and was a prominent worker in advocating the suspension of nuclear tests. But for him, I think, the most exciting time came when he was elected Member of Parliament from his family's home town, Mangalore.

Delhi in 1940 was still dominated by British officialdom, and even though New Delhi was not yet completed, people were already predicting an expensive disaster. There would never be enough government officials and ordinary citizens to fill it. Unlike most Indian cities, it was dead quiet at night. There was no "street life" as there is elsewhere in India—vendors selling *paan* or roasted chickpeas, groups of men squatting on street corners exchanging the news of the day. All the houses were separated by gardens; there weren't enough cars to create much traffic on any of the broad avenues. The local witticism at the time was "The only sound to be heard at night is the grinding of axes."

Mercifully, while my husband was away, I was not expected to take part in any of the official social life, and after the winter "season," I thought it a good idea to travel as much as I could with my daughters to acquaint them with their own country.

We first went to Kashmir in April, with a party of friends. Spring is Kashmir's most beautiful season, with the orchards in full bloom and the poppies and irises making a great show. Srinagar, the capital city, and its canals, its lakes, its *shikaras* (light gondola-shaped boats), its famous Moghul gardens, Shalimar and Nishat Bagh, and its exotic mixture of people in the bazaars—Tibetans wearing furs and felt boots embroidered in silver thread, their women jingling with turquoise and silver jewelry, the Kashmiris themselves in their robes and skull caps—were all new and fascinating to us. Our friends were congenial companions, ready to travel around the country by houseboat or on horseback or trek from one beauty spot to another. When we journeyed long distances from Srinagar, we hired horses, small hill ponies, surefooted and sturdy, and an army of coolies to carry tents, furniture, and foodstuffs. As soon as we reached a particularly lovely place and decided to stay a few days, tents were pitched, furniture set up, and food cooked with astonishing speed.

Poets and writers have adequately described the beauty of Kashmir and whatever I may say of the journey from Srinagar to Gandar Bal to Sonemarg to Thajiwas can never do it justice. It seemed more beautiful at each turn of the narrow hill paths we traveled. The snow line of the mountains accompanied us all the way till we reached Thajiwas, too small even to be called a

199

village. There, at the foot of a great glacier, we set up camp for a fortnight. Some of us wanted to explore the country around on our own, some took day-long walks with guides, and others rode hill ponies to the beauty spots.

The country about us was wild, with no habitation within easy reach. We found fallen trees which we dragged close to our tents and built a huge fire, which was constantly replenished with more dead wood and was not extinguished day or night. Every morning we gathered round this fire for breakfast, shivering in the early-morning mountain chill, and drank in the beauty of our surroundings with the hot coffee our cook provided. We made plans for the day's adventures as we gazed at the incomparable Himalayas, covered with blindingly white snow, the foothills massed with spring flowers.

Later we rented a houseboat in another lovely place closer to Srinagar and had the amusement of housekeeping in an entirely novel way. *Shikaras* laden with their varied wares—fruits, vegetables, carpets, shawls, all the beautiful things that Kashmir alone produces—passed by the houseboat, and we had only to make a sign for their boatmen to board our houseboat and display their fascinating and unusual merchandise. Friends of our family, also camping within easy reach of our houseboat, began to call on us, and through them we met more people, acquired new interests and found a wholly different kind of social life. Houseboats have no telephones, so you, or one of the houseboat servants carrying a note, walk to deliver an invitation, and most of your shopping or sightseeing is done in *shikaras*. But, although all of us loved the life in Kashmir, it is essentially a holiday life, and however enchanting they found it, both my girls began to fret about what they called their "real life."

Premila was nearly twenty years old and had grown into a beautiful girl. Santha, still long-legged and gawky at seventeen, was immersed in her studies and in storing up the many facts and impressions which she was to express in her first book, *Home to India* (after she graduated, much later, from Wellesley College in the United States). The eligible young men we had met in Delhi and Kashmir were naturally interested in Premila, and

200

Premila herself, understandably, began to take a new view of life at social functions. But Santha still hated the thought that her university career had been cut off before it had even begun, though she did interest herself in studying her own country while she waited for her father to return from South Africa.

After two months, we left Kashmir and traveled to Lahore, visited Calcutta, and spent some days in Santiniketan, where the great Rabindranath Tagore was the presiding genius of the university he had established. He had invited us to visit him and received us most graciously. Tagore was a remarkable old man, greatly revered by the whole of India, a poet who had translated his writings from Bengali into English and had won the Nobel Prize for his work. He was also a prose writer in both English and Bengali, an artist and a great internationalist, who took a vital interest in Indian politics and social reform, besides the work he did at his own university. We were his guests in Santiniketan and were able to see all the great work he had inspired in the villages round about, as well as in the university center.

His interest in poetry, music, painting, and a truly Indian education was as vivid at eighty as it had been when he was the young and radical son of a wealthy and aristocratic Calcutta family. In our honor he arranged an open-air program by his students and, old as he was, he listened very carefully to a particular song they sang. Suddenly, finding some wrong note in it, he joined in the singing in a rich, powerful voice, correcting their mistake. I don't know who was more thrilled, we in the audience or the students on stage, who were given further proof of his incessant, detailed interest in what they were learning. They had good reason to call him Gurudev, the divine teacher, and I felt it was a privilege for my daughters to have experienced this brief contact with him. He died a couple of years later.

In midsummer of 1940 we went back to Bombay to look for a home of our own until we knew what my husband's next post would be. We found an apartment on an estate on the shore of the Arabian Sea, with a great lawn and gardens and a swimming pool. We moved in with very little, since all our possessions had been left in London, and rapidly acquired some furniture but did not dare buy too much, as we didn't know how soon or where our next move would be.

Although we were happily settled in our own home after all our wanderings, the children were still rather uneasy, with too much time on their hands and at a loss to find something to do that seemed compellingly worth their while. At just about this time, the Government of India decided to start a department for documentary films, and Mr. Alexander Shaw, already known for his work in this field in England, was appointed to create the new department. He arrived in Bombay with his witty and beautiful wife, bringing a letter of introduction to me from a friend in England. I immediately invited him to our temporary home, where he met both my daughters. He politely asked Premila what she was doing. Somewhat to his surprise, she said bitterly, "Gradually turning into a cabbage." A few questions later he learned of her disappointment at not going to Newnham College and her corroding sense of idleness at having nothing to *do* in Bombay. The conversation ended with Alex saying, "My dear girl, come and work with us. I'm having the greatest trouble finding Indian workers who can understand my horrible English accent, and almost as much understanding theirs."

"But I can't *do* anything," Premila wailed.

"You can translate English English into Indian English, can't you?" Alex said sternly. "And you can take a secretarial course in the evenings."

So it was settled and Premila was thrilled to work for someone who would guide and help her in the new project he was setting up, although she was quite untrained for the job.

She started working almost immediately, and Alexander Shaw and his young wife became friends right at the start and have remained great friends ever since. It was a most happy association, for Premila loved the work she was learning—editing documentary films and traveling all over the country with the team of cameramen and filmmakers that Alex had assembled to collect material. Through this new occupation of Premila's our social circle grew bigger. Before we settled in Bombay we had very few friends there, but now a chance meeting at a party or an acquaintance who turned out to have similar interests often led to invitations exchanged and new friendships formed. I worried still about Santha and her interrupted education, but could take no decision as to how her life should be arranged until my husband's return, when we could talk the matter over.

CHAPTER 22

IN 1941 MY HUSBAND'S term of office as India's High Commissioner in South Africa came to an end. As soon as he returned to Bombay he was posted by the Government of India as Chairman of the Bombay Port Trust. At that time this office was more important than it normally is. The war was intensifying and much of the war requirements, men, ammunition, other military equipment, were being transported through Bombay, the best harbor on India's west coast and the closest to Europe. The port was carrying a very heavy load. But before he took charge of his new appointment, after long discussions between us and the children about the wisdom of sending them abroad in those troublous days, we decided that Santha should seek admission to an American college. She could not easily fit into any of the Indian universities and, of course, England was out of the question. We thought it would be a good idea if Premila also went to America and resumed her studies there. But she was twenty-one years old, and she decided against going to college in America, where students were admitted at an earlier age than in the British universities. She was happy with the work she was doing, and felt more settled generally than Santha did.

Santha applied to Wellesley College in Massachusetts and we had no real fears that she might be refused, as her reports from St. Paul's School in London showed that her career there had been consistently excellent. As soon as we received the acceptance from Wellesley, she and my husband left for Calcutta and Singapore, where Santha was to take the clipper to San Francisco, travel across America on her own, meet the Indian Trade Commissioner in New York (we had no Indian Embassy in the United States at that time), and travel to Wellesley to start college in late September. It was a long and arduous journey for a young girl who did not know America at all, had no family there and no friends, and whose only contact with India was her father's friend Mr. Malik, India's Trade Commissioner in New York, whom she had never met. However, she arrived at college safely and we were relieved to hear she had settled down happily. A few months after she got to America the attack on Pearl Harbor brought America into the war and made civilian traffic across the Pacific impossible for the duration of the war. Of course, she would not be able to come home for the summer, but we thanked God that she had arrived safely, was gradually becoming acquainted with a new and enthralling country, had found new companions, and was absorbing a new system of education and a new culture.

At first we were troubled by the expansion of the war after Pearl Harbor, largely because letters from and to America were delayed inordinately and exchange restrictions were imposed. We could not keep as closely in touch with Santha as we would have liked and, even more worrying, we were allowed to send her only a limited amount of money to meet her college expenses, and nothing at all to cope with her vacation expenses—such needs as winter clothes or such minor luxuries as a meal in a restaurant.

However, she made friends among her college mates, and I shall be eternally grateful for the proverbial American generosity and hospitality that made her friends open their homes to her for vacations and take an interest in helping her with the problems she faced. Americans remain among the people she loves best even now. She worked at different jobs during her holidays to avoid being a burden to her friends and to pay for things she could not have afforded otherwise. And during the long summer vacations she worked for the Office of War Information, where she had a wonderful opportunity to meet eminent writers, newsmen, and analysts of world affairs. In any case she had always wanted to be a writer, and the OWI helped to train her in reporting and improved her knowledge of public affairs considerably. In her infrequent letters she begged us not to worry about her or her finances. She was earning $50 a week for a six-day week. Thus, she was rich and having the time of her life.

In the meantime Premila at home was happy with her work in Alexander Shaw's new Office of Documentary Films. Her social circle was widening and she was rapidly making friends with young men and women of her own age in Bombay. Even before my husband returned from South Africa she had met Nitya Waglé, a young, handsome, highly intelligent Indian civil servant stationed in Ahmedabad, a couple of hundred miles north of Bombay. He often made the night's journey for holidays and weekends, as he had several relatives and friends in Bombay, and on each trip always made a point of seeing Premila.

He first came to our home one afternoon for tea and a swim in the pool with a mutual friend who had invited him, knowing this was to be an informal party of young people. I discovered when I talked to him that I had met his family and knew his eldest sister in Benares, where she was teaching in the same school of which Padmabai, my husband's eldest brother's wife, had been principal. I did not remember having noticed Nitya at the time, though he must have been about the school grounds where the young boys played games. In answer to my questions about his career since those long-ago schooldays, he told me about his success in the M.A. examination of Bombay University after his graduation from Benares, of his years at Oxford and his entry into the Indian Civil Service before he returned to India and was stationed in Ahmedabad.

From other sources I learned that he was considered one of the promising young men of the service. Nitya was a Brahmin, a Saraswath Brahmin as I and my husband were, but from Bombay State. Marathi was his family language, though he was fluent in Hindi because of his North Indian schooling. My home language was Hindi and my husband's was Konkani, so once again our common language was English, spoken at that time by all educated Indians.

Of all the young eligible men in Bombay at the time, Premila began to take a special interest in Nitya and he in her. Dutifully he waited for my husband's return from South Africa, and then rang me up to ask if he could call on us to pay his respects, as a junior officer belonging to the same service as my husband. My husband was pleased to meet him, thought him polite and well mannered, and considered his visit merely the expected procedure, a courtesy to a senior official likely to work in the capital city of the state to which the junior belonged. But it soon became clear that Nitya was becoming something more than just another in the string of beaux anxious to get to know Premila better.

CHAPTER 23

SOON AFTER WE were settled in Bombay in 1941 I resumed the social-welfare activities that had always interested me and joined several women's organizations such as the Women Graduates Union, the Maharashtra State Women's Council, and the Bombay branch of the All-India Women's Conference. I also worked for the School for the Blind, the School for Mentally Handicapped Children, the Society for the Rehabilitation of Crippled Children and other such organizations, mostly connected with women and children. There were many progressive women who were already working in Bombay, which is still the center of much social reform and many innovative programs, and I found it a pleasure to be associated with them. The field of social-welfare work was wide and varied.

The years from 1941 to 1947 were a difficult period for my husband. As the war in Asia expanded, as, in succession, Indo-China, the Philippines, Indonesia, Singapore, Malaya, and Burma fell to the Japanese, he was burdened in his job as Chairman of the Bombay Port Trust with the responsibilities of handling unprecedented pressures. Bombay had become virtually the only port able to bear the brunt of the massive military requirements in Asia. The Japanese threat to the east coast of India had diverted all military men and army equipment to Bombay, and this called for constant vigilance and expert organization. The Burma Front had become an important scene of action at that stage of the war, Calcutta and Madras had already been shelled by the Japanese, and all the extra flow of equipment to that theater of the war seemed to fall on Bombay.

I, in contrast, found myself with much free time for my social-welfare concerns. The All-India Conference, started in 1927, had met every year while I was abroad, and the meeting that year was in Calcutta. I was excited and exhilarated by the progress made during the years I had been away from home, and was ready to accept any new responsibilities that might be offered me. The enthusiasm generated by working with efficient and much-respected women, senior in age to me and more experienced in handling Indian public questions, made me realize that this was my true vocation, that I cared more about the true emancipation of Indian women than about anything else. With such a weight of illiteracy, orthodoxy, and outworn traditions to battle, our main difficulty was finding ways to reach out into the 550,000 villages in which our people lived, to provide them with adequate medical aid, simple nutritious food, and the most elementary social amenities. That eagerness to undertake something, however small it may be, to improve the lot of our village people still stirs me, old as I am, for I did then and do now believe that India can, given the opportunity, rise to her proper intelligent and constructive place in human affairs.

When I returned from Calcutta early in January 1942 with these feelings reinforced, Premila announced that she had decided to give up her job and get married to Nitya. I was filled with joy, for I knew by then that although Nitya was not a man of great means he had the sort of honesty, integrity, and uprightness that my husband possessed. I was convinced that their marriage would be successful and happy. Yet it was so unlike my own. No elders had arranged it. Premila and Nitya had fallen in love with each other. "In love"? The words were hardly considered decent in my youth.

We decided they should be married after the hot weather in October, as the climate of Ahmedabad, where Nitya was posted, was sticky and uncomfortable during the summer months. Every district officer had to travel over the village areas in connection with his duties, and I knew that Premila would find it difficult to live in such primitive conditions when she had always enjoyed the normal amenities of civilized life. She and I visited Nitya's headquarters and toured through some of the villages under his jurisdiction, to give her a taste of the life that she, as his wife, would have to lead for some years. I was strongly reminded of the early months of my marriage, the isolation, the barriers of language and interests.

As it turned out, she never had to endure such a grueling start to her marriage. Food supplies for the population of Bombay and the other parts of India were increasingly curtailed as the war went on, and the Bombay Government decided to introduce food rationing. This had never been done before, and a new department, organized on a big scale, needed trusted and efficient officials to handle the enormous task of storing, cleaning, and distributing food grains equitably for Bombay's 4.5 million people. Nitya was chosen to establish the rationing system and see that it worked, and he was immediately transferred to Bombay. Soon after he laid down the basis of his new work, he suggested, first to Premila and then to my husband and me, that their marriage date be advanced from October to April.

Premila was still working, and had given notice to Alexander Shaw that she would resign in June to give herself time to make preparations, choose a trousseau and order jewelry and other things for her wedding. Nitya overcame her objections by saying that a trousseau and jewelry could always be acquired after marriage, and she could continue to work as he himself would not be able to take more than a weekend off for their honeymoon. Of course he won, and Premila and Nitya were married on the 30th of April, 1942, and moved into a comfortable government apartment by the sea.

If things were working out beautifully for Premila and Nitya, conditions in India were getting more and more strained. Food

210

shortages because of the failure of the monsoon, especially in Bengal, began to create incredibly serious conditions for the civilian population. The Burma Front needed more men, more ammunition, and more of the services that would normally have been used for civilian purposes. Then, in 1943, India experienced one of the worst famines known to history in the state of Bengal. Three million men, women, and children died of starvation in unimaginably tragic conditions.

Bengal State depended a great deal on its water traffic along the great river Brahmaputra and its many tributaries, which interspersed the whole of that part of Bengal. That was how the villagers were accustomed to transport food and freight. The tributaries were where they fished, how they traveled. Because of the drought and the lack of food, thousands of people walked from the villages to the cities to look for work, their boats having been commandeered by the army for fear of Japanese spies, sabotage, and fifth columnists. The Japanese were within easy reach of the whole eastern boundary of India from Madras to Calcutta and had already begun to make menacing approaches. They were not far from the Bay of Bengal, and the military authorities could take no risks. In this situation civilian life seemed of little account. Millions died of starvation but the army was well fed and cared for and its requirements took precedence over the human wants of the suffering people.

As conditions worsened in Bengal, news stories of the terrible conditions, the mass exodus of the villagers from the drought-ridden areas, the hopeless misery of the homeless camping on the streets of Calcutta were all censored. But word travels fast in India, and we soon knew about the famine and about the diseases that always follow in its wake.

As one of the senior members of the All-India Women's Conference I was sent, with three or four other women, to travel over the famine-stricken area and bring back an authentic report of what exactly was happening. We traveled widely and witnessed nightmarish sights of children dead by the wayside, left there when they were too weak to walk and their parents too weak to carry them. Those refugees who survived arrived in an overcrowded city whose first priorities were the needs of the military for the war on the Burma Front. It was a common sight in Calcutta at that time for men, women, and children, having at last reached the city, to just lie down and die in the streets. A storm of protest arose all over India as the facts began to be reported, in spite of the strict censorship of the War Department, and eyewitnesses' accounts of the tragedies began to be heard.

The Central Government was at last moved to set up military hospitals with local assistance to bring some relief to these starving people, many of them already in the grip of the accompanying diseases, especially cholera, and the Viceroy, Lord Wavell, ordered that the military field hospitals be made available for them. We traveled through East Bengal, part of which later became East Pakistan and is now Bangladesh, and saw scenes I shall never forget. In the field hospitals in Calcutta, men and women watched for signs of their own approaching deaths. We saw children who had been attacked by jackals and other wild animals during their treks from the villages to the city. They were still alive and in agonizing pain. Cholera patients lay on the floor cheek by jowl in their own filth. There were not enough nurses or orderlies to clean up.

Our own report, added to the increasing evidence of the appalling conditions in Bengal, resulted in a vigorous campaign on the part of social workers. The All-India Women's Conference confined itself to collecting funds to save the children, to open homes for them and care for them. No one voluntary agency alone could bear the weight of all the work needed for the victims of this calamity, and so we concentrated our efforts on helping the children who had been left destitute and hopeless. We started the "Save the Children" fund and it was heartening when not only Indians but also donors from several foreign countries made valuable contributions to help this cause. Shrimati Vijaya Lakshmi Pandit was president of the A.I.W.C. at that time, and she and the standing committee, of which I was a member, began the work for these children—work that has continued all over the world wherever children are the victims of man-made or natural disasters.

212

Another great tragedy, not of course of the magnitude of the Bengal famine, struck the city of Bombay soon after. Thousands of human beings were affected and there was great loss, human and financial. My husband, as the Chairman of the Bombay Port Trust, was closely concerned with this calamity. On April 14, 1944, while he was at work in his office, there was a tremendous explosion that shook the city for miles around. I had invited some friends to lunch, and even five miles from the docks we not only heard the explosion, but the doors and windows of our house rattled badly. We all rushed out into the garden, wondering whether it could be an earthquake or some new type of military weapon being tried out. The sky was tinted pink in the distance from the fires, and then the telephone began to ring.

I was told that a ship containing a cargo of TNT had exploded in the harbor. Nobody knew whether it was sabotage or an accident. The only thing certain was that the ships in the immense harbor were shattered, the water of the harbor basin had emptied, and hundreds of dock workers were killed or maimed. The whole of the port area was ravaged as though it had been heavily bombed, and innumerable fires had started everywhere. One ship among several in the harbor was lifted with such force that its anchor was carried hundreds of yards away and deposited on the roof of a building.

My husband, of course, rushed to the port from his office and commandeered any vehicle he saw to help get the injured to hospitals. The nearest was an army truck, so as many casualties as it could hold were loaded into it. My husband directed the driver to go to St. George's, the nearest hospital. The driver, an army man from abroad, did not know the way to the hospital, so my husband jumped in beside him to direct him. They had barely left the area when a second, slightly less serious explosion took place, killing several men working to help the wounded. Among them was the manager of the Port Authority. My husband had had a narrow escape.

He came home late in the evening, tired and greatly distressed, but had a quick shower and a meal, and insisted on going back to the docks to help with the rescue work. Premila and I were racked with anxiety. Minor explosions were going on around the whole dock area, wherever the TNT had scattered. My son-in-law, Nitya, accompanied him, and it reassured us a little to think he would be prevented by Nitya from taking unnecessary risks in his determination to help the injured.

The damage caused by these explosions was enormous and for days afterward minor flareups continued to take place. The whole area had to be cordoned off for weeks, for it was impossible even to locate immediately the bodies of those who had died in this disaster. The stench of burning and decaying flesh pervaded large areas of the city, making it even more difficult to carry out clearing-up operations.

The first suspicion was that this major tragedy was a case of sabotage, but after prolonged inquiries, the supervisors decided that it was an accidental fire in the hold of the ship carrying a cargo of TNT which had caused the explosion. It took a long time to get the Bombay Harbor functioning efficiently again. In fact, even deliberate sabotage could hardly have crippled the port so effectively. The war came to an end in 1945, but the backlog of army operations continued for the Bombay Port workers till 1947.

CHAPTER 24

Until Mahatma Gandhi appeared on the Indian political scene and assumed leadership of the campaign for national freedom and social reform, the Congress party was led by highly educated Indians who understood Western political thought and the concept of democracy, and carried on a sophisticated and logical dialogue with the British rulers, claiming the right to self-government. But Mahatma Gandhi's approach was quite different. When he became the acknowledged leader of the Indian National Congress, he directed the movement not only to involve the well educated but also to reach down to the mass of the population of India—uneducated, illiterate but not unintelligent—and evoke their interest and support.

His identification with village India was dramatic. His clothes, his manner of life, the old Sanskritic principles on which his political agitation was based were recognized and understood by the poorest and most remote peasant. He put a new weapon into the hands of the unarmed masses and so created a new kind of movement against the foreign rulers. Truth and nonviolence would sustain them in defying the authority, no matter what hardships they were subjected to. Sacrifices had to be made,

215

whether of property or life, and these should be made without the desire for revenge.

For us, one of the most important things Mahatma Gandhi believed and preached was that men alone could never succeed in any national movement without the participation of women. He explained that men and women were the two wheels of the nation's chariot, and no progress was possible without the cooperation of both equally. The tasks he assigned to women were to enter public life, discarding their orthodoxy and ancient customs, to march in processions even when they were banned by the Government, to picket liquor shops and any stores that sold foreign goods, to face *lathi* charges by the police in public protest demonstrations and willingly to go to jail. He asked them to accept all these hardships without any retaliation, violence, or bitterness.

To put it mildly, his demands were staggeringly revolutionary. Yet Indian women came forward with a zeal and enthusiasm unprecedented among the uneducated and semi-educated. They massed together in processions and defied the ordinances prohibiting such demonstrations. They followed the guidance of the Congress committees and went to jail without any rancor. When the jails became overcrowded, they suffered a different kind of harassment from the police. They were loaded onto trucks, taken miles from their towns or villages, and left to find their way home as best they could. They made large bonfires of foreign cloth, and *khadi,* the handwoven, handspun coarse material—Gandhi's symbol—was worn not only by villagers, who had always worn it, but also by town and city dwellers to express their sympathy with the cause.

All this helped to create a new force in public affairs, for even uneducated women felt it was their duty to join in the nationwide struggle for independence. The unrest that was beginning to be felt by the illiterate and inchoate masses of India was given direction and guidance by Mahatma Gandhi, and they gained the courage to face sacrifices, even death, for the sake of the freedom of India and her right to be ruled by her own people.

This mass awakening in village India strengthened the

women's movement. News of the work of the All-India Women's Conference spread and attracted new recruits, particularly because the conference supported the national movement even though it continued to eschew party politics. Village India became important to the members of the educated classes, who had previously thought the cultural gulf between them too wide to bridge. Now women in remote areas were becoming aware of public affairs generally, and this widened the sphere of action of the women leaders, who so far had confined their work to the cities and larger towns. Branch organizations of the All-India Women's Conference were started in all provinces, and at each annual meeting of the main body greater and greater enthusiasm was evident. Our biggest drawback was that there was no common Indian language that could reach into all the different areas of the country, and we were limited to communicating with those women who had been educated in English or at least spoke and understood the language.

Conditions were still primitive and traditions powerful enough in rural India to make any approach to radical change difficult and slow. But, following Gandhi's deep concern for the welfare of the villagers and the emancipation of women, the All-India Women's Conference did make an important beginning. Branch organizations sought affiliation with the All-India organization through their own leaders and drew up programs of work for the underprivileged of their areas. The central committee members of the main organization helped by improving the programs and directing the work in different provinces with the greater experience they had already gained. And the conference continued to meet every year, outlining new and innovative projects for child care, adult literacy, maternal welfare. It encouraged education for women and small-scale and cottage industries, which were an important source of extra income for many millions of Indian villagers. Homes for the care of children, the orphans, the crippled and disabled, especially the victims of the Bengal famine, were opened, and generous donations were received from Indians and from foreign agencies.

One project was particularly close to my heart. Early in 1945, the A.I.W.C. was offered a fully fitted medical van, on condition that it be used to service remote village areas. This offer came from an old and dear English friend of mine, Mrs. Hilda Seligman, who as a young girl had been in India, had toured the villages with the official she was visiting and had been much moved by the poverty she saw, the malnutrition, the disease, the lack of clean drinking water and adequate health care. One day, some years later, during the war in 1944, standing at her window in London with some Indian friends, she watched a battalion of Indian soldiers marching down the street on that wet, snowy, dismal day, and she asked her guests where these men came from. She was told they had been recruited by the British from Indian villages. Many of them knew only their own warm tropical climate, where they lived half naked but in bright sunshine most of the year. They were completely unused to the cold, snow, and sleet of Europe and to the military uniforms and heavy boots they had to wear. Hilda Seligman could not get the two pictures out of her head—the dire poverty she had seen in the heat of India and, alongside it, these men from India tramping through London ready to give their lives for a Western cause. She wanted to do something concrete, however small, for those who lived in the distant villages of India, and so she wrote to the president of the A.I.W.C. and offered to give a medical van to help those villagers who lived out of reach of clinics, hospitals, and normal medical services. Would the conference undertake to place and maintain such a service?

At the A.I.W.C. standing committee meeting, this offer was placed before us. We argued about it and after much thought and discussion decided that the expense of maintaining such a project would be too great. It would require a doctor, a nurse, a chauffeur, a cleaner, and a dispensary, not to mention the high cost of petrol to tour even the nearby villages. No branch of the All-India Women's Conference was able to undertake it. This made me very unhappy. I saw the need for such a scheme and the advantage of getting leading urban Indian women directly interested in village conditions. Surely we could find the means to run this new project.

218

The war was over, but large sums of money were being collected for war widows and orphans through charity balls and fund-raising drives. At a lunch party I happened to sit next to one of the princes of an Indian state. In talking about the elaborate arrangements being made for the principal victory ball, he told me with great pride that he had donated a race horse to be auctioned for the fund.

"What would you expect as a fair price for such a race horse?" I asked.

"At least fifteen thousand rupees," he said . . . at that time about $3,000.

I remarked, "What a pity it is that people give so generously to a special appeal like the War Fund, but never think to contribute to a vital cause that is with us all the time."

He naturally asked what I meant, and I explained our great desire to help remote villages and Hilda Seligman's offer of a medical van. "We can't raise the necessary funds. We'll have to refuse the offer."

"What would such a venture cost the A.I.W.C.?" my lunch partner asked.

"About one thousand rupees a month, to begin with."

"Done," he said. "I'll send you a check for one thousand rupees on the first of each month for a year, and after that you will make your own arrangements."

I excitedly reported this offer to the standing committee. The van arrived from England soon after, and in June, 1946, we received our first check and began the work of our Village Mobile Medical Units. That scheme is still in existence, covering twelve tribal villages in the Thana area, north of Bombay, distributing medicines, treatment, and health education where medical aid had never been known before. The tribal people of the villages in the area we had chosen were called Warlies. Apart from chronic malnutrition, their chief scourges were malaria, bronchial diseases, and scabies. They had no clean drinking water, lived close together in clusters of huts for help and protection, and were, of course, most vulnerable as a result to the spread of any infectious disease.

The manners and customs of these particular Adivasis (a general term for tribal groups) are different from the ways of ordinary Indian villagers, and they speak a dialect which is a mixture of their own ancient tribal language and Marathi, the language of most of western India and the State of Maharashtra, where these tribes live. The women wear brass bangles from the wrist almost to the elbow and brass anklets from the ankle up to the middle of the calf. Their saris are short, pulled up between their legs, leaving their knees exposed. Their tight huddles of huts are scattered over the land for miles around. Mostly, they grow grass for hay, though there is some rice where the ground is arable, and they work in the teak forests by which they are surrounded. Cutting timber and grass is their chief occupation, and they are paid by the middlemen who buy their output according to the quantity they produce daily, because they do not own the land on which they work. Their religious rites and ceremonies are also different from those of other villagers. They believe in magic, in witch doctors and herbalists. On more than one occasion they have burnt a woman suspected of being a witch and of having caused their children to die. They are a simple people and for years were exploited by the more intelligent villagers who live in their neighborhood and treat them as inferiors and untouchables.

Enthusiastic about this project, I gladly accepted the presidency of the committee to deal with our mobile medical-care program. I traveled with a couple of members through the villages and acquainted myself with the conditions under which we would have to establish a welfare center. I was determined to find a way, at the start, to win the confidence of the Adivasis, and persuade them to accept modern medical treatment for their chronic ailments, and to wean them away from their belief in magical cures. The area we wished to cover was eighty-two miles from Bombay. The only way to get there was by taking a two-hour train journey and then traveling seven miles into the interior by motor van or jeep to reach the tribal villages.

Our work was deliberately intended only for those uncared-for landless laborers who worked for the surrounding Indian villagers. The landowners took strong exception to our project. They reminded us that the Adivasis had no proper medical aid in their own villages, and asked why we were so bothered about serving the "jungle dogs" who preferred the magic cures of the witch doctors. Still, we persisted in our determination to reach the tribal people, the outcasts.

My small committee and I engaged an enterprising woman doctor and a nurse. We rented a biggish hut of the tribal pattern, with a beaten-earth floor and thatched roof, made a few improvements in it, furnished it, and established our two workers there. Another similar hut housed a chauffeur and a cleaner, and also served as a shelter for the van. Dr. Natarajan, a public-spirited woman who had worked with the army during the war, was used to hardships and was very enthusiastic about our project. Having established our center and having equipped our small dispensary under her direction and advice, we rejoiced in the new experiences we were gaining in our frequent visits to Sanjan, the village we had chosen.

Then the monsoon came, and in that hilly part of the state it usually bring twelve inches of rain in three months. Because it is a jungle region, the snakes come out of their flooded holes and seek shelter in the huts. The rainwater spreading in great shallow lakes and swamps encourages enormous mosquitoes to make known their disturbing presence by whining all night. To my great consternation, the nurse suddenly turned up at my home in Bombay in a state of near collapse. She told me that she had seen three snakes in her hut the previous night and she could not work with us until something was done about the living conditions she and Dr. Natarajan had to face. I soothed her and assured her that we would do something to give both of them better housing.

My committee and I went back to the villages around the Adivasi area and this time met a number of landowners. One particularly generous and understanding gentleman, Mr. Mohite, listened to us and offered us an acre of land nearby as a gift.

We returned to Bombay determined to raise the money to build our own center, and once again personal friends came to our aid. One of them, the general manager of the railway, instructed his railway engineer to design and build a reinforced cement building where our workers could be housed. It was a small, simple structure with one wing to serve as the living quarters for the doctor, another for the nurse, and a central room for a dispensary and for treatment of outpatients.

I became deeply involved in this project and made repeated journeys to the village we had chosen, first to supervise the work of building, then to get to know the Adivasis, to understand their human needs and to bring back to city dwellers an account of the hardships that were the daily lot of these people. For example, there was a constant shortage of water in the areas they occupied, even though the monsoon brought torrential rain in the summer. The Adivasis had never learned how to store water, and since the land was hilly the heavy monsoon rain ran down the slopes, leaving the countryside parched the rest of the year. The women were forced to walk two or three miles to fetch pots of water for their needs.

Once again we collected funds to dig a well on our grounds for the benefit of our workers and the people who lived within easy reach of our medical center. We appealed for free medicines, vitamins, medical equipment, besides money donations to keep our new work alive. It took time to persuade the tribal people to trust our doctor and her remedies and advice. The superstitious hold of the witch doctors' magic cures was very strong. But from time to time cases reported by our doctor made us eager to extend our work: a young mother died of septicemia after a difficult confinement because the nurse and doctor could not provide adequately aseptic conditions in her hut; a newborn child died for similar reasons. We were determined to build a proper maternity ward for six women patients. We also built an infectious diseases ward for typhoid cases. This work was so far removed from the city population that it took a great deal of explanation of the village problems to get the sympathy, understanding, and finally the generosity of those who could donate to our work. I'm afraid that we all shamelessly exploited our friends.

222

Since those early days much has been done by the Maharashtra State Government to help the Adivasis of the area. The middlemen who kept the Adivasis in poverty have been dismissed, and now direct dealings for the purchase of timber and hay give the hard-worked Adivasis some extra money. Schools and hostels have been opened by the Government, and there is marked progress in every aspect of their lives. Our own work also continues, and only a few days ago, against much pleading from my committee to continue the work I had started with them, I forced them to accept my resignation. They made the condition that I would be available for advice whenever they needed me. Of course I agreed with pleasure, for this first village scheme was my baby, and while I live I shall continue to be interested in the progress of the work for the Adivasis and delighted that by now city women are fully aware that they owe a duty to the poorest areas of village India.

CHAPTER 25

I WAS ELECTED PRESIDENT of the All-India Women's Conference in December 1946. The term of office was one year, during which the president had to travel all over the country to help the provincial branches organize and expand the work in their neighborhoods. New groups of women seeking affiliation with the A.I.W.C. had to work on one or more projects for a period of at least three years before they could qualify for membership in the All-India organization. At the annual conference they reported on their work, and more and more members were enrolled to strengthen the movement. We were seeing the results of Mahatma Gandhi's propaganda as the membership of the A.I.W.C. climbed toward the one million mark.

Each year at the general conference the elected president delivered an address outlining her ideas about the work she wanted the branch representatives to undertake during the year of her stewardship. This address was always printed and delivered in English, which, as I have said, was the only language common to educated women from the different provinces of India. The year I became president, the conference was to be held at Akola, a small town where a very large gathering of women had assembled—so large that the meeting had to be held outdoors for the first time in the history of the conference—the majority of whom did not speak English. Already the demand was spreading that such women should by right be able to hear and understand the views of the speakers and whatever proposals and plans they were suggesting. The presidential address, they insisted, should be delivered in Hindi. Many of the women in Akola that year understood Hindi even though it might not have been their mother tongue.

As soon as the formal speeches of welcome were over, I stood up to deliver the president's address. At once a good many in the audience rose and demanded that I should address them in Hindi. This was acutely embarrassing for me. I held in my hand the printed address I was to deliver, copies had been distributed to the audience, and I had not prepared a speech in Hindi. I made several attempts to carry on in English in spite of the protests from the audience, but they simply would not allow it. There was no time to reorganize my ideas or think out effective phrasing, but there was no help for it. I was obliged to speak in Hindi. However, I did manage, not eloquently certainly, to satisfy the large numbers who had made themselves felt for the first time at this conference. There was some discontent among the South Indian delegates, the majority of whom did not understand Hindi, but they had the English version in their hands and that appeased them to some extent. In one way, in spite of my discomfiture, this scene was a good augury. It meant that women who so far had not been particularly interested in the activities of conference branches other than their own were beginning to feel entitled to take their places on the national level and work for a change in social patterns and on subjects of a wider political significance.

During my term as president of the A.I.W.C., I had a chance to see a great deal of the work already successfully established by the various branches. I traveled all over India, wherever women's groups were engaged in anything connected with the emancipation of women. I inspected nursery schools and nutritional centers for undernourished children and other places which provided programs in maternity and child care where hospitals were too overcrowded to maintain a maternity ward. I listened in on literacy classes, and saw projects providing vocational training for young women to enable them to earn some extra money to contribute to their household expenses. In every large city such work was already well established, and the women readily absorbed new ideas. It was exciting to find that in village areas, too, similar projects were developing, though more slowly.

That whole year was, for me, a combination of exhilaration and impatience. When I remembered that it was hardly fifty years before that my mother gave birth to her children with only the help of a *dai* to whom she paid five rupees, and how bitterly she was criticized for sending her daughters to school, I rejoiced in how far Indian women had progressed. But I also realized what a very small dent our work had made in the massive problems of Indian life and longed for some short cut, some faster way of reaching the poor, the illiterate, and the diseased.

In 1946 great changes were taking place in India. After the end of the Second World War, the British Government realized that India would have to be given her political rights at last. Lord Mountbatten was sent to work out with the Indian leaders the strategy for the transfer of power from British to Indian hands. During the years immediately before, even while the war was still going on, the demand for a division of the country had grown. The Muslim population, under the leadership of Mohammed Ali Jinnah, had already demanded that India be divided and a new country, called Pakistan, created. In two parts of India the Muslim population was slightly in excess of the Hindu population. The western area included the Punjab, the North West Frontier Province, and Sind; the eastern consisted of a long strip of Bengal along the Burmese frontier.

Mahatma Gandhi was strongly opposed to the division of the country, but the British Government was adamant about recognizing the Muslim demand. The rest of the Indian leaders, including Jawaharlal Nehru, agreed to the Partition of India as the price of Independence. In spite of Mahatma Gandhi's protests

226

the British terms were accepted, and on the 15th of August, 1947, with Lord Mountbatten still Viceroy (a designation later changed to Governor General), India attained full Independence. At a moving ceremony at the Red Fort in Old Delhi, the ancient capital of the Moghul Emperors, the Union Jack was lowered, the new Indian tricolor raised, and the Indian National Anthem, with words by Rabindranath Tagore, was played and sung. Amidst unprecedented rejoicing, at midnight, Pandit Jawaharlal Nehru, the first Prime Minister of India, made his stirring, much-quoted speech: "Long years ago we made a tryst with destiny and now the moment has come to redeem our pledge. . . ."

In June 1947, when my work with the All-India Women's Conference was in full swing, my husband was appointed India's first Ambassador to Japan. Santha was home from America. She had graduated from Wellesley College and had published her first book, *Home to India,* which had achieved great success. My husband had to leave almost at once for Tokyo and I could not accompany him, with my work as president of the A.I.W.C. only half done. Santha was free and eager to travel, so we decided that she should accompany her father as his hostess until December, when I would hand over my work in the A.I.W.C. to the new president.

All Indians lived through terrible, dark months after Independence. With the Partition of the country and the unexpected, cruel, and unhappy exchange of populations between Pakistan and India forced on the peoples of both countries, tragedies of a magnitude and intensity beyond the grimmest imagination of any leader were enacted. Approximately eight million people were uprooted from their homes in Pakistan because they were Hindus and Sikhs, and Pakistan was to be a purely Islamic state. In retaliation Muslims were forced to give up their homes in India to seek their fortune in the new country. Many went to Pakistan willingly, hoping for better opportunities and less competition. But all too often families were divided, religious persecution broke out, horrible atrocities were committed, and the bloodshed and death were as senseless as they were savage.

227

I cannot describe adequately the horrors of that time. Many historians have already recorded the tragic occurrences that followed immediately on Partition. The rejoicing of our nation on its liberation from nearly two hundred years of colonial rule was turned to mourning at the suffering of those of our people who were driven from their homes in Pakistan. All social workers, and naturally those who were already organized in associations dedicated to work for the underprivileged, turned their attention to assisting the eight million refugees from Pakistan. They were sent in batches to all parts of India, where camps were set up for them by the central and state governments. There the official and private social workers led the work of rehabilitating men and women and their families. It was a monumental task, for those who arrived in India had suffered irreparable loss, were brokenhearted from private tragedies—wives murdered, husbands slaughtered, daughters raped, children separated from parents—as well as the material misfortunes of property confiscated and homes looted. An unparalleled despair gripped them. They saw nothing in their future but sorrow, suffering, and tears.

Naturally, passions were aroused as the refugees flooded into India and cries for vengeance and retaliation were heard everywhere. Day after day, Mahatma Gandhi, who had dissociated himself from all governmental activities, devoted his time to bringing solace and comfort to the suffering. He tried in his usual evening prayer meetings, always attended by thousands, to soothe the anger and resentment of the victims of this massive disaster. His effort was to assuage the desire for revenge, for, he explained, revenge would naturally result in yet more violence. He told the crowds at his prayer meetings, in his simple, direct, and inimitable way, that they must learn the most difficult lesson of all: they should accept a philosophy of peace, nonviolence, and good will in spite of the cruelties they had endured.

For many thousands his voice alone was a kind of salve for their wounds. But there was a group of agitators who, although they revered Mahatma Gandhi, believed that his sermons on peace and forgiveness were emasculating the Hindus. They felt that the Muslim atrocities against the Hindu population in what had now become Pakistan should be punished. These extremists wanted to retaliate against the Muslims who continued to live in India, their homeland, rather than emigrating to the new country. India had declared itself a secular state and they had, in fact, every right to remain Indian citizens. But those fanatical Hindus would not accept this logic. On January 30, 1948, one of them fired the shot that killed the revered leader of the nation as he began his usual evening prayer meeting. The murderer came forward, touched Mahatma Gandhi's feet, apparently to show the deference he and his group felt toward this great man, and then assassinated him.

Never has a nation been so shaken, so incredulous, as the news of the Mahatma's death spread through India. All over the country anyone who could get to a radio listened silently to get details in special bulletins, which were broadcast every few minutes. Pandit Jawaharlal Nehru, in a heartbroken voice, at last spoke to the nation. Grief was mingled with his anxiety to reassure the country that a "Hindu madman," not a Muslim as many had feared the assassin would prove to be, had been responsible for the crime. Had it been a Muslim, no one could have curbed the violence that would certainly have resulted in a bloodbath all over India. It was small comfort for India's grief or, indeed, for the sense of bereavement felt by people all over the world. It took us all a very long time to get used to the idea that Bapuji, Dear Father, as he was called by many millions of Indians, was really gone from our lives.

CHAPTER 26

THE NEXT TWO years of my life were filled with travel in unfamiliar countries, with new experiences and new encounters with many different kinds of people. By now so many of far greater scholarship and a more profound understanding of Japan have written about those strange, contradictory times when the country was still under the Allied Occupation before the peace treaty had been signed that I hesitate to attempt a full description of life in Tokyo or an amateur assessment of the value of the SCAP regime.

However, a few impressions remain vivid in my mind, more because they taught me so much than because they are of any great intrinsic significance. When I arrived in Japan to join my husband and Santha, it was a cold, dark evening in February and I saw very little of my surroundings on the way from the airport. Until quite recently the Indian Embassy had not been allotted a house, and my husband and Santha had been staying in the Imperial Hotel along with a number of senior Occupation officials. Our house was partly Western in style and partly Japanese. It seemed comfortable and pleasant, and with the many maids, cooks, cleaners, gardeners, who were all lined up to welcome me, I thought it should be quite easy to run and that life in Tokyo would hold few domestic problems.

The next morning, when I looked around through the windows on all sides of the house, I received the first of many shocks to come. Everywhere I saw the horrifying evidence of the fire bombing of the city by American aircraft in the last stages of the war immediately before the unconditional surrender of Japan. Piles of debris on both sides of the road for miles increased the sense of desolation. Here and there a house, a chimney, a concrete building remained freakishly intact.

I had not been back to Europe since the war, though I had seen many photographs of the destruction in English cities. Still, I suppose one's first actual view of the ravages of indiscriminate bombing is bound to be etched far deeper in one's mind. Another thought, one that was to recur quite frequently, came to me then. Apart from our brief tour of Burma with the Simon Commission years before, I had never been in a country in Asia other than my own.

As the months of my stay went by, I can't, in all honesty, say that I came to feel any great affinity with the relatively few Japanese whom I met, but it hurt me to see an Asian country— one that had defeated most of the European colonialists in Asia —so humiliated by the West. It was difficult to see the Japanese in the light which they had hoped would illumine them—as liberators and saviors of shackled Asia. Gandhi and Nehru had both rejected their Pan-Asian appeal against the Western powers. But Subhas Chandra Bose, a leading Nationalist, had "defected" to Japan just before the war, and his many Indian followers combined to make an informal army which marched through Southeast Asia with the Japanese, picking up recruits from Indians settled in Indo-China, Thailand, Singapore, Malaya, and Burma. When they reached India, after the defeat of the Japanese, they were welcomed by the Indian populace as heroes. They claimed, with some truth, however flawed, that they had been the only Indians really to *fight* the colonialists with their own equipment—guns and ruthlessness. Thinking about all this in Japan didn't change my ineradicable faith in Gandhian principles, but I did begin to see Japan and all of Asia from a somewhat changed point of view. Now, after so many years, I still occasionally wonder who won and who lost that long war in Asia.

During the Occupation in Japan, our lives were severely limited by army regulations. This was brought home to me as soon as I arrived by Santha, who expressed her delight at seeing me and then added frankly, "Now I won't have to be the wife of a three-star general any more." I couldn't, at the time, imagine what she was talking about, but I soon learned that under the Military Occupation all diplomatic civilians were given courtesy army ranks to make the whole business of protocol simpler. For Santha, my arrival meant that she was no longer the "official first lady" of the Indian Embassy, and when we attended formal dinners, she could (if she was invited at all) sit with low-ranking friends closer to her own age instead of the generals and ambassadors with whom she had been paired for the previous eight months.

I also discovered that the Indian Ambassador, like the only other four ambassadors—British, French, Russian, and Chinese —were accredited, not to the Japanese Emperor or Government, but to General MacArthur, the Supreme Commander for the Allied powers in the Pacific. Accordingly, after my arrival, my husband and I were summoned to the American Embassy, now the MacArthurs' residence, for luncheon. Everybody knew that the MacArthurs entertained very sparingly, never giving a cocktail or dinner party, only inviting two or at the most three guests for luncheon. General MacArthur never accepted an invitation for a meal, and never attended a social function, however important, though he would sometimes allow Mrs. MacArthur to deputize for him. If a group of American Senators or Congressmen whom he could not ignore came to Tokyo, he would give them an "audience" in his offices in the Dai Ichi Building. He drove to and from his office in the morning and the afternoon. On each occasion his limousine was preceded and escorted by siren cars, and all the roads were cleared for his daily motorcades. Even the Emperor could command no such arrangements. At the time, in common with numerous Americans whom I came to know, I thought it all extremely ungraceful behavior. Now that I have seen so much of diplomatic life, I admit that perhaps the MacArthurs were wise.

The ADC on the telephone was scrupulously polite but made it perfectly clear that we should come for luncheon at one o'clock sharp and leave at two-thirty sharp. The General liked a little siesta before he returned to work. We arrived promptly, were met by an ADC, shown into the drawing room, where Mrs. MacArthur received us and chatted with us for a few minutes. We heard a siren scream up the drive and drone into silence in front of the house. Then there was much slamming of car doors and finally General MacArthur strode in, looking uncannily like his photographs, handsome and determined, except, with his cap off, it was clear that he was balding fast. Mrs. MacArthur always called him, in company, "General"—sometimes "General, dear" or "General, darling"—never "Douglas." This seemed to me less astonishing between husband and wife than it did to many of my American friends. That day, Mrs. MacArthur ran to meet him at the door. "Oh, General, how *are* you?" she said in her soft southern accent, kissed him, and then allowed the ADC to introduce us formally.

Over lunch General MacArthur was an affable and a brilliant conversationalist, and showed great concern about the work he was doing to rehabilitate Japan and reconstruct every aspect of the traditional social systems to bring them into line with a democratic way of life, or to change or reject the old authoritarian structure which Japan had inherited from the past. His talk flowed in such a stream, sincere, informed, enthusiastic, that it gave us very little opportunity to say much. We listened, however, with great interest. My husband did try to talk about India's relations with Japan in the future, but General MacArthur only briefly acknowledged that they might be of importance, but not at the moment and not in the immediate future.

As I settled into Occupation life in Tokyo, my biggest frustration came from the "non-fraternization" rules that were still in effect. Japanese homes, restaurants, theaters, and cinemas were all "off-limits" to us. No Japanese could be invited to any hotel where foreigners lived because these were considered army billets. We couldn't shop in Japanese markets or stores for fear of the inflation in prices, especially of fresh fruit and vegetables, that might result. All our needs had to be met by the American and British PX and commissaries. Since none of us were allowed to have any financial dealings with the Japanese, we all used military scrip for money, which the Japanese were not permitted to accept. The canned or dehydrated food, the shortage of sugar, the appalling—almost inedible—quality of rice, the difficulties of transportation would all have been much less irksome if we could have come to know the Japanese people to some extent.

We had a few advantages as diplomats, and Santha had used them to get permission to teach English at the Jiyu Gakuen, the Freedom School, run by an eminent educationalist, Mrs. Hani. Santha had assured the authorities that she would not accept payment for her work, and as there was an acute shortage of English teachers since the war (the second language taught in schools for some years had been German), she was not depriving a qualified Japanese of a job. Through this work she had managed to make friends with some of the students and their parents, but none of them would accept an invitation to tea or a meal, because they were too timid to come to the Indian Embassy or too embarrassed to explain that they had no way of getting there. Buses and trams were jammed. We used to see queues of people waiting for hours on street corners before they could manage to squeeze onto a bus to return home from work. I often wondered how the mothers carrying their babies strapped to their backs saved them from being crushed to death.

The Indian community in Japan was very small, consisting almost entirely of businessmen and traders settled for the most part in Kobe and Osaka, both important commercial centers. Naturally, my husband had to visit them, discuss their problems, and explain the new relationship between Japan and an independent India. They were endlessly hospitable to us, gave us parties and feasts and showed us the marvels of Kyoto and Nara

234

as well as their own cities. A grimmer memory for me was that, each time we went to a railway station to take our places in the first-class compartment reserved for us, I saw the crowds of shabby Japanese with tired faces who had been waiting on the platform—often for days—to find accommodation in the third-class carriages. The first class was for Occupation personnel only.

There were, as well, several thousand Indian soldiers and officers stationed mostly around Yokohama as part of the Allied Occupation Forces. They were still under the command of the Australian general who headed the Commonwealth troops, but since the previous August 15th, to their huge delight, they had been permitted to parade under the Indian tricolor instead of the Union Jack and had changed their shoulder patches to the orange, green, and white of our national colors. When my husband and I visited them, or when officers and their wives came to Tokyo, they always entertained us lavishly, explaining that the army was a good deal better off than the civilians for food, transport, and special treats (like the delicious long-grained rice of North India and fresh spices). In return they dropped in on us any time at all, very properly treating the Embassy as part of their homeland, simply for the pleasure of seeing that there really *was* an Indian Embassy in Japan.

In spite of the many beautiful things I saw, the lovely country-side and the exquisite interiors of Japanese palaces and homes, in spite of the kindness of those few Japanese I came to know, all of them businessmen who had commercial relations with India, I was not really sorry when my husband's year in Japan came to an end and he received orders to go to Washington as the Indian Ambassador to the United States of America. It was years before I saw Japan again, but I always carried with me an admiration for the serenity of its people in defeat, the courtesy, the ability to make something elegant out of the poorest materials, and, most of all, the way they made an art of appreciation —cherry blossoms, a full moon, autumn leaves, the first snow, any natural wonder drew from them a deep response to beauty.

Santha also went ahead with her father to keep house for him in Washington until I could settle some family matters in India and join them. Premila and her husband Nitya Waglé had been married during the war and had been able to take only a week-end for a honeymoon before they returned to their jobs. Premila had stopped working for the Documentary Film Unit when her first child, a daughter, Asha, was born in 1944. Two and a half years later she gave birth to a son, Nikhil, and I had promised that I would take care of both my grandchildren on my return from Japan while Premila and Nitya took their first real vacation in Europe after six years of marriage. I couldn't bear to disappoint them by asking them to postpone their long-delayed holiday, so I took the children with me to Washington. By then I knew how big a part entertaining and being entertained play in the diplomatic life, and I employed an English governess to come with us. Asha and Nikki were not at all happy with her, being used to the indulgent ways of their beloved ayah in Bombay, and the governess, in turn, disapproved of me, feeling, in the entrenched English tradition, that her word, not mine, should rule the nursery. However, we all knew that it would be a relatively short-lived arrangement, for Premila and Nitya would be coming to Washington after their European tour.

The Indian Embassy is a beautiful building, beautifully situated on McComb Street. After I had paid and received the usual ceremonial calls, our lives became hectic with parties and receptions on a much grander scale than anything I had known. The diplomatic community was enormous, the members of Government even more numerous, and since my husband had official dealings with many of them, our social life often involved two or three parties in one evening. In spite of this feverish pace, we did meet interesting and congenial people who remained friends long after we had left Washington.

As if there wasn't enough to excite us in our first visit to America—our new surroundings, the beauty of the countryside around Washington, our new acquaintances—1948 was also a presidential election year. Like everyone else in America we sat riveted most of the night listening to the election results coming in, thinking how different it was from the English or Indian voting system. And like many others we were delighted to see the "underdog," Harry Truman, win against Thomas Dewey, the "certainty."

A few weeks earlier, Santha had left for China, where she was joining three friends to travel in Asia. They were determined to go to the far northwest of China and then to cover as much of Asia as they could. This gave us some very anxious moments. The Communist revolution in China had already caught fire and was spreading with alarming rapidity all over the country. We got no news from Santha for a long time and became more and more apprehensive every day. Then a woman I met, a top executive of Pan-American Airways, undertook to help me. The Pan-American planes were still flying to and over China and might be able to radio for information. A few days later my new friend phoned me with the happy news that the travelers were all right, were not in the Communist zone, were hitchhiking south and, she guessed, could not communicate because there were no postal facilities in that area.

From Hong Kong, Santha and her friends went on to Indo-China, Thailand, Malaya, Singapore, and Indonesia. It seemed to me that they were courting disaster, for all of Southeast Asia was in a state of turmoil and revolution, but there was no arguing with my adventurous and headstrong daughter in those days. The trip took much longer than any of the group expected, and by the time Santha came back to Bombay, my husband and I had returned from Washington and he had taken up his duties in his new posting as Governor of the Reserve Bank of India.

CHAPTER 27

ONE SMALL INCIDENT from our time in Washington stays in my mind. I was taking my four-year-old granddaughter, Asha, up for her afternoon nap when I noticed a particularly good photograph of Jawaharlal Nehru which hung at the bottom of the stairs.

"Do you know who that is?" I asked Asha.

"No, who is it?"

"That's the Prime Minister of India."

Asha stared at the photograph, very puzzled. Then she said, "But, Gran, why do you call him the 'Crying Minister'?"

I laughed and gave her an explanation that she could hardly have understood. But her question set me thinking about my old friend, fellow Kashmiri Brahmin, and beloved national leader. I recalled the fourteen years he had spent in jail, the apparently insurmountable opposition he had braved, the joy of achieving Independence, so quickly overcast by the bloodshed and misery of Partition and by the murder of Mahatma Gandhi—a calamity that robbed him of his guide and inspiration. And now he had the enormous burden of leading India, that vast, complicated mixture of peoples and languages, of princes and beggars, of intellectuals and illiterates, into a workable democracy. In a way, Asha was almost right—if not the "Crying Minister," Jawaharlal Nehru might well be called the "Sorrowful (though brave) Minister" of India. All these random thoughts went through my mind, and I realized that I missed India very much indeed. This wasn't merely homesickness; rather, I felt that my true life was there, my work, my people, my world. We had off and on lived abroad for fifteen years, had traveled extensively; now it was time to go home.

When my husband was offered the job at the Reserve Bank, we discussed this assignment very thoroughly. We both felt that it was a great opportunity to serve our newly independent country in a more basic way than by representing India in an ambassadorial capacity abroad. Although my husband had done an outstanding job in his various foreign assignments, he did not particularly enjoy diplomatic life. Since the early days of his service with the Finance Department he had hoped to pursue his work in that field. Here was his chance, and it would be exciting and exhilarating to play a part in the building of a country so long under colonial rule. I too was thrilled at the thought of returning home and once again taking an active part in the women's movement and in social-welfare projects.

Our headquarters were again in Bombay, where we were entitled to the official residence of the Governor of the Reserve Bank, a commodious two-story house with seven bedrooms and bathrooms upstairs, a formal drawing room and dining room downstairs, and a charming, informal sitting room opening onto a lovely terrace and garden. There were, besides, two office rooms. It was a perfect house for entertaining—of which we had to do a great deal—as it was spacious yet intimate, and the garden was a special joy. My husband's predecessor was a gardener and botanist of great skill and imagination, and he had filled it with rare and beautiful plants.

By lucky chance our new residence was only a ten-minute walk from the house that Premila and Nitya and their family occupied. My grandchildren, Asha and Nikki, walked down the road with their ayah every morning at eight o'clock and had breakfast with us before my husband went to his office, and then the children were taken to their school. We both loved the children dearly, enjoyed their company for an hour each morning, and yet I was left free all day to arrange my household and social duties and resume my welfare work.

As soon as we were established in our new home in Bombay, I looked around to see what changes had taken place in my absence, and where and to what extent my services could be used. The high spirits in which I had returned home were dashed to the ground when I realized that conditions around us showed no perceptible improvement. New government housing was receiving attention, but while buildings were gradually being erected, the slum conditions in industrial areas seemed worse than before. Unskilled labor for new buildings was being drawn from those neighboring villages which could spare manpower, but no provisions had been made for housing these newly employed people, or to provide them with light, water, and sanitation. Colonies of squatters were springing up in vacant spots in the city. The men and women were employed, it is true, but they lived in deplorable conditions. They set up dwellings for themselves of thatch, tin, old crates, and even cardboard. Their ramshackle enclaves became plague spots, poisoning the environment of the open spaces of the city.

We were used to the old slums of Bombay. The *chawls,* tenements for the very poor, had existed ever since the development of industries, factories, and mills in the days of the British. We knew that these could not be wiped out in a day. But here was a worsening situation, for the evil was not confined to the industrial areas of the city but was spreading all over wherever new building projects were undertaken. Children swarmed about the huts, naked, undernourished, uncared for while the parents were at work. More were being born every day into those squalid conditions, to live like maggots in a pile of refuse.

I had no trouble renewing my contacts with the All-India Women's Conference, with the All-India Women Graduates Union, and the National Council of Child Welfare. The only problem lay in trying to decide on which of the enormous needs

Procession during a village family planning conference in 1950

of India's poor I should concentrate my own small efforts. Looking back now, I can pinpoint exactly the events that brought me to a decision.

A fellow welfare worker took me to visit a tenement family; the man was a mill worker who lived with his wife and three children in one dark, poorly ventilated room. The woman was a TB patient, lying in one corner of the room, coughing painfully, spitting blood on the floor. Her three children, aged five, three, and one, sat around her. The five-year-old was trying to help her mother. The three- and one-year-olds were rickety and unable to move around much. The woman herself was pregnant again. I asked her why she did not go to the municipal hospital in that area. She replied that she was too weak to take three children with her, two of whom would have to be carried, to seek medical aid. She still had to cook for her family. Her husband did the shopping.

A similar case was that of another mill worker who had a wife and four children—two boys and two girls. The girls seemed normal, but both the boys were mentally handicapped. The woman was pregnant again, and her husband's fear was that if the child were a boy he too would be mentally defective. It seemed to be a pattern in his family. Could I help him, he asked, to have the child aborted rather than take the risk of another son? I could not help him, for at that time an induced abortion was a criminal offense.

In the *chawls,* no provision had been made for adequate ventilation in the one room a whole family occupied. If they cooked in the privacy of their room, the smoke blackened their walls and caused them to cough and choke and retreat with streaming eyes into the open passageway between rooms, where they would relight their small charcoal stoves and thus expose their children to the risk of being burned as they ran in and out. And yet in these conditions more and more children were being born to an almost unbearable life.

It was when I thought over these glimpses of slum life that it became perfectly clear to me that, however much our social workers tried to improve conditions, nothing could be accom-

242

plished while unlimited numbers of children continued to be born in crowded houses where expansion was impossible. Many women I had talked to were tired of childbearing and were desperate at each new pregnancy. The only consolation handed them by their elders was, "It is God's will, so accept it with grace." I knew then that I had found a new purpose in life. There was no question in my mind but that I should work for family planning single-mindedly and intensively. The limiting of our population was a fundamental and pivotal necessity if we were to make the gigantic task of social and economic improvement successful.

The idea of birth control, as it was then called, had been introduced many years ago. In fact, in 1936, the A.I.W.C. had invited Margaret Sanger, the great American pioneer in birth control, to speak on the subject at the annual conference. She had been received with great interest and respect by the mixed audiences she had addressed, not only at the conference but afterward in several of the larger cities of India where she traveled. Even earlier than Margaret Sanger's visit, the Government of Mysore State, under its enlightened Maharaja, had made tentative proposals for setting up clinics for the limitation of population in the interest of bettering economic conditions in homes, improving the health of mothers and children and the care of families generally. This work had not received sufficient support and had died out shortly after. Various official reports on labor and industry had recommended family planning as desirable for improving the health of workers, and several individual social workers, most prominent among whom was a Professor Karve, had opened small clinics in their homes, where the simplest methods of birth control were taught privately. One or two prominent workers had written articles for newspapers on the subject and had been penalized by the authorities for their unorthodox views, for at that time the officials concerned, both British and Indian, frowned on birth control.

In 1949 the independent Government of India was engaged in formulating the First Five-Year Plan for the country so newly enfranchised. For this purpose, a National Planning Commis-

243

Prime Minister Nehru admiring the author's medal, awarded by the President of India

sion was appointed by the Central Government, and consultations were held between official and nonofficial leaders to lay down the priorities to be considered in creating the foundation for the social and economic development of the country. We, as social-welfare workers, were naturally concerned with the plans for social change, health, education, sanitation, and a better standard of living, not only in the cities but also in the villages. Eighty percent of our population were illiterate and lived in rural areas, our maternity and infant mortality were high, and our standard of living almost the lowest of all civilized countries.

India would soon begin to receive the assistance of the United Nations agencies, especially WHO and FAO, and, predictably, as conditions of health and sanitation would improve, maternal mortality and infant deaths would decline. Killer diseases such as plague, smallpox, and malaria, among others, would receive concentrated attention. The advance of medical science and the discovery of penicillin and antibiotics were helping to save lives, and the projects of the FAO were already providing help with malnutrition. It all would have promised a marvelous era for our country, with the obliteration of the endemic problems of disease and starvation, but for the fact that the demographers were forecasting the increasingly rapid growth of the population along with the measures that were helping to save lives. In short, we had to be prepared for what has come to be known as the "population explosion."

India's population had been growing at the rate of five million per year. It now rises by fifteen million per year, but even then we knew that this increase in numbers would make it impossible for the Government to keep up, to improve existing conditions fast enough to raise standards of living through economic development—a slow affair at best—in time to match or benefit the increased population.

I felt very strongly that family planning should be a priority program. Advocates of birth control had openly voiced their fears for the future, but had received no encouragement. It was necessary to make a concentrated effort to bring the subject prominently before the Planning Commission—not only as a general welfare measure but also as a concrete program, with special financial backing and provision for training personnel with governmental support rather than through voluntary welfare organizations. It was with this conviction that I embarked on creating a new organization of both men and women to spread the message of family planning, to approach scientists for help in drawing up a program of work and guiding us in its execution.

First we had to find professionally qualified men and women willing to spare time for such work; then we had to find a group of volunteers, a suitable place to work in, and finally—crucially —the initial finances. We could not work exclusively through the existing women's organizations with which I was connected because it was important to have men on the new committee. I met two specialists, Dr. A. P. Pillay, an eminent doctor in sexology and in male diseases, and Dr. V. N. Shirodkar, a renowned gynecologist, and I sought their help. I then asked my husband if he would give me the ground-floor office in our home. He was at first reluctant to let me use an official residence for private voluntary work, especially as, at that time, the Government had no decided policy about family planning, and the Health Minister of the Central Government and the Chief Minister of Bombay were openly opposed to any such program. His position was awkward. He himself agreed that the time had come for volunteers to campaign for measures to contain the threat of even greater overpopulation, yet he was not sure that, as a government official, he could give me active support in this project. However, he did finally give his consent and the room in the Bank House was my first office.

I saw my task as twofold: to find professional men and women willing to donate their scientific knowledge and to mobilize public opinion. It was the first project I had ever undertaken that would require the assistance of experts in many fields—physicians, demographers, economists, researchers, biologists, gynecologists, and, of course, specially trained social workers.

With what now seems to me incredible brashness, born of ignorance, I invited a group of men and women to my home, and there we discussed our ideas for action and established the Family Planning Association of India. Dr. Pillay and Dr. Shirodkar accepted the joint directorship of the organization, and I collected the first life membership fees from each one of the group that formed our first committee. This was to be the nucleus of the fund I meant to start to cover our initial expenditures. My next move was to approach the Planning Commission of the Government and draw their attention specifically to the subject of population control. We drafted a memorandum expressing in strong terms the urgent need for this work and sent it to the Planning Commission. Meanwhile, we looked around the crowded city of Bombay for a suitable place to establish our first clinic.

After much hunting, I heard that the Western Railway had recently built a welfare center, where the wives of railway officials were intending to start social-welfare programs for railway workers. Their plans had not yet materialized, and I was able to persuade the railway manager to allow me to rent the premises until the officials' wives were ready to use them. Having got our committee, my office, and our clinic premises set, we had to find people to campaign among the underprivileged and to educate both men and women about the necessity of limiting their families. There were no trained publicists to start with, but as we called our new clinic the Family Welfare Center, many of the slum dwellers in our neighborhood came to visit our doctor for medical help of all sorts. Here we began to educate them in the simplest, least-threatening terms about the need for controlling the size of their families. There is no religious objection to family planning in India, but habit and old fears are almost as difficult to overcome.

In the meantime, it was necessary that our small group in Bombay, which had ambitiously called itself the Family Planning Association of India, should justify this title. We felt that the time had arrived when the control of population had become so urgent that it had to be recognized as the basis for all economic planning for the country. This fact, so apparent to us, was not given anything like its proper emphasis in the National Planning

247

Premila in 1952

Santha in 1952

Commission. Strong forces in the state and in the Central Government were definitely opposed to the introduction of family planning in the health programs being formulated, despite the fact that demographers from abroad as well as Indian experts were warning us of the terrible spiral India was entering. The equation was simple and frightening. Children who normally would have died before reaching maturity would live to reproduce. The millions carried away by plague, smallpox, and malaria would be saved by the new remedies already available. The death rate would be lowered. Life expectancy, which was twenty-six years in 1947, would rise. The problem of population growth would become more serious and more unmanageable each year. To us it seemed grimly obvious that any promise of improvement in living conditions through the programs being framed by the Planning Commission for economic growth, better agricultural methods, expansion of industry and social services would be hopelessly undermined by the increasing, unplanned-for millions who would be born in India.

To test the extent of the interest in our new program we organized the first All-India Family Planning Conference in 1951. We hoped to invite respected and well-informed people to read papers, join in discussion groups, and attract enough public attention to make a considerable impact on the Government and impress on the official planners the fact that all economic growth would be nullified unless they gave population control a high priority. We wanted the widest possible understanding of the remorseless mathematics of the situation as well as the human cost of neglecting the problem. National health, child welfare, nutrition, and economic betterment could not be achieved unless a limit was placed on the number of children in each home, programs for mass education toward that end were put into effect, and provision was made for clinical services for the prevention of unwanted births.

Dr. Shirodkar, an old friend, was already one of our directors and readily gave us his support. Dr. Pillay was a hard, cynical, highly qualified man. He was interested in the whole idea, but he had no faith in women social workers. At our first meeting

250

at my home, I had conceded from the start that from the medical and scientific point of view we knew very little about family planning. Still, we were convinced that we could generate some action to curb this towering problem and awaken the authorities to its urgency. Dr. Pillay laughed at my enthusiasm. He said, "You are only a socialite. As the wife of the Governor of the Reserve Bank of India, you may attract some attention, but you will never be able to work in depth in this difficult field." His words seemed to me a direct challenge and I think now that his remark was the reason I called the first All-India Conference as soon as the initial work in Bombay had been set in motion.

As the president of the new organization, I with my committee issued invitations to as many doctors, both civil and military, demographers, economists, and social workers in every state of India as we could reach. Further, we invited those in the universities of each state who were interested in allied subjects to attend an All-India Conference under the auspices of the association in Bombay.

The subject of birth control had been discussed seriously in the past by some, derisively by others. Even in my student days I had heard the story of a well-known lawyer who had no children, and a friend of his, a judge of the High Court in Madras, who had thirteen, and how they had called a drawing-room meeting to discuss the possibility of forming a eugenics society to draw up programs for birth control. A good deal of discussion took place, much of it antagonistic. When one gentleman who was strongly opposed to the idea said, "You gentlemen are not qualified to talk about this subject. One of you does not know anything about birth, and the other obviously knows nothing about control," the meeting broke up on a hilarious note and nothing was accomplished.

So many years later we were making an effort to deal seriously with the question. We knew very little about modern contraceptives or how they should be used. We had very few trained doctors, and those few had, at some stage, received their training abroad. Years earlier, in 1936, when Margaret Sanger had visited India and talked about birth control, a few clinics had been opened here and there, but as no contraceptives were available in India at that time, they soon faded out or changed their emphasis. A few condoms were imported from abroad, but when the Second World War broke out in 1939 these imports were stopped, and all the work in this field died. Here and there some doctors advised women to try the simplest method, at one time advocated by Marie Stopes. This was to use crude, unprocessed cotton soaked in oil before sexual intercourse. But most women who wanted to limit their families found this method displeasing and soon discarded it.

When we called our first Conference on Family Planning it was as much to clarify our own thinking on the subject and to be able to present workable programs as to ask for support from the medical and scientific community and cooperation from social workers. What we wanted to establish was a scientific and practical course of action. We wanted to initiate projects to educate illiterate men and women on the desirability of smaller families and on methods of spacing the births of children and limiting their numbers.

CHAPTER 28

ONE HUNDRED AND TEN qualified men and women accepted our invitations to a two-day session of the All-India Conference on Family Planning in Bombay, traveled at their own expense, and made their own arrangements for accommodations and transport in this large city. It heartened us greatly to know that the delegates came from all the states of India. We were thus assured that the subject was indeed of interest to the thinking public, and that we would have the cooperation of many active participants if only we could raise enough public funds to start programs in different parts of the country.

We in the Family Planning Association sent a memorandum on "The Growth of Population in Relation to the Growth of Economic Development" to the National Planning Commission for consideration by the commission's Health Department. This was acknowledged, and I, as the president of the Family Planning Association of India, was invited to sit on the Advisory Health Panel of the National Planning Commission. Such panels of nonofficial men and women were invited to contribute their views on all subjects covered by our First Five-Year Plan. I was immensely encouraged by this invitation. It indicated that the

The first All-India Family Planning Conference, 1951 *(Asian Photos)*

Health Department of the Government had accepted the importance of the problem and was giving me the opportunity of putting our case before the powerful Planning Commission, despite the opposition of the Chief Minister of the Maharashtra State, of which Bombay is the main city, and the Union Health Minister in our Central Government in Delhi. I tried to keep my courage up by remembering the struggle and antagonism that early pioneers in the field had encountered.

In the early years of this century, Margaret Sanger in America and Marie Stopes in England had been met with fury and ridicule for suggesting that a woman had the right to bear children only when she wanted them and was able to give them a decent upbringing. I remembered also my own mother's life of drudgery as every two years of her marriage she produced another child, feeling that this was her natural destiny. However, the world had changed a great deal since her day and since the time when Margaret Sanger was refused permission to enter Japan because she was too well known as a leader of the birth control movement to be allowed to address Japanese audiences. Now the interest in preventing unwanted children and in population control had grown in many countries of Europe. Sweden and the Netherlands were outstanding for their private practitioners and public support, and a number of other European countries had begun to accept the desirability of contraception, though the subject was officially frowned on by their governments. But we, in India, had little knowledge of this increasing interest in the field of population studies in Europe, although we had been sympathetically interested for years, largely because of our admiration for Margaret Sanger.

To our astonishment this first All-India Conference on Family Planning attracted great attention abroad and was reported in many foreign papers. Soon afterward I had a cable from Margaret Sanger, who had seen a Paris report of the Indian conference, asking if I could arrange an international conference on family planning in India. My colleagues and I were so excited by this recognition of our first effort on the part of so eminent a person that we cabled back our readiness to accept her proposal for the next year, 1952, just about fifteen months after our first All-India Conference. The support of those who had for years fought "to establish the right of bearing only wanted children" in America and Europe would boost our new effort considerably.

We realized that this venture would involve us in very hard work, not least because at that time we were unfamiliar with even the names of the outstanding men and women abroad who were already working for the cause, and we depended on the international committee in Europe to recommend the eminent people who should be asked to present papers on the many subjects relating to the social, medical, demographic, and scientific aspects of family planning.

At this time I was serving as president of the Bombay branch of the Women Graduates Union and was fostering new projects for them and closer contacts with colleagues in other Indian cities. I also headed the Child Welfare Association. In addition, of course, I had my duties at home, which included the entertaining that the wife of a Governor of the Reserve Bank is expected to do and taking care of foreign house guests as eminent as the Governor of the Bank of England and his wife, Lady Hermione Cobbold, who came to stay with us for a week, Walter Lippmann and his wife and daughter, Mr. and Mrs. Bernstein of the International Bank, Hamilton Fish Armstrong and his charming wife, and a great many others from India and abroad. All these visiting celebrities had to be suitably entertained, and parties had to be arranged for them to meet interesting Indian bankers, economists and journalists. We made some lasting friendships, and I deeply appreciated the opportunities to develop these new relationships, but I marvel now at the energy and enthusiasm I must have had in those days, because my family also demanded some of my time. Santha had married Faubion Bowers in France in 1951, and she came with her husband to spend some months in our home. They traveled to Kashmir and returned to Bombay for Santha's confinement. Her son, Jai, was born in Bombay on September 24, 1952.

I had taken on what seemed an impossible task: simultane-

256

ously organizing the international conference on family planning in November and another on child welfare in December of the same year. We still had only the one small office in the Reserve Bank house, which we divided into two sections. The programs being arranged for the two conferences were entirely different, and we wanted no confusion or overlapping. It was important that the subject of family planning should receive more publicity than the Conference on Child Welfare.

Family planning was a new and controversial subject for the general public, but the close relationship of population growth to the development of the country's economic resources had been so emphasized that even the Health Minister, Raj Kumari Amrit Kaur, who was not in favor of family planning through contraceptives, had agreed that a representative of WHO be invited to travel over India, carry out a research study, and make recommendations about these intertwined subjects to the Government. She had, however, made it a condition that if such a study proved that birth control was necessary for India to raise the standard of living for her people, only the rhythm method of contraception should be recommended. In her opinion this was the only "moral" way, however ineffective it proved to be.

Even with his hands so tied, Dr. Abraham Stone, an ardent admirer and fellow worker of Margaret Sanger and a well-known supporter of contraception in America, accepted the WHO assignment and came to India in 1951 to make his survey. He traveled widely, assessed the situation, and, of course, came to the same conclusion as all the demographers, national and international. He was my guest for the three days he spent in Bombay, and my friends and I, all involved with organizing the first International Conference on Family Planning, had heated arguments with him. We blamed him for accepting a limited assignment on such an important question. He in fact agreed with us that the rhythm method, though scientifically sound under ideal conditions, could not succeed in our villages, where 80 percent of our population lived, where illiteracy was rife, where calendars and thermometers were unknown, where people reckoned time by phases of the moon, and menstrual charts could not be

With Dr. Abraham Stone, in 1951 *(Foto-Husch)*

kept to determine the "safe" period for a woman.

Yet he had traveled all over India, had been impressed by the enormous population and the increasing rate of growth in an underdeveloped country, and had realized the massiveness of the problems. He reported that in his opinion immediate measures for birth control must be taken even if only the rhythm method was permitted. He hoped that in the future he could return to India and express himself more definitely and freely on the use of contraceptives, unhampered by the Health Minister's conditions.

The International Child Welfare Conference was noncontroversial, and the Prime Minister, Pandit Jawaharlal Nehru, consented to inaugurate it. He had always been particularly interested in child care, and wherever he went, at every public function, he used to be surrounded by adoring crowds of children, who always greeted him with ringing cries of *"Cha Cha Nehru ki Jai"* ("Victory to our Uncle Nehru"). He always responded with some affectionate gesture that thrilled the children. He would throw them garlands that had been given him or pat the nearest ones on the back, or speak briefly to them of his interest in them and encourage them in their studies.

We also had the cooperation of all the welfare organizations, both official and voluntary, national and international. It was the first time that the Indian Child Welfare Association was host to the international organization, and everyone wanted us to appear in a good light. Even the Health Minister, who did not like us because of our continued activities with family planning work, agreed to attend and address the meeting. Maternity and child welfare were very much her responsibility in the ministry. Thanks to all this, the conference was a great success and gave a new spurt to child-welfare work.

The Conference on Family Planning, however, was more complicated. In preparing for this, I dutifully wrote to the Health Minister, asking her for a message. She replied that, since she did not approve of contraception except through abstinence or the rhythm method, she could not give her support to our conference. I was sure that the Prime Minister was sympa-

259

thetic, but I knew that it would not be diplomatically possible for him to commit himself and flout his Health Minister until a decision was taken by his Government. I did not, therefore, approach him.

Still, we had to have an eminent person to inaugurate this conference, one whose patronage would be of importance to a young organization engaged in a new field of work. I wrote to Dr. Radhakrishnan, whom I had known years ago when I was a young college student in Madras and he was a young assistant professor in the same college. Later, already established as a scholar of philosophy, the author of books on comparative religion, and a brilliant speaker, he had, as I have said, been our guest when he visited South Africa during my husband's term there as India's High Commissioner. At this time, when I asked him to open our Conference on Family Planning, he was Vice-President of India. I explained how important we thought this conference was going to be to the future of our country and outlined our objectives.

I had an immediate reply. He sympathized with the cause we were espousing, but as the Government had not taken a decision on the subject of accepting family planning as part of the official Health Plan, he felt he should not accept our invitation. I refused to be disheartened and wrote again, pointing out that the whole subject was under consideration by the central ministry and that Dr. Stone had been deputized to carry out a survey by the WHO at the request of the Indian Government. I suggested that the report of a person of Dr. Stone's position and status would certainly influence Government policy. To our great joy and satisfaction, Dr. Radhakrishnan reconsidered and agreed to open our conference.

We had already issued invitations to all our Asian neighbors —Pakistan, Ceylon, Nepal, Japan, Indonesia, Malaya, Singapore, and China, as well as Egypt, Israel, and all the European countries, and America. About 150 delegates from abroad had registered, and nearly 400 from India. Money was our great problem, for we had practically no working capital, but just in time we received a donation of $5,000 from Mrs. Ellen Watu-

260

mull of the Watumull Foundation, who was a great friend of Margaret Sanger, and we collected another 25,000 rupees from the sale of advertisements in the brochure we issued explaining the purpose of the conference, publicizing the program, and listing the names of the eminent speakers.

We could provide a few of the delegates with private hospitality—some of those from abroad and some from India—but we could not assume their travel expenses or pay for those who were accommodated in hotels. All we could afford was the cost of the hall during the week of the conference, secretarial expenses, printing of the papers to be presented by the speakers, and transportation from the main hotels to the conference hall. We did, however, provide for one entertainment by persuading the Mayor of Bombay to hold a reception for all the delegates. The rest of the conference was all our own amateurish, hastily-put-together work.

Before the opening of the Family Planning Conference we had arranged for a training course for our Indian doctors. A great many of them, like us, had no idea of the latest contraceptive devices used abroad, or of the techniques in using the different types required in different cases. At our clinic in the Railway Colony where we had first begun work our patient load was too small to provide enough "cases" for the training classes we were proposing to hold, and so we paid women to come to the clinic daily, once our conference started, and the expert doctors from abroad agreed to teach the Indian doctors attending the conference.

When registrations began to come in, we were surprised by the number received from our neighboring Asian countries, where family planning was still a new subject. Between 1947 and 1949, several countries that had been under foreign rule had become independent, and they were all beginning to realize that population growth resulting from improved health conditions was assuming menacing proportions. Economic development projects in each of these countries would limp along but could not keep pace with the soaring numbers of human beings. Western countries, whose grasp of the implications of growing popu-

261

lations in underdeveloped countries, mostly in Asia and Africa, was far more thorough than ours, were anxious in a different way. They were concerned with the frightening implications of runaway population growth in underdeveloped countries because of the strain this would cause in the developed nations and the problems it would pose in the context of world population growth. They sent delegates to the conference to increase their knowledge of research work in Asia.

The conference opened on the appointed day, and the packed auditorium, the international character of the occasion, and the importance of the subjects to be discussed filled us with high excitement. The hall was crowded to overflowing, the balconies were so jammed that people were leaning over each other, and just as many could find standing room only. The doors finally had to be closed as more and more men and women were trying to get in. We had not expected such a response; otherwise we could have had loud-speakers set up for those who could not get in. But the greatest thrill of all was when Dr. Radhakrishnan got up to make his inaugural address. Tall, dignified, eloquent, he spoke with authority in supporting our cause, quoting from the Sanskrit scriptures the sanction that the Hindu religion gave those who wished to plan their families, and stressing the necessity of doing so as a duty to their progeny. He was cheered to the echo, and those who were present on that occasion still remember the great dynamic and emotional impact made on the audience by his speech. He was given a spontaneous standing ovation, and we sat back with relief and satisfaction, feeling that an auspicious start had been made on the new and difficult campaign we had to undertake.

The delegates from Europe, who for years had been encountering opposition from the Catholic Church, were greatly heartened by the fact that the vast population of the East raised no objections during the deliberations that followed the inaugural session, even though, outside the conference hall, small groups of Catholic men and women were handing out leaflets against the program and clamoring to be given a place on our platform to put forward the Catholic point of view against family planning.

While the conference plenary sessions and group meetings were going on, day after day, Indian doctors and nurses crowded the classes being given at our new clinic by a number of leading doctors from abroad, among them Dr. Abraham Stone and Dr. Lena Levine from America, and Dr. Helena Wright from England. By the end of the conference we had a core of trained medical staff who could serve the Family Planning Association of India and, in their turn, train others in similar courses. For the first time Indians were instructed in the variety of contraceptives available and their correct usage.

The main contraceptives being advocated in India before the conference were the cheap, oil-soaked cotton pads suggested by Dr. Marie Stopes, which I have mentioned, and a palm-sized sponge soaked in a concentrated solution of salt recommended by Dr. Charles Gamble of the United States. The followers of Mahatma Gandhi, of whom the Indian Health Minister was one, insisted that abstinence was the best solution or, at worst, the rhythm method, over which there had been so much controversy when Dr. Abraham Stone's report was presented to the Government.

At the end of the conference, at the final meeting of the heads of the national delegations who had attended, it was suggested that the International Committee on Population, which had so far worked only in four countries, the United States, England, Sweden, and the Netherlands (although other countries, especially in Europe, were interested in the subject), be established as a full-fledged International Planned Parenthood Federation. I was nominated to be co-president with Margaret Sanger of this new international organization, and a business meeting was arranged for the following year in Stockholm to frame a constitution, decide the aims and objectives, rules, and regulations, elect the officers of the new international body, and outline the program of work to be undertaken in the building up of national units that could qualify for affiliation to the main federation.

With Margaret Sanger at the 1952 International Conference *(R. N. Ahuja & Co.)*

We met in Stockholm in 1953 and I was strongly urged to stand for election as president, but I declined this opportunity because there was far too much work to be done in India, where even the surface of our problems had not been scratched. Although I was willing to continue as a member of the standing committee, I wished to devote my time and energy to building up branches of the Family Planning Association in different parts of India. I hoped for guidance from the central office, but I knew that the major work in India—organizing programs that would fit into the social and cultural patterns of our large cities, smaller district towns, and even, perhaps, the village areas—must be undertaken by Indians. And it was a massive task, even though we were certain that the Government would accept family planning in time.

Early in 1953 the Planning Commission of the Central Government published its report of the First Five-Year Plan and definitely accepted family planning as part of its overall program. To our great pride, India thus became the first independent country officially to accept family planning as part of its national health program. Three million three hundred thousand rupees was allocated for organizing family planning work at the central administrative level and through the state health ministries. But the Health Minister still objected to the use of contraceptives and organized three centers in village areas for a three-year experimental project. Local workers and some WHO workers were assigned to teach women the rhythm method. They introduced a rather fanciful device—green and red beads threaded on a string. The green beads represented the infertile days of a woman's menstrual cycle and were to be moved one a day till they reached the red beads, which indicated the fertile days when sex relations with her husband should be avoided to prevent conception.

We opposed the whole program strongly because it took no realistic account of the facts of village life, which Dr. Abraham Stone had observed earlier: the villagers could read neither a calendar nor a thermometer. The beads themselves could not always be kept out of the reach of children, and in any case

265

calculations would be difficult no matter how carefully they were explained. Sure enough the program did fail, but only after wasting three years and a great deal of money, since the scheme required the help of highly paid workers from abroad.

Soon after the Government's acceptance of the concept of family planning, I was appointed to the Family Planning and Research Committee of the Ministry of Health. All the programs approved by the Government laid down strict rules controlling all voluntary agencies seeking Government grants for their work, and we often argued hotly with Government representatives about the details and the general approach. But within the guidelines we did the best we could. For the clinics we established we engaged full-time and part-time trained personnel. Realizing that the education of the poorer classes was fundamental to our efforts, we trained social workers to reach out to both literate and illiterate men and women to teach them the need for spacing children and to convince them of the benefits of such planning: that it would not only improve the health of mother and child but would lead to their economic betterment, enable them to educate their children and thus give them the chance for a better life. Gradually we moved further and placed proposals before the authorities for the introduction of family planning courses in all medical colleges, nurses' training schools, and social-science colleges, to provide trained personnel for the future and create a new consciousness among professional workers in the areas of medicine, nursing, and social welfare.

I traveled all over India, accepting every invitation to speak that came my way—at Rotary Clubs, women's meetings, Lions Clubs, social-welfare associations—and I went into the villages wherever possible. I spoke to audiences of women accompanied by small children and seated on the ground at open-air meetings. Usually there were a few men in the background, embarrassed to come too close, but eager to listen to what was being said. I welcomed discussions on the subject, especially in the less sophisticated areas. I found that my audiences were frank and uninhibited and, considering that they were mostly illiterate, I was amazed at how intelligently they argued the pros and cons of small families. I was again impressed by the great advantage that India has over most other societies where family planning is at issue: the majority of the population has only very rarely shown a moral, a religious, or an ethical objection to birth control. At my meetings it was quite evident that two major questions needed answers: How do we prevent unwanted births? And what becomes of our social structure if our young couples do not produce children?

Very early in our work we were surprised to find that many men and women approached us, not for family limitation, but for problems of infertility. Childless couples claimed that if happy families were what we were aiming for, those who had no children should receive our attention so that they too might find happiness in parenthood. This was to us a very valid argument, and we immediately gave it our attention. We opened the first infertility clinic under the guidance of our old champion, Dr. Pillay, a specialist in that field. At the outset there were more infertile couples seeking the help of our doctors than those wanting to limit their families, and we had to find extra, qualified staff to deal with the several hundred patients who came to us within our first year.

When the Second Five-Year Plan came up for serious discussion, the Government at last woke up to the fact that new procedures would have to be adopted if an impact was to be made on population growth. To our great satisfaction, a larger sum of money was allocated and the ineffective rhythm method was abolished as the sole approved form of contraception. A new program was accepted, linking family planning with maternity and child-welfare work in all the governmental health centers, from the primary clinics in rural areas to the maternity departments of all hospitals in large cities and in district towns. In order to receive the official grants, our voluntary organization continued to carry on the educational programs sanctioned by the Government. But now we also established some innovative projects outside the pattern approved by the Health Ministry, with funds obtained from private sources.

Adlai Stevenson's 1955 visit to Bombay *(USIS)*

CHAPTER 29

OTHER ASIAN COUNTRIES had begun to recognize that the problem of exploding population growth must be quickly and intensively tackled. Japan was the leader in the Far East. Apart from the usual post-war surge in births, a great many Japanese who had settled abroad in China, Manchuria, and Korea were forced to return to Japan, and drastic measures had to be adopted to curb the population and enable the nation to rebuild its shattered economy. The first new Government after the Peace Treaty was signed in 1952 and the Allied Occupation was disbanded followed India's example by legalizing family planning and advocating the limitation of children to three per couple.

Japan had always been a highly disciplined and literate country, provided with adequate medical facilities even in the villages. A deeply patriotic nation, when the Japanese understood that controlling population was in the interest of reconstructing their ravaged country, their response was immediate. Since it would take too long to train doctors and their patients in the use of contraceptives and while work was being done to provide and propagate contraceptive methods, Japan chose the short cut of legalizing abortion, the first country of all those beginning to study the demographic picture of underdeveloped countries to sanction abortion officially. Every couple was encouraged to terminate a fourth pregnancy. Abortion was a crash program on a scale that gave Japan immediate results, and this method of controlling numbers was accepted by the people with no opposition.

In 1955 Japan invited the International Planned Parenthood Federation, now a well-established organization with headquarters in London, to an international conference in Tokyo. The figures presented at this conference by the Japanese demographers showed that Japan had succeeded in reducing the growth of its population from 2 million per year to 1.3 million and reported that over a million abortions in government hospitals had been successfully carried out.

So, although India was the first country to accept family planning as a government policy, Japan was the first to show a dramatic result of the policy, though at the time it was much criticized by the delegates of several of the other nations present at this conference. Soon after, the government of Pakistan followed India's lead and proclaimed its support of family planning, but other governments were not prepared to accept the program officially, owing to religious prejudices. However, voluntary agencies were nonetheless encouraged to organize clinics and train doctors for family planning. Eminent demographers were predicting the consequences of a doubling of the world's population from three billion to six billion by the end of the century unless drastic measures were taken by every country in the world, and the necessity for controlling human fertility was being realized in some of the Western countries. But the whole movement was aimed especially at the underdeveloped countries, where the situation was critical.

As the All-India Family Planning Association, of which I continued to be president, was receiving more and more government aid, our work was spreading, and some of the progressive states were responding even more readily than we had hoped. They were willing to organize educational and clinical work with our assistance. But the less progressive areas were quite indifferent to the support being offered, in spite of our efforts to arouse interest and the offers of financial grants from Government.

We began to organize All-India Conferences in different parts of the country to keep the propaganda alive and to enlist more workers and encourage them to set up their own regional programs and apply for government grants. We hoped, in this way, to relieve social workers of the time-consuming and anxious business of raising funds and free them for more intensive work in their special fields.

As voluntary workers our relationship with government officials was a happy one on the whole, though at our conferences we sometimes publicly criticized certain official procedures that, in our opinion, hampered our work. Government officials were invited to our meetings, responded to our invitations, and, invariably, an important personage connected with the Government inaugurated these conferences. We also invited representatives of the United Nations agencies at work in India, such as WHO, FAO, UNICEF, UNESCO, ECAFE, (now ESCAP), especially those agencies with a direct or indirect interest in population problems. Invitations were also sent to the representatives of various grant-giving bodies, such as the Rockefeller Foundation and the Ford Foundation, and representatives from neighboring countries were invited to attend.

One of the effects of these all-India meetings was that local workers in many parts of the country began to start branches of the Family Planning Association of India with the assistance of social workers and medical men and women in their areas. They sought affiliation with the parent body and were warmly welcomed. We had now grown so large that the small room in my husband's official residence could no longer contain the people to handle our official correspondence, keep files, handle overseas inquiries, keep track of new publications, and so on. We therefore rented a room in the center of the city, but working there was no joy, since there were three typewriters rattling away all day, visitors being received, information being given, new projects being discussed—all in the midst of the clatter.

271

Fortunately, we learned in 1955 that a large apartment in the heart of the city was falling vacant. Its occupant, who was connected with the Reserve Bank of India, was moving into new premises built for him and several other of the bank officials in a large block of buildings. I immediately wrote to the Secretary of the Health Department of the Government of India, describing our predicament and persuading him to help us to get the commodious and rent-controlled apartment. (The rent was only 500 rupees a month.)

He and other officials sympathetic to our cause backed our request, and we were allotted the apartment, but we still needed money to pay some rent in advance and to move from our one-room office. Once again I fell back on the personal generosity of a friend. I wrote to Mr. J. R. D. Tata, a well-known industrialist and a great supporter of family planning, and I immediately received from him a check for 10,000 rupees, which smoothed our way and gave us the chance to begin expanding our work. It was a splendid and timely gift, for we were in desperate need just then. At last we felt truly established and able to carry out our plans for new projects.

In 1954 I had been invited to make a lecture tour in America, and I accepted the invitation gladly. I thought it would be interesting to convey to audiences there some of the excitement we in India were experiencing in nation building and the part we were playing in the social-welfare field. Our contact with America during the period of British imperialism had been a tenuous one, and I looked forward to getting better acquainted with the people of a country which my daughter, Santha, loved, which had made her so welcome, and where many of her closest friends from college days lived.

I was excited by the prospect of talking to them about our problems, seeking their moral support, understanding, and sympathy in our efforts. My only previous experience of America, as an ambassador's wife, had been limited for the most part to what I could see and do in Washington and had not left me with the feeling that I really knew or understood Americans.

Now, I thought, a lecture tour would change all that.

The subject I chose was a general one, "The Social Revolution in India," so that I could explain to American groups, women's clubs, university students, town-hall forums, and Unitarian church groups the different aspects of our First Five-Year Plan, and our hopes for the future of our country. The question of population control naturally figured in my assessment of the general situation in India and the future prospects of its developing economy. We were on the threshold of a new era of independence and were, then, full of optimism, though we knew we had a long way to go to develop our economic resources and change our social patterns.

I traveled the length and breadth of America from New York to Los Angeles, and from Minnesota to Georgia, a very strenuous program, but extremely interesting to me from many points of view. I talked seriously to university groups about the enormous scope of the First Five-Year Plan, which had to take into account a population of nearly 500 million, 80 percent of whom lived in the 550,000 villages of India, of the weight of illiteracy and underdevelopment that the planners faced, of the determination to establish a democratic system even though progress might be quicker under autocratic rule. Old, established traditions had to be eradicated. Primary education had to be provided for this massive population, at that time growing at the rate of seven million per year. Equally important programs had to be started to help agriculture, industry, social services, and the development of the economic potential of the country to raise the standard of living. In fact, my purpose was to impress on these groups the gigantic tasks we were undertaking and to convey to them some of the excitement and enthusiasm we Indians felt. One day in the not so distant future, we hoped, India would develop on its own momentum without foreign aid.

Often at the end of such meetings time was allotted for questions. I cannot describe the disappointment and the sense of deflation I felt when the questions from the floor were: "Can you explain to us how the Indian sari is worn?" or "What is the significance of the red spot on the forehead that Indian women

273

wear?" or "How is it that you speak English with an English accent?"

In the case of the American women's clubs I came up against strong objections to any mention of family planning. Before the meetings my hostesses insisted that I promise not to mention population control, as it was a subject that the Catholic members of their organizations would not tolerate. Much as I explained that it was a vital subject to a developing country seeking to raise its standard of living and assured them that I would speak of it only as an Indian concern and that my talk need have no reference to American prejudices, I failed to convince them. I had to soft-pedal what to us was an extremely important subject.

I had been lecturing in Tucson, Arizona, Margaret Sanger's home town, and she had very kindly offered to accompany me to Santa Barbara for my next engagement. There the president of the Women's Club talked to both Margaret Sanger and to me about her own and her committee's objection to any mention of population growth. The meeting was waiting, the audience had assembled, and I was ready to go onto the platform, when, at the last moment, the ban was imposed. Margaret Sanger was hotly indignant. She walked out of the hall, leaving me to manage as best I could. I talked about the conditions we social workers had to tackle in India and merely skirted round the subject of our massive and growing population and the extra burdens it placed on our people. It could have been a stormy meeting; instead, it was rather dull. But the next day the local paper carried a very strong article by Margaret Sanger which touched off a highly charged controversy that went on for weeks in letters to the editor. But I left Santa Barbara the next morning for Pomona University, my next assignment, and could not follow it.

Such incidents in the thirty-six cities I visited amused and infuriated me, in turn, but I went home with a better knowledge of America, the country and the people, their problems and their deep-seated prejudices and fears. I also met extremely intelligent men and women who sympathized with the work India had undertaken and were willing to help. Some universities organized special studies on India and other under-

274

developed countries, and others behaved with warmth and friendliness. On the whole, I enjoyed the tour, but I decided, although I received repeated invitations, never to undertake another. I did not think my lectures penetrated deep enough or could help to educate Americans about the vital issues of another country.

CHAPTER 30

S OON AFTER THE Government of India began to put the First Five-Year Plan into effect, a central Social Welfare Board was appointed by the Social Welfare Department, with Mrs. Durgabhai Deshmukh, an outstanding, dynamic worker, as chairman. She had served as a member of the Planning Commission, and her new appointment required her to choose recognized social workers from different states of India to help with the Community Development Department and its pilot projects in village areas. The overall scheme was that the country should be divided into units of a hundred villages each, where programs of total development would be started—health, sanitation, medicine, literacy, primary education, agricultural development, including the use of better seed and better handling of the soil, improved care of cattle, milk production, poultry farming. Every aspect would be considered in a total effort to improve the conditions in which village India lived. Along with the education given the men of the villages by Community Development workers, a women's wing would be established to involve illiterate women. Community Development women would work to inspire confidence in these village women and persuade them to trust the outsiders who were trying to improve maternity and child care through primary health centers and instruction in improved nutrition. They were also to establish adult education for women and primary education for children.

In central areas experimental farms were to demonstrate new scientific methods of farming, the value of new and improved seeds, and the correct use of manure and fertilizers. Teams of specialists would demonstrate how to improve the breed of cattle by artificial insemination, how to take better care of poultry and other farm animals. The whole project was, in a way, the beginning of the "Green Revolution." All this work needed constant supervision, and the central Social Welfare Board members were required to travel periodically over these rural areas to supervise, solve problems, and make suggestions.

I willingly accepted the invitation to join this board, knowing it would give me the opportunity to get into the village areas and, with the help of those in charge of primary health centers and maternity and child welfare clinics, to introduce family-planning education. Durgabhai Deshmukh was a great supporter of family limitation and gave wholehearted support to the new projects we were suggesting and the new education we were trying to push into the villages. But we found that the doctors at the village health centers were too busy with maternity and child-welfare problems to give much time to educating and motivating young mothers to space their children and limit their families.

One such health center served several villages and the women had to walk long distances to get the medical attention they or their children needed. They worked all day with their menfolk in the fields and had to wake at daybreak to prepare meals for the family. They carried their little bundles of food—a couple of *chapatis,* a vegetable, some pickles—to the fields and ate at the midday break. Their children played or helped as they worked, and the baby was often left in a makeshift hammock made of an old sheet tied to a branch of a tree. From time to time the mother took a break to nurse the baby. They returned in the evenings tired and dusty and after a quick wash settled down immediately to preparing the evening meal for the family and attending to the domestic chores in their homes.

There was no opportunity for social workers to carry on a substantial educational program among these women, to persuade them to visit the medical center regularly. If only clinics could be placed within easy reach of their homes, I thought many, many times, it would be easier for them to accept the guidance of the family-planning workers and take advantage of the simple contraceptive appliances offered to them.

All this was very frustrating, but we could do nothing about it. There was a dearth of doctors, of trained midwives, of social workers, of transportation, and even of appliances for contraception, and although some elementary training in family planning was given Community Development workers, it just was not enough. We had to take into account the irrefutable facts. The villagers lived in huts crowded with family, where they had no storage places and no privacy. They had to walk long distances to the health center. The climatic conditions were difficult—the heavy rains during the monsoon, the burning heat during the summer—and even if we could create motivation strong enough to overcome all these impediments, the appliances themselves, most composed of rubber, perished very soon. It is no wonder that, in spite of the intensive work we did to educate them, the enthusiasm we were able to create faded quickly and we did not make the progress we had hoped for.

I talked to meetings of village women in different states of India and learned more than I expected. Illiterate as they were, the arguments they advanced were reasoned and thoughtful. Children, they told me, were necessary in every household, especially boys, who would grow up to carry on the responsibilities of their fathers, tend their fields, and support the aged members of their families. All those who were incapable of work because of old age, or other disability, had to be provided for in a joint family (which is still the social structure of village India). It was sons only who would be charged with the burden of the unemployed or those incapable of gainful employment within the family. Daughters would be married and have responsibilities in their husbands' homes. No government unemployment dole or old-age pensions were available, so every household had to have sons. Child mortality in villages was high because of the lack of balanced nutrition, sanitation, and medical aid. Therefore, many sons were desirable since some of them would surely die before they reached manhood. Besides, children helped their parents by tending to the grazing of goats and cattle or weeding and doing other light work in the fields, and the girls helped with washing utensils and clothes and with cooking for the family.

My only answer to these arguments was that spacing children would result in healthier mothers and children, and such large families would no longer be necessary. Children would not succumb to the usual ailments when they were strong enough to resist infections. The Government would provide better sanitation and health conditions for village families, and the death rate would be lowered. I found that women who had borne several children were more ready to accept advice on contraception, but how could we make it easier for them to get to the health centers and receive help in solving their difficulties?

The attitude of women in different states of India varies according to the traditions of the villages to which they belong. The women in some South Indian states are freer and more willing to accept new ideas, while in the northern villages I found the women more conservative and inhibited, clinging to traditional patterns and resisting any change. When I talked to them the only response I could get was "Our fathers and mothers lived as we live and our children will live as we do." These attitudes are reflected in the better progress in family planning programs made in states like Maharashtra, Kerala, Mysore, as compared with Bihar, Uttar Pradesh, Rajasthan, and Himachal Pradesh. The exception, however, is the Punjab, where the standard of living is better than in other states and the villagers more ready to improve it and therefore more willing to accept new patterns.

A couple of years after I joined the Central Social Welfare Board, I was appointed chairman of the Social and Moral Hygiene Committee inquiring into the immoral traffic in women. This was a startling and interesting assignment. Four other women members of the board and I toured the whole of India, collecting information on brothels and on other forms of sexual exploitation in all the important towns in each state. We visited eighty cities and were assisted everywhere by district magistrates, chiefs of police, and social workers, all alerted before our arrival to give us the facilities we required for our investigation.

We traveled for several months and learned extraordinary facts about Indian life, which, in our sheltered, middle-class families, came to us with shocking impact. In the brothels we visited, for example, we were surprised by how many different reasons women had for taking to prostitution and submitting to the exploitation of procurers and pimps. Some had entered willingly and some unwillingly. We talked to young girls who had been enticed from the villages to the cities and were reluctant to return even if they had been given such a chance. They told us that at home they lived in poverty, darkness, and a continual round of hard work. In the city they loved the bright lights, the opportunities for entertainment—a cinema, a fair, a chance to sit in a coffee shop and watch the world go by. The money they earned they sent back to their families in the villages to help their parents, brothers, and sisters. They knew a time would come when they themselves would have to go back, prematurely old, diseased, and discarded. But in the meantime they enjoyed the gaiety and glamour of city life.

We also met women so depressed and miserable at heart that they spent their days writing on sheets of paper the words "Rama" and "Sita," sacred characters from the ancient epics whom they worshiped. They wrote in very small lettering—a thousand times on each sheet—then tore up the sheets into tiny pieces with one name on each fragment, which they embedded in small globules of dough and fed to the fishes. All this was their form of worship. As they answered my questions, I learned that, yes, they earned their livelihood by prostitution but they were deeply religious and lived by a moral code of their own. They would never be seen in broad daylight in any manner that could be considered indecent by Indian standards, such as some respectable women affected on the streets. In fact, they were shocked by modern society women, who wore "seductive" garments such as tight-fitting slacks or diaphanous saris. They themselves moved around during the day simply and sedately clad, and dressed to attract a clientele only when exhibitionism was in order for the purpose of their profession.

In certain communities, however, the traditions were totally different as well as unfamiliar to us. Among them it was recognized that the daughters of a family should be trained from childhood for the profession of singing and dancing. The men were trained to be the musicians who accompanied their sisters in performances. All of them were considered professional artists, and those who visited their houses expected a serious concert or dance recital. However, it was not considered immoral for any of these trained women to take a paramour, change him for another if she so desired, to earn money for herself and the men of the family who provided her instrumental accompaniment. These women were proud to be highly trained, and the reputation of an outstanding performer quickly spread. Like a Japanese geisha, she would have a large clientele from whom she chose her favorite. The men of the family married and led normal lives with their wives, but the tradition was carried on when their children were born, for again the girls were trained as dancers and singers and the boys as musicians like their fathers. The women were always free—never married—and led independent lives. If children were born of their relations with their paramours, they belonged to the mothers and not to the fathers.

In sordid contrast to those communities, we also came across the so-called "rescue homes," which claimed to provide for destitute girls and women, and even received government grants for the maintenance of their inmates. Our investigation into some of these houses unearthed the brutal facts that the girls were really kidnapped, kept in locked houses, and sold to men who ran brothels in different parts of the country. The system was simple, ingenious, and appalling. A man would offer

281

marriage to a girl in the home through the manager, who arranged for him to see all the inmates. He would choose the one he thought best suited for his purpose, and put down a fee of 200 or 250 rupees. He then took the girl to a magistrate, made a declaration that he wished to marry her, signed a marriage certificate, gave her some jewelry and a couple of showy garments, and took her away to another state. Usually, the girl, with no dowry to offer and no family to make inquiries, was quite willing to accept any proposal of marriage. This could happen again and again, the same man appearing under different names and collecting the girls for the brothel he owned. Since the girls could neither read nor write, and since no magistrate could or would bother to find out the details of the girls appearing before him, they became the prey of such characters and there was no redress for them.

After our journeys I wrote a report for the Central Social Welfare Board, which was published, and the Government took action in ordering better supervision of the homes for destitute women. They also implemented other suggestions we made after our detailed research. However, that study for the Social and Moral Hygiene Committee was a side interest, and I soon got back to the Family Planning Association and the programs that were beginning to take shape.

CHAPTER 31

A S NEW FAMILY-PLANNING clinics were opened, we
were faced with new situations. In one small town near Madras
we opened a center and appointed a woman doctor to attend to
women suffering from gynecological ailments. In the course of
her work she was to advise her patients about family planning
and tell them that she could help them to prevent unwanted
pregnancies. Soon after she had established herself, her clinic
was crowded with pregnant women all clamoring for a termina-
tion of their pregnancies, since they understood that she could
help them to prevent unwanted children. The doctor wrote to
me at our headquarters asking what she should do. Of course
I told her that, since induced abortions were illegal, she should
advise her clients to wait until the birth of the babies they were
expecting and then teach them the use of contraceptive appliances.

She reported back that she had to face much resentment and
disappointment from the women at her refusal to help them.
They accused her of holding out false promises to them. Because of this experience, we began to consider seriously the
question of demanding legislation on abortion, and the subject

was discussed in the closed sessions of our meetings, but at that time we did not have the courage to advocate the legalizing of abortion publicly. We feared that strenuous opposition might adversely affect our work. That there were many illegal abortions taking place in both towns and villages was common knowledge, but it was hard to prove.

The question of sterilization of the male and female was more readily acceptable, especially vasectomy, the easier of the two operations and one that required no hospitalization of the patient. By this time, as our annual population increase kept steadily mounting, more and more anxiety was being expressed in official circles. A much larger allocation of money was made in the Second Five-Year Plan, and state governments were instructed to intensify family planning programs. Our population was now increasing by seven million per year and the projections made by demographers were little short of catastrophic.

National and United Nations health programs had shown dramatic results. Life expectancy had steadily increased since independence. Plague, smallpox, cholera, and malaria were rapidly coming under control. Prompt help could now reach areas of the country stricken by famine, drought, or floods. With the curtailing of infant and maternal mortality, it was expected that within the next fifteen years or so those children who would otherwise have died before the age of six would live to reproduce and make our population future bleaker and bleaker.

It was only at the end of the Second Five-Year Plan that the Central Government at last showed a sense of emergency. The Central Health Ministry was divided into a Ministry of Health and a Ministry of Family Planning. The Health Minister was in overall charge, but the Minister for Family Planning had his own official staff to allow greater concentration. New schemes were introduced and hotly debated, of which perhaps the most controversial was the offer of cash incentives to men who accepted sterilization and also to those who motivated others to have vasectomies performed. The offer of transistor radios—an unusual and much-prized item in India at the time—caused particular consternation abroad.

With Mrs. Mary Lasker and Mrs. Frances Ferguson *(Jerry May)*

Dr. Rajendra Prasad, President of India, conferring the Padma Bhushan Award on the author in April, 1959

I had the honor, about this time, of being awarded the Albert and Mary Lasker Award for Service in the Cause of Planned Parenthood. I flew to America, proud as a peacock, yet humble as a churchmouse, feeling unworthy of such recognition, and attended a large and glittering function at which the awards were given to several of us who had achieved distinction in various fields. There I had the pleasure of meeting Mary Lasker, a great friend of Margaret Sanger's. Since a meeting of the American Planned Parenthood Federation was to be held in Puerto Rico soon after, I accompanied Margaret Sanger there and, after a few days, we flew to Jamaica. The Jamaican workers were in the process of forming their own family-planning organization and impressed us with their dedication and the extensive but realistic programs they had outlined. It was a marvelously inspiriting trip for me, and I returned home refreshed to the heavy work of organizing the next All-India Family Planning Conference.

This time we met at Lucknow in Uttar Pradesh, where Mrs. Sarojini Naidu, the outstanding politician, well-known poet, great orator, and my girlhood idol, was the Governor of the state. She gave us her patronage wholeheartedly and we felt we had penetrated another state where no organized work was being done but where professional workers were interested in building a branch organization.

We were especially encouraged when the Health Minister of the Chinese Government, a woman who was visiting India, expressed a wish to attend the 1957 All-India Conference in Calcutta. Some months earlier, a Chinese delegation led by Chou En-lai had visited India officially and been received by Pandit Jawaharlal Nehru with great cordiality. The whole of India, wherever they traveled, had given them a warm welcome, and along the roads crowds waving Indian and Chinese flags shouted, *"Hindi Chini Bhai Bhai"* ("Indians and Chinese are brothers)."

On public occasions Chou En-lai spoke with great respect about Pandit Jawaharlal Nehru, referring to him as an older brother, and expressing the hope that China would follow

India's example in framing the policies of its newly independent country. When the party visited Bombay our Prime Minister accompanied them and they were the guests of honor at a big reception held by the Bombay Government. Pandit Nehru introduced me to Chou En-lai at this function and in doing so mentioned to him that I was the president of the All-India Family Planning Association. At this introduction Chou En-lai paused in greeting the other guests to ask how our work was getting on. I answered briefly, aware of how many other people were waiting to meet him. He said, "You know we also have a population problem in China."

These words encouraged me greatly, and later when the Chinese Health Minister asked to attend the conference in Calcutta, we began to think that if China too were to frame a government population policy, our hands in India would be greatly strengthened. We were, after all, the two biggest nations, in terms of population, in the world.

When, in the year following our Calcutta conference, the Chinese Government invited a delegation of six Indian women to attend the Liberation Day celebration on the first of October, I was formally asked by the External Affairs Department if I would care to lead the group. Of course I accepted with alacrity. I do not know whether this invitation to me was linked with the interest in family planning Chou En-lai had indicated. Perhaps his had been only a polite party remark, but I hoped he had meant it more seriously.

I embarked on this journey to China with great excitement. Although family planning was my main interest, I had last seen China in 1948 on my way to Japan when Chiang Kai-shek was still in power and Shanghai was a shambles, with the Communists pushing from the north and an unmanageable influx of desperate refugees crowding into a city already stretched beyond its capacity in housing, food, and medical care. At that time I had been left with the impression of chaos, although several voluntary agencies had sprung up to render assistance. Through one of them I had come to know Madame Sun Yat-sen, the sister-in-law of Chiang Kai-shek and also the widow of the rev-

Lunch as Mme Sun Yat-sen's guest in Shanghai, 1958

With Mao Tse-tung in 1958

ered founder of modern China, who was known to be *persona non grata* with the Nationalist Government for her supposed Communist sympathies. She was working very hard to help the refugees in their distress.

On that occasion I had stayed a few days in Shanghai, had seen something of the conditions there, something of her work, and had admired the earnestness of her efforts, the genuine concern she expressed, and the unsparing drive she and her colleagues put into relieving the sufferings around them. In 1958, therefore, I was keenly interested to see how the country had developed during the ten years of the Communist regime. I wondered what changes had taken place and how people belonging to an ancient culture with traditions somewhat similar to those of India had reacted to the new ideas and policies.

Having had to walk a short distance from Hong Kong across the famous bridge which separates the two territories, supervised by the guards, we were given transport to enter Canton. There we were met by Communist officials and taken to the airport to fly to Peking. On October 1, 1958, the tenth Liberation Day celebrations were held with great pomp. Mao Tse-tung, Chou En-lai, and all the high officials of the Chinese Government as well as the honored guests from other countries took their places on the high platform. It was a most imposing ceremony, with the great walls of the Forbidden City in the background and disciplined young members of the new China marching in a seemingly endless procession. Army, Navy, Air Force, services of all kinds, nurses, schoolchildren, on and on they marched, turning only to salute their leaders.

At a great reception which followed, I among others had the honor of being introduced to Mao Tse-tung, and a photographer happened to take a picture of my meeting with him. All the young Chinese who accompanied us during our tour were awed, when they saw the pictures, by the one in which I was talking to the great leader. I was considered particularly lucky to have actually shaken hands with him.

We stayed in Peking for a week and were taken to see all the new developments in the city and its surroundings as well as the splendors of the palaces and monuments. We visited palaces, schools, factories, prisons, children's play centers, the theater, and the traditional places of entertainment, where daily performances were held to encourage the artistic side of life—music and dancing, singing and drama. Everywhere we were presented with figures and statistics about the improvements since the new republic had been established. We met and talked to young men, young women, students and workers. We questioned them and found that they answered in almost identical words, telling us how much damage imperialism had caused and how much progress had been accomplished since liberation.

We talked about population control and were taken to the small group meetings of men and women who all lived on the same street and who met regularly to discuss various subjects. They were all interested in family planning and ready to consider ways and means. These street committees helped to educate by word of mouth and to spread information about the contraceptives that were being produced. Posters and placards were also displayed. I was very much impressed with the thoroughness of the system that could organize the work from street to street and in such detailed and diverse ways. In turn I told them about our government projects and the voluntary work that was being done in India, but it was clear to them, as it was to me, that their form of government could exert pressures and controls on its people that India could not. At that time we were still committed to noncoercive, democratic, and, alas, slower methods.

I found Shanghai so greatly changed that I could hardly believe my eyes. Instead of the hopeless tangle of traffic and people, there were order and discipline on the streets, in the markets, on the playing fields. People walked quietly and purposefully. There was no shouting, no pushing and shoving, no dawdling and gossiping, no quarrels on the slightest pretext, as in 1948. The money market was stable, the currency was fixed, there appeared to be no black market, and the prices of articles in the shops were clearly displayed. The brothels had been closed down, the streets were clean, and everything

290

seemed hygienically neat and tidy. Early every morning the parks and sports grounds were packed with young people playing games seriously and in an ordered way. Both men and women were expected to work. Hostels were provided for them, and simple but wholesome food was served. Young married women with children were also expected to work, and their children were placed under the care of their grandmothers, who were not young enough to contribute otherwise to the work the country required. We were told that young men and women were "persuaded" to go into the villages and work with the uneducated, illiterate villagers to help them adopt progressive ideas and learn modern methods of agriculture. I couldn't help wondering what our young people would say if they were ordered to do similar work in our villages.

In Shanghai I was especially interested in the Children's Palace. The president was Madame Sun Yat-sen. She had visited India after liberation and on each occasion we had met with great cordiality, for Santha, my daughter, was a friend of hers. I had retained a great admiration for her from the days, a decade earlier, when I had first seen her work. We had exchanged gifts, and I still remember the piece of Chinese brocade she gave me and the two boxes of jasmine tea she brought me when she came to India. I greatly looked forward to meeting her again.

She received our big party of delegates very correctly. Although I knew she spoke English fluently she addressed me formally in Chinese, and an interpreter extended her welcome to me. I felt hurt and embarrassed, because my first instinct had been to put my arms around her and greet her warmly and affectionately. But I sensed it was not the right thing to do on that occasion and replied, equally formally, in English and waited till the interpreter translated what I had said to her. She went with us around the Children's Palace, and I was greatly impressed with the intelligent combination of work and play in which the children were engaged after school hours.

The whole of this enormous palace was divided into sections where every kind of attraction was provided: music, dance, singing, dramatics, needlework, games, carpentry, painting, and the

291

children were allowed to choose whatever class they wished to attend. The most expert professionals in drama, music, singing, and the other arts gave the children performances periodically, —opportunities they would never normally have had—in order to encourage them and keep their interest alive in whatever they were doing. The children themselves arranged a very charming show for us, and after that we sat down to a meal. It was then that Madame Sun Yat-sen gestured to the interpreter to place me by her side. As soon as the interpreter moved away, she turned to me with much warmth and asked, in English, "And how are you and how is your daughter Santha?" This broke the ice, and we chatted gaily through the meal.

After three weeks in China, I came back greatly impressed by all I had seen, but, like many visitors to that land, I also had disturbing doubts. Why were we obliged to keep so strictly to the program? Why could we never go out without an escort? How was it that group after group of young and not-so-young people we met gave almost exactly the same answers to our questions? No one seemed to have an even slightly different opinion to offer, and there never was a word of criticism about any of the policies we discussed. However, I was very grateful to have had this opportunity to see how a Communist regime works, and often wondered if our Indian way of life, tradition-bound, religion-oriented, and custom-ridden, could in any circumstances be altered so drastically as the Chinese. And, if so, what the cost would be.

CHAPTER 32

O N MY RETURN to Bombay, our Family Planning Office
was already humming with activity, for we had invited the International Planned Parenthood Federation to a World Conference at Delhi in February 1959, the second to be held in India.
By this time the large Government conference hall, Vidya Bhavan, had been built, containing committee rooms and facilities
for interpreters. Invitations went out to all countries, and eminent speakers were invited. Among others, we sent a cordial
invitation through the Chinese Embassy to the Health Minister
of China, asking her to bring a delegation with her. After a long
delay, we got a curt reply from the Chinese Ambassador in Delhi
saying he regretted China could not send a delegation to the
Conference. China was no longer interested in family planning,
and therefore was not anxious to encourage the use of contraceptives! For years after, no information about Chinese population figures could be obtained by the outside world.

This came as a shock to me, as I was still glowing with enthusiasm about the Chinese handling of their family-planning program. We were told there had been a change of policy and were
obliged to accept that disheartening verdict. Still, we went on

with our preparations for the world conference, and Prime Minister Nehru agreed to inaugurate it. Applications from many countries poured in; some of these delegates were scientifically advanced and others would be coming from countries that were still grappling with the elementary problems of population control.

Margaret Sanger, the president of the federation, was at this time so ill that her doctors and her son, who was also a doctor, strongly advised her not to attend the meeting in Delhi. The strain of the long journey and the excitement of a world conference might well be too much for her. But she could not resist the temptation to be present at a conference where the Prime Minister of a country the size of India, a man whose stature was already recognized by the whole world, was to associate himself publicly with a cause so dear to her heart. She was determined to take all the risks. She saw such a meeting as the vindication of the calumny she had suffered and the culmination of the years of hard work and struggle she had carried on so nobly to establish the right of women to decide the size of their families and to refuse to bear unwanted children.

She traveled with a devoted friend, in short stages, from Tucson, her hometown, to Honolulu, to Tokyo, to Hong Kong, to Bangkok, to Calcutta, arriving in Delhi a few days before the opening of the conference. There we received her and put her to bed immediately. At each halt on her journey she had rested, consulted doctors, at times had oxygen administered. She was, of course, exhausted, and when we met her we found her so ill and tired that we were desperately afraid that she might not, after all, be able to attend the inauguration. We put her under the care of a doctor and refused to allow any visitors except her close associates; meanwhile, we went on with the last-minute rush of preparations for the opening of the conference.

On the day of the inauguration, to our amazement, Margaret Sanger got up from her sickbed, dressed in a smart new dress, put on a jaunty hat, and presented herself at the Vidya Bhavan a little before the Prime Minister was due to arrive. We placed her in a small adjoining room to await the chief guest in order to save her from undue excitement. Then I went down a few steps to meet the Prime Minister and welcome him. I whispered to him that Margaret Sanger was awaiting him in the anteroom to the main hall and that she had traveled to India at great risk to her health to be present at this meeting.

Jawaharlal had met her many years ago, knew all about her, and admired her greatly. On hearing my news, he ran up the steps like a schoolboy, put his arms around Margaret in greeting, and gently led her into the hall where the great gathering was waiting for him. It was a most touching and unforgettable scene: the Prime Minister ignoring all formality, Mrs. Sanger glowing with pride, and the huge audience standing up, cheering and applauding.

After the Prime Minister's opening speech, Margaret Sanger was inspired to get up and say a few words, graciously acknowledging the honor done her and expressing her satisfaction that this conference promised to be an important milestone in the movement. Shortly afterward she retired as president to become president emeritus, and in her place Mrs. Elise Ottesen Jensen, an eminent pioneer in the field, was elected president of the I.P.P.F.

During the days that followed, several controversial subjects were discussed openly for the first time. Could Japan's government policy of abortion be accepted universally by the International Planned Parenthood Federation? Could sterilization of the male or female, as accepted by the Government of India, be encouraged and recommended as I.P.P.F. official policy? To what extent could intra-uterine devices succeed? Which were the most effective and safe types? Could the International Planned Parenthood Federation recommend any particular contraceptive devices that might be controversial from the point of view of religion or morality? Should every country affiliated with the I.P.P.F. make decisions on these matters for itself? Or should the I.P.P.F. accept the responsibility of these decisions as central policies? What was the position to be taken about the pill? Should the I.P.P.F. support it although countries like Japan and India were not prepared to recommend it except under

295

strict medical control? These and many other questions were debated.

All our proceedings that year combined just the right mixture of debate, accomplishment, and future planning, and I still remember that conference with all the vividness of the excitement I felt at the time. The most important and most honored man in my country, Jawaharlal Nehru, and the most important and most honored woman in the movement I had espoused, Margaret Sanger, came together on an occasion that foreshadowed the worldwide success we were to achieve. It is a moment that I cherish to this day.

In a way this was the climax of my story, or rather the story of my involvement in public life. Of course my work for family planning in India and abroad continued for the next twenty years—I continued to be president of the All-India Family Planning Association and served on various boards and panels—and although there were difficult and demanding times, we knew that nothing could now stop the momentum of the work we had begun.

CHAPTER 33

M Y HUSBAND RETIRED from the governorship of the Reserve Bank of India after long and distinguished service to our country. We were glad to give up all the official entertaining, to lead a quieter social life, and to see more of our children and grandchildren.

By this time the financial condition of the International Planned Parenthood Federation had improved enough to afford a commodious office in the center of London, Lower Regent Street, and appoint a Secretary General, an administrator who had retired as Governor of Mauritius and was keenly interested in the population problem. Sir Colville Deverell helped to spread the message of the Planned Parenthood Federation across the world through his extensive travels, his meetings with high government officials in different countries, and the contacts he made with all the United Nations agencies.

The Federation had laid down important principles in its constitution, which also allowed for amendments to accommodate changing conditions. We declared our belief that the knowledge of planned parenthood was a fundamental human right and that it was only through achieving a balance between the population of the world and its natural resources and productivity that human happiness, prosperity, and peace could be achieved. The aims of the organization were (1) to advance the education of the countries of the world in family planning and responsible parenthood in the interest of family welfare, community well-being, and international good will; (2) to increase the understanding by people and governments of the demographic problems of their own countries and the world; (3) to promote education about population growth and limitation, sex education, and marriage counseling; (4) to stimulate appropriate research in the biological, demographic, economic, eugenic, physiological, and social implications of human fertility and sterility, and to collect and make known such research; (5) to stimulate and assist the formation of Family Planning Associations in all countries; (6) to stimulate and promote family planning in all countries through other appropriate organizations; (7) to encourage and organize the training of all appropriate professional workers, such as medical and health personnel, educators, social and community development workers, in the implementation of the objectives of the federation, and to organize regional or international workshops, seminars, and conferences.

It was no easy task to supervise the work being done in these regions, to attend regional conferences, to suggest ways and means of encouraging new ventures under trained guidance, and to maintain a relationship between governments and voluntary associations, particularly since our work had now spread to every continent.

At the 1963 conference of the International Planned Parenthood Federation, Mrs. Ottesen Jensen retired as president and I was elected in her place. Year after year, more and more countries applied for membership and everywhere the conditions, religion, customs had to be studied to slant the work of motivation and education appropriately. During my first four years as president I traveled extensively, attending conferences, fulfilling speaking engagements, and encouraging work in our field wherever possible.

In Rome I had several interviews with archbishops and monsignors who, at that time, were debating the explosive question of birth control at the Vatican Conference. They received me kindly, talked about the Will of God, blessed me, and presented me with Catholic medals, hoping I would see the light one day, but gave no practical advice as to how this world problem could be solved. I attended a conference in Madrid on an allied subject —family organization—but could make no dent in spite of repeatedly stressing the importance of family planning in family organization and despite the support of my Egyptian and African friends and even of a few Spanish delegates, who courageously spoke up in favor of planning families.

My visit to Israel was an eye-opener. Their progress since they had achieved independence was unbelievable, and I admired their dedicated efforts to build a new country on Western lines. The only occasion on which I felt distressed was when I was introduced to the Health Minister and naturally talked about the control of population. I pointed out how important it was in a small country that was still accepting immigrants from all parts of the world. The Minister strongly disagreed with me. "Six million Jews were destroyed under the Hitler regime," he said, "and Israel has to make up these losses. It is our policy to reward those mothers who produce large families." We parted on that discordant note and I realized that any family planning in Israel would have to be on a voluntary basis for many years to come.

The next international meeting was to be held in 1967 in Santiago, Chile, and a great deal of really intensive work had to be done to bring together representatives from all over the world, especially from South America, where Catholicism had its strongest hold. It was an audacious move and was to be one of the most extraordinary occasions in the history of our organization. Several eminent scientists from the Catholic countries had not only consented to attend the meetings, but were also prepared to speak on radically controversial subjects. I naturally looked forward eagerly to this meeting, since it would also have involved my first visit to South America.

But in January of that year, my husband had a bad fall, broke his upper femur, and was rushed to the hospital immediately. The doctors decided that an operation would help him recover more quickly than if his leg was put in a cast. In that case, he would have had to lie in one position for a long time, and at his age this could cause complications. The operation seemed the wiser course.

The operation was successful, and within a month we were able to bring him home. But, as the time for the Chile conference drew nearer, I was still worried about his health. He suffered from neuritis, his eyes were giving him trouble, and, not being able to read, he was lonely and depressed. He gradually began to draw away from friends, and his only interest seemed to be our children, Premila and our son-in-law in Bombay; their son, who had started work in Bombay; and Santha, whose marriage to Faubion Bowers had broken up and who had come from America to live with us. Her problems, the fact that she was unhappy, that her son was in a boarding school in America, caused him anxiety. As time went on he required more and more care. In these circumstances I could not possibly leave Bombay to attend the conference in Santiago, and I cabled my regrets to the secretary general and the organizers of the Chile committee.

The conference in Santiago was a historic meeting, and proved to be a great success. For the first time delegates from every country of South America attended, some with the open consent and backing of their governments and some representing merely the voluntary work that was being done by forward-looking demographers and doctors who had initiated programs for family planning in spite of the opposition of their Catholic governments. Besides the South American countries, Europe, North America, Asia, and Africa were represented, and the general feeling was that the International Planned Parenthood Federation had reached an important milestone that marked the way to further and more steady progress in the future.

My four years as president of the I.P.P.F. were over. The president must be elected every two years at a governing body meeting and may be re-elected only twice. I had first been elected in 1963, and had been re-elected at the governing body meeting held in 1965. When, after the conference in Santiago, I received a cable informing me that I had been elected for the third time, I felt greatly honored that, in spite of my absence, I was still considered eligible to continue my presidency, even though I could no longer undertake journeys that would keep me away from home for long periods.

When I did go abroad, both my daughters were in Bombay to keep my husband company and give him the care he needed. For the next two years he was a semi-invalid. In spite of a cataract operation, he could read only for short spells and this was a terrible deprivation for someone whose chief pastime had been reading. He felt cut off from all activity. His health declined gradually and he died on December 13, 1969, after only a week's illness. I, both our daughters, and our grandson Nikhil were with him.

He was a man so family-oriented that he rejoiced in the success of his children and grandchildren, suffered when they were unhappy, and could deny them nothing that was in his power to give. He was happy at Premila's successful marriage and had shared her disappointment when she could not go to Cambridge University. He glowed with pride at Santha's success at Wellesley College and, as her books came out, he treasured them on a special shelf in his room. He was silently, miserably anxious when her marriage broke up, and unfortunately he did not live long enough to see her happily married again. His grandchildren, Asha, Nikhil, and Nandita in India, and Jai, Santha's son in America, were perfect in his opinion and could do no wrong. He felt all their triumphs and failures as if they were his own.

After my husband's death, the tributes to him that poured in, expressing a sense of loss and offering condolences, filled a large case, which I have preserved, for someday my great-grandchildren may be interested to know about the qualities of a man so highly and warmly regarded by relatives, friends, colleagues, and even strangers.

My older sisters and I (Bishan on my right, Kamala on my left)

CHAPTER 34

In THE COURSE of my long life I have been fortunate enough to receive many awards, but I find that some have a special meaning for me. The Padma Bhushan, which was announced in the Republic Day honors list of 1959 and presented to me by the President of India, was the first I was given by my own Government.

The Watumull Foundation Distinguished Service Award in 1967 had a different meaning for me. Apart from my delight in the honor, I was reminded that it was Mrs. Ellen Watumull's foundation that had given the Family Planning Association of India, in its early struggling days in 1952, $5,000 to make it possible to arrange our first international conference.

In yet another way, I cherish the Society of Man's Award for Peace, which I received at a splendid and brilliant assembly in New York. The citation read: "In recognition of her deep respect for human life and her sustained work in establishing those basic conditions which are fundamental to peace." I felt both proud and humble and could conceive of no higher praise.

Finally, in 1974, the silver jubilee year of the Family Planning Association of India, after ill-health had forced me to retire from active work, tributes came pouring in from all over India. The most important, from Prime Minister Indira Gandhi, said, "While we live, while we work, while we talk, an inaudible metronome is ticking—the metronome of rising population. Each day India's population goes up by about 30,000; each month by a million. I think it is time to pause and think over the implications."

I was overjoyed by the public acknowledgment of the importance of our work and deeply touched by the personal appreciation shown me on this great occasion. I was given a beautiful plaque, a silver triangle, point downward, which has become the symbol of family planning in India. It is mounted on a highly polished wooden stand with a silver plate on which the following words are engraved:

SHRIMATI DHANVANTHI RAMA RAU

In grateful appreciation of determined and
   dedicated service in the cause of
   Family Planning

From: The President, Members and Staff of
   the Family Planning Association of India.
   Silver Jubilee Year 1974

It is the final tribute I will ever receive and it will always be a precious possession during the rest of my life. I shall leave it to my children, my grandchildren, and my great-grandchildren, in memory of the love and affection I was fortunate enough to receive from my associates in the work I was able to do during our years together.

There is an old tradition in India that when men and women have passed the different phases of growth, from babyhood to old age, it becomes a duty for them to practice detachment and renunciation in preparation for the end of life. It is usually the ambition of those who have completed their duties in life to pray that there should no longer be a reincarnation but that the soul should merge with the Almighty. In my case, although as a Hindu this belief was impressed upon me from childhood, I now find that I cannot accept it. I feel I should like to be born again and again and again, to work in my country as I have tried in this life, in however small a way, for the eradication of the social and economic evils and injustices which still afflict the vast masses of India.

I also have a less high-minded reason. On the 17th of December 1973 my first great-grandchild arrived, Aisha Pearl, the daughter of Nikki and his American wife, Mary Jane. I spend some time with her almost every day, for I adore her and she enthralls me. I am sure I must have been as much impressed with the day-to-day changes in looks, in perception, in the movements of my own children and grandchildren, but that was so long ago. Now it comes as a new revelation to watch the growth of this child. She is a little over nine months old, and she has made progress in a remarkable way. She crawls, she sits, she stands with support, and for the first time, two days ago, she took three steps on her own before she dropped to her crawling position. I think she shows astonishing intelligence. She looks around a room and a sudden gleam appears in her eyes; she has spied something interesting she would like to investigate, but that might involve some risk. She is prepared to take the risk and makes a beeline for that particular attraction, single-mindedly and swiftly, while we watch, trying to follow the workings of her mind. Quietly she is removed from what might involve danger. She does not seriously mind, for immediately she is looking toward the other side of the room and wondering what new adventure she should embark on, and what strategy she should employ to evade the attention of her elders.

What will she be like when she grows up? Will she retain her fearlessness? Will she focus her immense energy and her sharp intelligence on the things she considers really worth pursuing? Will she preserve her enthusiastic interest in all she sees in the world about her? I wonder. And perhaps that loving curiosity is as valid a reason as any other for wanting to be born again.